The Book of Lamentations

THE NEW INTERNATIONAL COMMENTARY
ON THE
OLD TESTAMENT

Series Editors

The Book of LAMENTATIONS

John Goldingay

William B. Eerdmans Publishing Company
Grand Rapids, Michigan

Wm. B. Eerdmans Publishing Co.
4035 Park East Court SE, Grand Rapids, Michigan 49546
www.eerdmans.com

Published 2022
Printed in the United States of America

28 27 26 25 24 23 22 1 2 3 4 5 6 7

ISBN 978-0-8028-2542-1

Library of Congress Cataloging-in-Publication Data

Names: Goldingay, John, author.
Title: The book of Lamentations / John Goldingay.
Description: Grand Rapids, Michigan : William B. Eerdmans Publishing Company, [2022] | Series: The new international commentary on the Old Testament | Includes bibliographical references and indexes. | Summary: "A commentary for scholars and pastors on the biblical book of Lamentations, with an emphasis on reading it as authoritative Christian Scripture"—Provided by publisher.
Identifiers: LCCN 2021028284 | ISBN 9780802825421
Subjects: LCSH: Bible. Lamentations—Commentaries.
Classification: LCC BS1535.53 .G645 2022 | DDC 224/.307—dc23
LC record available at https://lccn.loc.gov/2021028284

Contents

Series Editor's Preface

"Do you *understand* what you're *reading*?"

What a question!

With this opening line, Philip, one of Christianity's first evangelists, approached a seeker from Africa, who had been in Jerusalem to worship. Somewhere along the Gaza Road, on his return trip to Ethiopia, the stranger was reading a portion of the Old Testament. Philip asked the question when he heard him "reading" the ancient text, an activity that almost certainly involved verbalizing the text by reciting it aloud (*anaginōskō*; Acts 8:30). An "angel of the Lord" had sent Philip to meet the Ethiopian for this very opportunity (8:26–29).

Realizing that the seeker was reading a difficult text, and yet also realizing how vitally important it was to the stranger's faith, Philip distinguished between reading and comprehending. "Understanding" is different from simply pronouncing the text aloud; comprehension involves grasping the significance of what is read (*ginōskō*).

Such a deep-level understanding of ancient Israel's Scriptures has always been the goal of The New International Commentary on the Old Testament. Since 1965, the editors of this series—Edward J. Young, Roland K. Harrison, and Robert L. Hubbard Jr.—have guided the series and its authors with the sole purpose of aiding the reader to gain understanding of the text. They have left us a treasured gift. Today a wide readership of scholars, priests, pastors, rabbis, and other serious students of the Bible turn to NICOT volumes for assistance in reading the ancient text.

The aim of the series has always been "to publish biblical scholarship of the highest quality" (to quote the preface of my predecessor, Professor Hubbard) and to do so respectfully from a position of faith seeking understanding. The series appeals to readers across the entire spectrum of theological or philosophical perspectives, and always with the conviction that the Old Testament is more than great literature from the past. Its authors engage the range of traditional methodologies, always sensitive to newer innovations in recent scholarship, and always remembering that the books of the Old Testament constituted the first Bible for the earliest Christians.

Specifically, the NICOT authors believe the books they are writing about—ancient Israel's Scriptures—are God-breathed (*theopneustos*) or "inspired" and therefore "useful for teaching, for reproof, for correction, and for training in righteousness" (2 Timothy 3:16). This high regard of and respect for the authority of Scripture characterizes what has come to be known as "evangelicalism," together with conversionism, activism, and crucicentrism (according to noted historian David W. Bebbington). While the term "evangelical" today requires considerable qualification, the movement it denotes is of God and is still much needed in the Church universal. The authors of the NICOT come from diverse theological branches of the Church, and yet they hold firmly to this conviction that the Old Testament continues as God's means of grace for the Church today. In its pages, and by means of its message, God calls readers into an ever-deepening relational intimacy, inviting all who read (*anaginōskō*) to understand (*ginōskō*).

In response to Philip's question, the Ethiopian seeker admitted that he could not possibly read the ancient text with understanding "unless someone guides me" (Acts 8:31). He was aware of his need to have someone come alongside him to help him acquire the knowledge he desired. He invited Philip to join him in his chariot (and thus in his reading experience), and once he finally understood the Old Testament text, he immediately asked to be baptized (Acts 8:31–38).

This exchange illustrates the difficulty of reading for true understanding, the need for a faithful guide in one's reading, and the power of the ancient text to lead one into saving faith. The goal of each NICOT volume is to be such a guide. Readers around the world have invited the volumes of this series into their reading experience. The ancient text may seem obscure and distant. But God is still at work in its power, and reading it for understanding still makes a life-changing difference for the reader, as it did for Philip's new Ethiopian friend.

Bill T. Arnold

Abbreviations

AB	The Anchor Bible
ABR	*Australian Biblical Review*
ACCS	Ancient Christian Commentary on Scripture
AcT	*Acta Theologica*
AIL	Ancient Israel and Its Literature
ANET	*Ancient Near Eastern Texts Relating to the Old Testament*. Edited by J. B. Pritchard. 3rd ed. Princeton: Princeton University Press, 1969
AOTC	Abingdon Old Testament Commentaries
Aq	Aquila's Greek translation, as documented in F. Field, *Origenis Hexaplorum quae supersunt*, 2 vols. (Oxford: Clarendon, 1867)
ArBib	The Aramaic Bible
AS	*Aramaic Studies*
AS	Assyriological Studies
b.	(followed by the name of a tractate) Babylonian Talmud
BASOR	*Bulletin of the American Schools of Oriental Research*
BDB	Brown, F., S. R. Driver, and C. A. Briggs. *A Hebrew and English Lexicon of the Old Testament*. Reprinted with corrections. Oxford: Clarendon, 1968
BEATAJ	Beiträge zur Erforschung des Alten Testaments und des antiken Judentum
BEHER	Bibliothèque de l'École des hautes études: Sciences religieuses
BETL	Bibliotheca Ephemeridum Theologicarum Lovaniensium
BHS	*Biblia Hebraica Stuttgartensia*. Edited by K. Elliger and W. Rudolph. Stuttgart: Deutsche Bibelgesellschaft, 1983
BHQ	*Biblia Hebraica Quinta*. Edited by A. Schenker et al. Stuttgart: Deutsche Bibelgesellschaft, 2004–
Bib	*Biblica*
BibInt	*Biblical Interpretation*

BibInt	Biblical Interpretation Series
BibOr	Biblica et Orientalia
BibSem	The Biblical Seminar
BKAT	Biblischer Kommentar, Altes Testament
BW	Bible and Women
BZ	*Biblische Zeitschrift*
CBQ	*Catholic Biblical Quarterly*
CBR	*Currents in Biblical Research*
CHANE	Culture and History of the Ancient Near East
COS	*The Context of Scripture*. Edited by W. W. Hallo. 3 vols. Leiden: Brill, 1997–2002
CTAT	*Critique Textuelle de l'Ancien Testament*. By D. Barthélemy. Vol. 2. Göttingen: Vandenhoeck, 1986
CTQ	*Concordia Theological Quarterly*
CurTM	*Currents in Theology and Mission*
DCH	*Dictionary of Classical Hebrew*. Edited by D. J. A. Clines. 9 vols. Vols. 1–5, Sheffield: Sheffield Academic, 1993–2001; vols. 6–9: Sheffield: Sheffield Phoenix, 2007–2016
DG	*Davidson's Introductory Hebrew Grammar: Syntax*. Ed. J. C. L. Gibson. Edinburgh: T&T Clark, 1994
DJD	Discoveries in the Judaean Desert
DSS	*The Dead Sea Scrolls*. Edited by F. García Martínez and E. J. C. Tigchelaar. 2 vols. Repr., Leiden: Brill, 2000
DTT	*A Dictionary of the Targumim, the Talmud Babli and Yerushalmi, and the Midrashic Literature*. By M. Jastrow. New York: Choreb, 1926
EvT	*Evangelische Theologie*
ExAud	*Ex Auditu*
FAT	Forschungen zum Alten Testament
FOTL	Forms of the Old Testament Literature
GK	*Gesenius' Hebrew Grammar*. Edited by E. Kautzsch. Translated by A. E. Cowley. 2nd ed. Oxford: Clarendon, 1910
GPBS	Global Perspectives on Biblical Scholarship
HALOT	*The Hebrew and Aramaic Lexicon of the Old Testament*. L. Koehler, W. Baumgartner, and J. J. Stamm. Translated and edited under the supervision of M. E. J. Richardson. 4 vols. Leiden: Brill, 1994–1999
HAR	*Hebrew Annual Review*
HBM	Hebrew Bible Monographs
HBT	*Horizons in Biblical Theology*
HCOT	Historical Commentary on the Old Testament
HS	*Hebrew Studies*

HThKAT	Herders Theologischer Kommentar zum Alten Testament
HTR	*Harvard Theological Review*
HvTSt	*Hervormde teologiese studies*
IBC	Interpretation: A Bible Commentary for Teaching and Preaching
IBHS	*An Introduction to Biblical Hebrew Syntax*. B. K. Waltke and M. O'Connor. Winona Lake, IN: Eisenbrauns, 1990
IBS	*Irish Biblical Studies*
ICC	International Critical Commentary
IDS	*In die Skriflig*
Int	*Interpretation*
ITC	International Theological Commentary
JANESCU	*Journal of the Ancient Near Eastern Society of Columbia University*
JAOS	*Journal of the American Oriental Society*
JBL	*Journal of Biblical Literature*
JCS	*Journal of Cuneiform Studies*
JHebS	*Journal of Hebrew Scriptures*
JM	Joüon, P. *A Grammar of Biblical Hebrew*. Translated and revised by T. Muraoka. 2 vols. Rome: Pontifical Biblical Institute, 1991
JNSL	*Journal of Northwest Semitic Languages*
JR	*Journal of Religion*
JSOT	*Journal for the Study of the Old Testament*
JSOTSup	Journal for the Study of the Old Testament Supplement
LamR	Lamentations Rabbah, as translated in H. Freedman and M. Simon, eds., "Lamentations Rabbah," in *Midrash Rabbah*, vol. 4. (London: Soncino, 1977)
LHBOTS	Library of the Hebrew Bible/Old Testament Studies
LXX	*Septuaginta: Id est Vestus Testamentum graece iuxta LXX interpretes*. Edited by A. Rahlfs and R. Hanhart. Rev. ed. Stuttgart: Deutsche Bibelgesellschaft, 2006
MC	Mesopotamian Civilizations
MG	Mikraot Gedolot (the "Rabbinic Bible"), as published in A. J. Rosenberg, *The Books of Lamentations, Ecclesiastes*, vol. 2 of *The Five Megilloth* (New York: Judaica, 1992)
MT	Masoretic Text; MT^A refers to the Aleppo Codex, MT^L to the Leningrad Codex
NAC	New American Commentary
NCB	New Century Bible
NIB	The New Interpreter's Bible. Edited by L. E. Keck. 12 vols. Nashville: Abingdon, 1994–2004
NIBCOT	New International Biblical Commentary on the Old Testament

Or	*Orientalia* (NS)
OTE	*Old Testament Essays*
OTL	Old Testament Library
OTS	Old Testament Studies
PG	Patrologia Graeca [= Patrologiae Cursus Completus: Series Graeca]. Edited by J.-P. Migne. 162 vols. Paris, 1857–1886
PL	Patrologia Latina [= Patrologiae Cursus Completus: Series Latina]. Edited by J.-P. Migne. 217 vols. Paris, 1844–1864
4QLam	Manuscript fragments of Lamentations from Qumran Cave 4; see F. M. Cross, "4QLam," in E. C. Ulrich et al., *Qumran Cave 4.XI: Psalms to Chronicles*, DJD 16 (Oxford: Clarendon, 2000), 229–37
5QLam	Manuscript fragment of Lamentations from Qumran Cave 5; see J. T. Milik, "Lamentations," in *Les "Petites Grottes" de Qumrân: Exploration de la Falaise: Les grottes 2Q, 3Q, 5Q, 6Q, 7Q à 10Q, le rouleau de cuivre*, ed. M. Baillet, J. T. Milik, and R. de Vaux, DJD 3 (Oxford: Clarendon, 1962), 174–78
RB	*Revue biblique*
ResQ	*Restoration Quarterly*
RevExp	*Review and Expositor*
RTR	*Reformed Theological Review*
SBLDS	Society of Biblical Literature Dissertation Series
SBLStBL	Society of Biblical Literature Studies in Biblical Literature
SBT	Studies in Biblical Theology
SemeiaSt	Semeia Studies
SJOT	*Scandinavian Journal of the Old Testament*
SSN	Studia Semitica Neerlandica
Sym	Symmachus's Greek translation, as documented in F. Field, *Origenis Hexaplorum quae supersunt*, 2 vols. (Oxford: Clarendon, 1867)
SymS	Symposium Series
Syr	The Syriac translation of the Old Testament, as printed in D. M. Walter, G. Greenberg, G. A. Kiraz, and J. Bali, eds., *The Syriac Peshiṭta Bible with English Translation: Lamentations, Prayer of Jeremiah, Epistle of Jeremiah and Epistles of Baruch* (Piscataway, NJ: Gorgias, 2013)
TDOT	*Theological Dictionary of the Old Testament*. Volumes 1–8 edited by G. J. Botterweck and H. Ringgren. Volumes 9–15 and volume 17 edited by G. J. Botterweck, Helmer Ringgren, and Heinz-Josef Fabry. Volume 16 edited by Holger Gzella. Translated by J. T. Willis et al. 17 vols. Grand Rapids: Eerdmans, 1974–2021

Tg	Targum, as printed in A. Sperber, *The Hagiographa*, vol. 4a of *The Bible in Aramaic* (Leiden: Brill, 1968)
Theod	Theodotion's Greek translation, as documented in F. Field, *Origenis Hexaplorum quae supersunt*, 2 vols. (Oxford: Clarendon, 1867)
TOTC	Tyndale Old Testament Commentaries
TTH	*A Treatise on the Use of the Tenses in Hebrew*. By S. R. Driver. 3rd ed. Oxford: Clarendon, 1892
TThSt	Trierer theologische Studien
TynB	*Tyndale Bulletin*
Vg	Vulgate Latin translation, as printed in R. Weber, ed., *Biblia Sacra Iuxta Vulgatam Versionem* (Stuttgart: Deutsche Bibelgesellschaft, 1969)
VT	*Vetus Testamentum*
WBC	Word Biblical Commentary
YNER	Yale Near Eastern Researches
ZAW	*Zeitschrift für die alttestamentliche Wissenschaft*

Bibliography

Albrektson, B. *Studies in the Text and Theology of the Book of Lamentations with a Critical Edition of the Peshitta Text.* Studia Theologica Lundensia 21. Lund: CWK Gleerup, 1963.

Alexander, P. S. *The Targum of Lamentations: Translated, with a Critical Introduction, Apparatus, and Notes.* ArBib 17B. Collegeville, MN: Liturgical, 2007.

Allegro, J. M., with A. A. Anderson. *Qumrân Cave 4.I (4Q158–4Q186).* DJD 5. Oxford: Clarendon, 1968.

Allen, L. C. *A Liturgy of Grief: A Pastoral Commentary on Lamentations.* Grand Rapids: Baker, 2011.

Anderson, D. "Medieval Jewish Exegesis of the Book of Lamentations." PhD diss., University of St. Andrews, 2004.

Bailey, W. A. "Lamentations." Pages 19–133 in *Lamentations, Song of Songs.* By W. A. Bailey and C. Bucher. Believers Church Bible Commentary. Harrisonburg, VA: Herald, 2015.

Baillet, M., J. T. Milik, and R. de Vaux. *Les "Petites Grottes" de Qumrân: Exploration de la Falaise: Les grottes 2Q, 3Q, 5Q, 6Q, 7Q à 10Q, le rouleau de cuivre.* DJD 3. Oxford: Clarendon, 1962.

Bergant, D. *Lamentations.* AOTC. Nashville: Abingdon, 2003.

Berges, U. *Klagelieder.* HThKAT. Freiburg: Herder, 2002.

Berlin, A. *Lamentations: A Commentary.* OTL. Louisville: Westminster John Knox, 2002.

Berrigan, D. *Lamentations: From New York to Kabul and Beyond.* Lanham, MD: Sheed and Ward, 2002.

Bier, M. J. *"Perhaps There Is Hope": Reading Lamentations as a Polyphony of Pain, Penitence, and Protest.* LHBOTS 603. London: T&T Clark, 2015.

Blayney, B. *Jeremiah, and Lamentations: A New Translation with Notes Critical, Philological, and Explanatory.* 2nd ed. Edinburgh: Oliphant, 1810.

Boase, E. *The Fulfilment of Doom? The Dialogic Interaction between the Book of Lamentations and the Pre-exilic/Early Exilic Prophetic Literature.* LHBOTS 437. London: T&T Clark, 2006.

Boda, M. J., C. J. Dempsey, and L. S. Flesher, eds. *Daughter Zion: Her Portrait, Her Response.* AIL 13. Atlanta: Society of Biblical Literature, 2012.

Bracke, J. M. *Jeremiah 32–52 and Lamentations.* Westminster Bible Companion. Louisville: Westminster John Knox, 2000.

Brady, C. M. M. *The Rabbinic Targum of Lamentations: Vindicating God.* Studies in the Aramaic Interpretation of Scripture 3. Leiden: Brill 2003.

Broughton, H. *The Lamentations of Ieremy.* Amsterdam [?]: 1608.

Brunet, G. *Les Lamentations contre Jérémie: Réinterpretation des quatre premières Lamentations.* BEHER 75. Paris: Presses Universitaires de France, 1968.

Bugenhagen, J. "Threni Ieremiae." Pages 545–65 in *In Ieremiam Prophetam Commentarium.* Wittenberg: Seitz, 1546.

Calvin, J. *Commentary on Jeremiah and Lamentations.* Translated by J. Owen. 5 vols. Repr., Grand Rapids: Christian Classics Ethereal Library.

Clines, D. J. A. "Lamentations." Pages 617–22 in *Eerdmans Commentary on the Bible.* Edited by J. D. G. Dunn and J. W. Rogerson. Grand Rapids: Eerdmans, 2003.

Cox, H., and S. Paulsell. *Lamentations and the Song of Songs.* Belief: A Theological Commentary on the Bible. Louisville: Westminster John Knox, 2012.

Davidson, R. *Jeremiah and Lamentations.* Vol. 2. The Daily Study Bible. Edinburgh: Saint Andrew, 1985.

Dearman, J. A. *Jeremiah and Lamentations.* NIV Application Commentary. Grand Rapids: Zondervan, 2002.

Dobbs-Allsopp, F. W. *Lamentations.* Interpretation: A Bible Commentary for Teaching and Preaching. Louisville: Westminster John Knox, 2001.

Ellison, H. L. "Lamentations." Pages 693–733 in *The Expositor's Bible Commentary.* Edited F. E. Gaebelein. Vol. 6. Grand Rapids: Zondervan, 1986.

Fuerst, W. J. *The Books of Ruth, Esther, Ecclesiastes, The Song of Songs, Lamentations.* Cambridge Bible Commentaries on the Old Testament. Cambridge: Cambridge University Press, 1975.

Gerstenberger, E. S. *Psalms, Part 2, and Lamentations.* FOTL 15. Grand Rapids: Eerdmans, 2001.

Gladson, J. A. *The Five Exotic Scrolls of the Hebrew Bible: The Prominence, Literary Structure, and Liturgical Significance of the Megilloth.* Lewiston, NY: Edwin Mellen, 2009.

Gordis, R. *The Song of Songs and Lamentations: A Study, Modern Translation and Commentary.* Texts and Studies of the Jewish Theological Seminary of America. New York: Ktav, 1974.

Gottlieb, H. *A Study on the Text of Lamentations.* Acta Jutlandica 48. Århus: Det laerde Selskab, Århus Universitet, 1978.

Gottwald, N. K. *Studies in the Book of Lamentations.* SBT 14. London: SCM, 1954.

Guest, D. "Lamentations." Pages 394–411 in *The Queer Bible Commentary*. Edited by D. Guest, R. Gross, and M. West. London: SCM, 2006.

Harrison, R. K. *Jeremiah and Lamentations: An Introduction and Commentary*. TOTC 21. London: Tyndale, 1973.

Hays, C. B. *Hidden Riches: A Sourcebook for the Comparative Study of the Hebrew Bible and Ancient Near East*. Louisville: Westminster John Knox, 2014.

Hens-Piazza, G. *Lamentations*. Wisdom Commentary. Collegeville, MN: Liturgical, 2017.

Hillers, D. R. *Lamentations: A New Translation with Introduction and Commentary*. AB 7A. 2nd ed. Garden City, NY: Doubleday, 1992.

House, P. R. "Lamentations." Pages 278–473 in *Song of Songs, Lamentations*. By D. Garrett and P. R. House. WBC 23B. Nashville: Nelson, 2004.

Huey, F. B. *Jeremiah, Lamentations: An Exegetical and Theological Exposition of Holy Scripture*. NAC. Nashville: Broadman, 1993.

Hunter, J. *Faces of a Lamenting City: The Development and Coherence of the Book of Lamentations*. BEATAJ. Frankfurt: Lang, 1996.

Ibn Ezra [Abraham ibn Ezra]. "Commentary A" and "Commentary B." Pages 155–97 in "Medieval Jewish Exegesis of the Book of Lamentations." By D. Anderson. PhD diss., University of St Andrews, 2004.

Joyce, P. M. "Lamentations." Pages 528–33 in *The Oxford Bible Commentary*. Edited by J. Barton and J. Muddiman. Oxford: Oxford University Press, 2001.

Joyce, P. M., and D. Lipton. *Lamentations through the Centuries*. Blackwell Bible Commentaries. Chichester: Wiley, 2013.

Koenen, K. *Klagelieder (Threni)*. BKAT 20. Neukirchen: Neukirchener, 2015.

Kotzé, G. R. *The Qumran Manuscripts of Lamentations: A Text-Critical Study*. SSN 61. Leiden: Brill, 2013.

Kraus, H.-J. *Klagelieder*. 2nd ed. BKAT 20. Neukirchen: Neukirchener, 1960.

Lalleman-de Winkel, H. *Jeremiah and Lamentations: An Introduction and Commentary*. TOTC 21. Downers Grove, IL: InterVarsity, 2013.

Landy, F. "Lamentations." Pages 329–34 in *The Literary Guide to the Bible*. Edited by R. Alter and F. Kermode. London: Collins, 1987.

Lee, N. C. *The Singers of Lamentations: Cities Under Siege, from Ur to Jerusalem to Sarajevo*. BibInt 60. Leiden: Brill, 2002.

Lee, N. C., and C. Mandolfo, eds. *Lamentations in Ancient and Contemporary Cultural Contexts*. SymS 43. Atlanta: Society of Biblical Literature, 2008.

Linafelt, T. *Surviving Lamentations: Catastrophe, Lament and Protest in the Afterlife of a Biblical Book*. Chicago: University of Chicago, 2000.

Longman, T. *Jeremiah, Lamentations*. NIBCOT. Peabody, MA: Hendricksen, 2008.

Mandolfo, C. R. *Daughter Zion Talks Back to the Prophets: A Dialogic Theology of the Book of Lamentations*. SemeiaSt 58. Atlanta: Society of Biblical Literature, 2007.

———. "Lamentations." Pages 451–55 in *The New Interpreter's Bible One Volume Commentary*. Edited by B. R. Gaventa and D. Petersen. Nashville: Abingdon, 2010.

Mayer, J. *A Commentary Upon All the Prophets*. London: Millar and Cotes, 1652.

Melton, B. N., and H. A. Thomas, eds. *Reading Lamentations Intertextually*. London: T&T Clark, 2021.

Mintz, A. *Ḥurban: Responses to Catastrophe in Hebrew Literature*. New York: Columbia University, 1984.

Mitchell, M. L. "A Reading of the Imagery of Lamentations." PhD diss., McGill University, 2004.

Nguyen, K. L. *Chorus in the Dark: The Voices of the Book of Lamentations*. HBM 54. Sheffield: Sheffield Phoenix, 2013.

Nowell, E. *Song of Songs, Ruth, Lamentations, Ecclesiastes, Esther*. New Collegeville Bible Commentary: Old Testament 24. Collegeville, MN: Liturgical, 2013.

O'Connor, K. M. "Lamentations." Pages 278–82 in *Women's Bible Commentary*. Edited by C. A. Newsom, S. H. Ringe, and J. E. Lapsley. Rev. ed. London: SPCK, 2014.

———. "Lamentations." Pages 553–926 in *The New Interpreter's Bible*. Edited by L. E. Keck. Vol. 6. Nashville: Abingdon, 2001.

———. *Lamentations and the Tears of the World*. Catholicity in an Evolving Universe Series. Maryknoll, NY: Orbis, 2002.

Parry, R. A. *Lamentations*. The Two Horizons Old Testament Commentary. Grand Rapids: Eerdmans, 2010.

Parry, R. A., and H. A. Thomas, eds. *Great Is Thy Faithfulness? Reading Lamentations as Sacred Scripture*. Eugene, OR: Pickwick, 2011.

Paschasius Radbertus. *In Threnos sive Lamentationes Jeremiae Libri Quinque*. PL 120:1059–256.

Peake, A. S. *Jeremiah and Lamentations*. Vol. 2. Century Bible. London: Caxton, 1911 [?].

Provan, I. W. *Lamentations*. NCB. London: Marshall, 1991.

Re'emi, S. P. "Lamentations." Pages 73–148 in *Amos and Lamentations: God's People in Crisis*. By R. Martin-Achard and S. P. Re'emi. ITC. Edinburgh: Handsel, 1984.

Renkema, J. *Lamentations*. Historical Commentary on the Old Testament. Leuven: Peeters, 1998.

Rong, L. *Forgotten and Forsaken by God (Lam 5:19–20): The Community in Pain in Lamentations and Related Old Testament Texts*. Eugene, OR: Pickwick, 2013.

Rosenberg, A. J. *The Books of Lamentations, Ecclesiastes*. Vol. 2 of The Five Megilloth. New York: Judaica, 1992.

Salters, R. B. *Jonah and Lamentations*. Old Testament Guides. Sheffield: Sheffield Academic, 1994.

———. *Lamentations: A Critical and Exegetical Commentary*. ICC. London: T&T Clark, 2010.

Schäfer, R. "Lamentations." In *General Introduction and Megilloth*, ed. A. Schenker et al. *Biblia Hebraica Quinta* 18. Stuttgart: Deutsche Gesellschaft, 2004.

Simeon, C. "Lamentations." Pages 319–39 in *The Entire Works*. By C. Simeon. Vol. 9. London: Bohn, 1844.

Slavitt, D. R. *The Book of Lamentations: A Meditation and Translation*. Baltimore: Johns Hopkins University Press, 2001.

Streane, A. W. *Jeremiah and Lamentations*. Cambridge Bible for Schools and Colleges. Cambridge: Cambridge University Press, 1913.

Theodoret. *Thrēnoi*. PG 81:779–806.

Thomas, H. A. "Poetry and Theology in the Book of Lamentations: An Examination of Lamentations 1–3 Using the Aesthetic Analysis of Umberto Eco." PhD diss., University of Gloucestershire, 2007.

Toussaine, D. *The Lamentations and Holy Mourninges of the Prophet Ieremiah*. London: Bate, 1587 [?].

Trapp, J. *A Commentary or Exposition upon These Following Books of Holy Scripture: Proverbs of Solomon, Ecclesiastes, the Song of Songs, Isaiah, Jeremiah, Lamentations, Ezekiel and Daniel*. Kidderminster: Simmons, 1660.

Tyler, J. J., ed. *Jeremiah, Lamentations*. Reformation Commentary on Scripture. Downers Grove, IL: InterVarsity, 2018.

Vermigli, Peter Martyr. *Commentary on the Lamentations of the Prophet Jeremiah*. Kirksville, MO: Truman State University, 2002.

Villanueva, F. *Lamentations: A Pastoral and Contextual Commentary*. Carlisle: Langham, 2016.

Webb, B. G. *Five Festal Garments: Christian Reflections on the Song of Songs, Ruth, Lamentations, Ecclesiastes and Esther*. Nottingham: Apollos, 2000.

Wenthe, D. O., ed. *Jeremiah, Lamentations*. ACCS. Downers Grove, IL: InterVarsity, 2009.

Westermann, C. *Lamentations: Issues and Interpretation*. Edinburgh: T&T Clark, 1994.

Wright, C. J. H. *The Message of Lamentations*. The Bible Speaks Today: Old Testament. Nottingham: Inter-Varsity, 2015.

Ziegler, J., ed. *Ieremias, Baruch, Threni, Epistula Ieremiae*. Septuaginta: Vetus Testamentum Graecum 15. Göttingen: Vandehoeck, 1957.

Introduction

On the ninth day of the fourth month in the eleventh year of the reign of Zedekiah King of Judah, the wall of the city of Jerusalem was breached, and the city surrendered to the besieging Babylonian army (Jer 39:2; 52:6). In terms of Western dating, the year is usually taken to be 587 BC; the fourth month, the month of Av, overlaps with July and August. Each year Jewish communities thus commemorate the fall of Jerusalem on this day, which is also by tradition the day that saw the fall of Jerusalem in AD 69 and a sequence of other disasters to the Jewish people.[1] And on this day, Jewish communities chant the five poems that make up the Lamentations scroll. Lamentations is thus used in worship more than the other Megilloth (Song of Songs, Ruth, Ecclesiastes, and Esther—together they are "The Five Scrolls"). The poems are "recited with intense devotion"[2] in the evening of this day, intoned by a reader with the congregation following along quietly.[3]

In Jewish tradition, the title of Lamentations is *Eichah*, the first word in the scroll—the word for "how." But the Babylonian Talmud's list of the scrolls that make up the Scriptures, which comes in *b.* Baba Batra 14b–15a, refers to it as *Qinot* ("laments"), and the Greek translation and thus the Latin and English translations likewise call it Lamentations. The scroll comprises five poems grieving and protesting and praying over the 587 disaster.

1. D. R. Slavitt tells this story, closing with "after the ruin of the Temple, we could never again be surprised—not even by Auschwitz" (*The Book of Lamentations: A Meditation and Translation* [Baltimore: Johns Hopkins University, 2001], 3–58).

2. P. S. Alexander, "'Translation and Midrash Completely Fused Together'? The Form of the Targums to Canticles, Lamentations and Qohelet," *AS* 9 (2011): 98.

3. See further E. R. Stern, "Lamentations in Jewish Liturgy," in *Great Is Thy Faithfulness? Reading Lamentations as Sacred Scripture*, ed. R. A. Parry and H. A. Thomas (Eugene, OR: Pickwick, 2011), 88–91.

I. BACKGROUND

The background of Lamentations thus lies in the fall of Jerusalem in 587 BC, in the knowledge about Yahweh and his relationship with Israel that the authors bring to this event along with the questions it raises for Judahites, and in the practice of prayer that they bring to it.

"Lamentations is as historical as the Song of Songs is ahistorical; it marks, with untampered immediacy, the focal calamity of the Bible."[4] For a century and a half, up until 587, Judah had been under the distant oversight of the Mesopotamian empire-of-the-day—of Assyria for most of the period, of Babylon for the last decades. During these last decades, a more determined imperial assertiveness by Nebuchadnezzar, the Babylonian king, clashed with a greater inclination on Judah's part to affirm its independence, and in 597 and again in 587 this clash issued in a siege of Jerusalem, in the deposing and exile of a Judahite king (Jehoiachin, then Zedekiah), in a plundering of the temple, and in a forced migration of Jerusalemites to Babylon. The 587 siege brought the destruction of the city and the devastation of the temple.

Any such experience would be traumatic for the people involved. For the populace of Jerusalem and Judah, it brought an extra level of trauma because it clashed with what they took to be the implications of their knowledge about Yahweh and about his relationship with them. He had committed himself to Jerusalem, to its temple, and to the line of Davidic kings; he had now not maintained that commitment. The five poems also bring to the event another strand of knowledge about Yahweh and his relationship with Judah, one expressed in the Torah (especially Deuteronomy), in the preaching of Jeremiah in Jerusalem, and in the preaching of Ezekiel among the 597 migrants to Babylon. The other side of Yahweh's commitment to Israel was his expectation that Israel would be committed to him. In terms that Lamentations does not use,[5] there was supposed to be a covenant between Yahweh and Israel. An abandoning of Israel's commitment could lead to an abandoning of Yahweh's.

A further background to Lamentations is a practice of prayer expressed in the Psalms. This practice presupposes a freedom on Israel's part to grieve and protest before Yahweh about things that happen to it and to plead for a reversal and for Yahweh to act against its attackers—even if it has to grant that it had deserved what happened. Other ancient Near Eastern peoples made the same assumption about prayer. In particular, they too sometimes grieved

4. F. Landy, "Lamentations," in *The Literary Guide to the Bible*, ed. R. Alter and F. Kermode (London: Collins, 1987), 329.

5. As R. B. Salters notes in "Yahweh and His People in Lamentations," in *Covenant as Context: Essays in Honour of E. W. Nicholson*, ed. A. D. H. Mayes and R. B. Salters (Oxford: Oxford University Press, 2003), 347–48.

over disasters that came to a city; we have a number of examples of these city laments.[6] They may personify the city, grieve over its destruction caused by a god, talk of the god abandoning the city, portray a goddess weeping over the destruction of her sanctuary, curse its destroyers, promise that the god will return, envisage the city rebuilt, and give praise for that rebuilding.

> The destruction is presented as terrible and utter, affecting the city's inhabitants, buildings, infrastructures, and agricultural life. The city loses its wealth, honor, and fertility. All social institutions collapse: priests abandon their offices; shepherds burn their pens; men neglect their wives and sons. Vivid descriptions are devoted to horrifying sights of bloodbath, piles of corpses, cut-down limbs, and dead, helpless victims abandoned by their loved ones. The climax of the process of devastation is the destruction of the temple with its accessories, the cessation of the cultic practice, and the exile of the temple's divine inhabitants.
>
> On the theological level, the City Laments describe the devastation as the decision of the great gods, executed by two primary agents of destruction: the storm in the cosmic realm and the enemy in the human realm. As a consequence of the great gods' sentence, which is presented

6. See, e.g., the Lamentation over the Destruction of Sumer and Ur in C. B. Hays, *Hidden Riches: A Sourcebook for the Comparative Study of the Hebrew Bible and Ancient Near East* (Louisville: Westminster John Knox, 2014), 375–88; the Lamentation over the Destruction of Ur, trans. S. N. Kramer, in *ANET*, 455–63. See further Kramer's *Lamentation over the Destruction of Ur*, AS 12 (Chicago: University of Chicago, 1946); and, more recently, C. J. Gadd, "The Second Lamentation for Ur," in *Hebrew and Semitic Studies: Essays Presented to G. R. Driver*, ed. D. W. Thomas and W. D. McHardy (Oxford: Clarendon, 1963), 59–71; also R. Kutscher, *Oh Angry Sea = (a-ab-ba hu-luh-ha): The History of a Sumerian Congregational Lament*, YNER 6 (New Haven: Yale, 1975); M. W. Green, "The Eridu Lament," *JCS* 30 (1978): 127–67; M. W. Green, "The Uruk Lament," *JAOS* 104 (1984): 253–79; M. E. Cohen, *The Canonical Lamentations of Ancient Mesopotamia*, 2 vols. (Potomac, MD: Capital, 1988); P. Michalowski, *The Lamentation over the Destruction of Sumer and Ur*, MC 1 (Winona Lake, IN: Eisenbrauns, 1989); S. Tinney, *The Nippur Lament: Royal Rhetoric and Divine Legitimation in the Reign of Isme-Dagon of Isin (1953–1935 BC)* (Philadelphia: University of Pennsylvania Museum, 1996); "Lamentation over the Destruction of Sumer and Ur (1.166)," trans. J. Klein, *COS* 1:535–39; N. Samet, *The Lamentation over the Destruction of Ur*, MC 18 (Winona Lake, IN: Eisenbrauns, 2014); P. Attinger, "Une nouvelle édition de la Lamentation sur Ur," *Or* 84 (2015): 41–74 (a review of Samet's work). More explicitly in connection with Lamentations, see W. C. Gwaltney, "The Biblical Book of Lamentations in the Context of Near Eastern Lament Literature," in *Scripture in Context II: More Essays on the Comparative Method*, ed. W. W. Hallo, J. C. Moyer, and L. G. Perdue (Winona Lake, IN: Eisenbrauns, 1983), 191–212; C. Westermann, *Lamentations: Issues and Interpretation* (Edinburgh: Clark, 1994), 1–23; F. W. Dobbs-Allsopp, *Weep, O Daughter of Zion: A Study of the City-Lament Genre in the Hebrew Bible*, BibOr 44 (Rome: Pontificio Istituto Biblico, 1993); F. W. Dobbs-Allsopp, "Darwinism, Genre Theory, and City Laments," *JAOS* 120 (2000): 625–30; Hays, *Hidden Riches*, 375–96.

> as irrevocable, the patron deities are forced to abandon the city prior to the destruction. This abandonment is often accompanied by the lamenting of the city's patron god and/or goddess about the bitter fate of his or her city and shrine. . . .
>
> An additional important feature is an optimistic epilogue, referring to the restoration of the temple and the return of the deity to his holy abode. In most of the City Laments, the epilogue also includes a description of a ritual performed in the restored shrine, involving the recitation of a prayer and an offering of a lament.[7]

The poems in Lamentations both compare and contrast with these city laments. The laments are a millennium older than Lamentations and come from hundreds of miles away, and we cannot know how the authors of Lamentations might have been acquainted with their way of praying.[8] But the comparison still draws attention to aspects of Lamentations. One could almost see in Lamentations "an allusion to, or even a parody of, the very kind of sanctuary-razing ceremonies for which the Mesopotamian city laments and *balag*s were originally composed. . . . The parody brings into relief the distinction between Lamentations and the classic city laments from Mesopotamia. The latter eventually look forward to renewal and rebirth."[9] In contrast, Lamentations is more resolutely focused on the facts of what has happened. It does not presuppose the existence of a plurality of deities among whom responsibility for what has happened can be shared and who can take different attitudes to it.

II. UNITY OF COMPOSITION

Readers of the English Bible who turn over the page from Jer 52 to Lam 1 find themselves reading about the same events. The subject is still the fall of Jerusalem in 587, and Lam 1 offers another Judahite account of the event, the product of another author's thinking that might facilitate the Judahite community's own reflection. But Jer 52 (like the rest of the Jeremianic nar-

7. Samet, *Lamentation over the Destruction of Ur*, 3, 4.

8. See, e.g., Dobbs-Allsopp, *Weep, O Daughter of Zion*; Hays, *Hidden Riches*, 392–95.

9. F. W. Dobbs-Allsopp, "R(az/ais)ing Zion in Lamentations 2," in *David and Zion: Biblical Studies in Honor of J. J. M. Roberts*, ed. B. F. Batto and K. L. Roberts (Winona Lake, IN: Eisenbrauns, 2004), 46, 47. The *balags* were a slightly later type of lament, still a millennium older than Lamentations. E. L. Greenstein suggests that the background of Lamentations is similarly the rebuilding of the temple ("The Book of Lamentations: Response to Destruction or Ritual Rebuilding?," in *Religious Responses to Political Crises in Jewish and Christian Tradition*, ed. H. G. Reventlow and Y. Hoffman, LHBOTS 444 [London: T&T Clark, 2008], 52–71).

rative about the fall of Jerusalem) is prose, while Lamentations is poetry. Jer 52 incorporates hard facts, names, and dates, and in that way both offers interpretation and stimulates the imagination. Lamentations incorporates imagery and accounts of people's feelings. It offers interpretation and stimulates the imagination in another way. Notwithstanding Lamentations' historical reference, one commentator recalls diving into the poems looking for historical data and finding that he "came up almost completely empty."[10]

A. THE UNITY AND INTERRELATIONSHIP OF THE POEMS

Lamentations' unity of composition finds expression in the way each of the five poems responds to the fall of Jerusalem and each comprises twenty-two short stanzas; the figure corresponds to the number of letters in the Hebrew alphabet. Together, the poems manifest a tight formal unity unparalleled by any other work in the Scriptures. Their alphabetical form makes for a further comparison with ancient Near Eastern works.[11] One may make various guesses as to the aim or result of this arrangement.[12] It gives the poet a structure to work with. It makes the poem easier to remember. It covers its subject from A to Z. It thus allows for comprehensive expression of grief but suggests a containment that holds this expression within bounds.[13] We may think it "somewhat startling to discover that a book that portrays such radical disorientation should be one of the most ordered works in the Old Testament,"[14] but it makes sense in the context of a community where there are both the "spatial void" and the "ideological void" to which Lamentations attests.[15] The poems' form begins to enable people to find some order.[16] It creates an alternative "linguistic space" where survival might be possible

10. D. R. Hillers, "History and Poetry in Lamentations," *CurTM* 10 (1983): 155.

11. See J. Brug, "Biblical Acrostics and Their Relationship to Other Ancient Near Eastern Acrostics," in *The Bible in the Light of Cuneiform Literature: Scripture in Context III*, ed. W. W. Hallo, B. W. Jones, and G. L. Mattingly (Lewiston, NY: Edwin Mellen, 1990), 283–304.

12. See, e.g., R. B. Salters, "Acrostics and Lamentations," in *On Stone and Scroll: Essays in Honour of Graham Ivor Davies*, ed. J. K. Aitken, K. J. Dell, and B. A. Mastin, BZAW 420 (Berlin: de Gruyter, 2011), 425–40.

13. P. J. Owens, "Personification and Suffering in Lamentations 3," *Austin Seminary Bulletin: Faculty Edition* 105 (1990): 77.

14. B. G. Webb, *Five Festal Garments: Christian Reflections on the Song of Songs, Ruth, Lamentations, Ecclesiastes and Esther* (Nottingham: Apollos, 2000), 60.

15. C. M. Maier, "Lost Space and Revived Memory: From Jerusalem in 586 B.C.E. to New Orleans in 2009," in *Interpreting Exile: Displacement and Deportation in Biblical and Modern Contexts*, ed. B. E. Kelle, F. R. Ames, and J. L. Wright, AIL 10 (Atlanta: Society of Biblical Literature, 2011), 194.

16. G. C. Anderson, "Lamentations 2:1–13," *Int* 69 (2015): 78–80.

when geographical space is impossibly distressing.[17] Given the "tension" between "the emotional expressions of grief and the rigid shape in which they are embedded," the poems interact with the reader on both an emotional and a rational level; they are both emotional and well thought out.[18]

Within this framework of twenty-two units, the first four poems are alphabetical in a more precise sense. In Lam 1 and 2, every fourth line begins with a new letter of the alphabet;[19] in Lam 3, in addition, each line within each group of three begins with the same letter (this poem is consequently divided into sixty-six verses); in Lam 4, every third line begins with a new letter. (In Lam 5, there is no sequencing of letters, simply the structure of twenty-two lines.)[20] The first four poems are thus often described as acrostics. MT treats each three-line or two-line unit in Lam 1–4 as a semi-separate entity (marked by a *setumah*, a section marker), and in the commentary I do the same. Each of the poems is complete in itself, but one poem may sometimes give indications of picking up phrases from another poem (see, e.g., 2:4, 11). What the sequence of alphabetical poems suggests is "not completeness but repetition; with the acrostics' structure, the community's suffering repeats over and over, from beginning to end, from *aleph* to *tav*, as psychological trauma repeats into the lives of survivors, making the trauma continually present," never finding completion or closure.[21] Yet maybe the poems could function to bring together a fragmented community around a shared way of looking at their experience.[22]

The poems mix *qatal* and *yiqtol* verbs (and participles and noun clauses); I follow LXX and Vg in mostly translating *qatal* verbs with English aorists, taking them to refer to the event of destruction rather than the ongoing situation.[23] It is possible to guess at differences between how near each poem is to the fall of Jerusalem. For instance, Lam 2 and Lam 4 convey a sense of white-hot closeness to the event itself, Lam 1 is more wistful, Lam 3 incorporates more

17. U. Bail, "Wehe, kein Ort, nirgends . . . : Überlegungen zum Sprachraum der Klagelieder Jeremias," in *Journal of the European Society of Women in Theological Research* 7 (1999): 81–90.

18. E. Assis, "The Alphabetic Acrostic in Lamentations," *CBQ* 69 (2007): 716, 717, 719.

19. To be more precise, 1:7 and 2:19 each have four lines, so there are sixty-seven lines in each poem, and Lam 3 alone has exactly twenty-two times three (H. A. Thomas, "Poetry and Theology in the Book of Lamentations: An Examination of Lamentations 1–3 Using the Aesthetic Analysis of Umberto Eco" [PhD diss., University of Gloucestershire, 2007], 209).

20. W. H. Shea argues that this arrangement mirrors that of the 3-2 rhythm in a line ("The *qinah* Structure of the Book of Lamentations," *Biblica* 60 [1979]: 103–7).

21. D. Janzen, *Trauma and the Failure of History: Kings, Lamentations, and the Destruction of Jerusalem*, SemeiaSt 94 (Atlanta: Society of Biblical Literature, 2019), 93.

22. E. Boase, "Fragmented Voices," in *Bible through the Lens of Trauma*, ed. E. Boase and C. G. Frechette, SemeiaSt 38 (Atlanta: Society of Biblical Literature, 2016), 49.

23. But B. D. Giffone suggests that *qatal* may be more common in alphabetic poems because it provides more scope for meeting the requirements of the alphabetic structure ("A 'Perfect' Poem: The Use of the Qatal Verbal Form in the Biblical Acrostics," *HS* 51 [2010]: 49–72).

measured reflection, and Lam 5 raises questions about whether the community's suffering is to go on forever. But the nature of poetic composition means it is hazardous to infer an actual chronology from these differences.[24]

B. POETIC FORM IN THE POEMS

Lamentations has a poetic profile that runs through all five chapters, and it also shares many features with other poetic books such as Job, Psalms, and Proverbs. In each of those three scrolls, the opening words provide some orientation to the whole; Lam 1:1–2 similarly forms a telling beginning to this scroll, whether or not it was composed first. Lam 1:1–4 constitutes a textbook embodiment of many features of First Testament poetry.

aleph 1How the city sat down alone,
 one that was great with a people.
She became like a widow,
 one that was great among the nations.
Princess among the provinces,
 she came into slavery.
bet 2She cries, cries in the night,
 so her tears are on her cheek.
For her, there is no one comforting
 from all her friends.
As all her neighbors broke faith with her,
 to her they became enemies.
gimel 3Judah went into exile away from humbling,
 away from greatness of servitude.
Though she sat down among the nations,
 she did not find rest.
All her pursuers, they caught up with her
 among the narrows.
dalet 4The paths to Zion are mourning
 for lack of people coming to an assembly.
All her gateways are desolate,
 her priests are crying out.
Her girls are sorrowful,
 and she herself, it's hard for her.

24. Cf. D. R. Hillers, *Lamentations: A New Translation with Introduction and Commentary*, 2nd ed., AB 7A (Garden City, NY: Doubleday, 1992), 10; J. Middlemas, *The Troubles of Templeless Judah*, Oxford Theological Monographs (Oxford: Oxford University Press, 2005), 182.

A key formal feature of poetry in the Hebrew Bible is to work in sentences that average between four and eight words and divide into two parts, which I call cola. A sentence or line is then a bicolon, with two, three, or four words in each half.[25] In English translation, the lines have more words because Hebrew compounds words more than English does. In this commentary, I lay out the lines in light of their comprising two parts, indenting the second colon. Given that an individual word in Hebrew has one stressed syllable (whereas in English a word such as "individual" has two stressed syllables), the number of individual words in a line is a key factor in establishing the line's rhythm: generally, the number of the words is the number of the stresses. But another factor nuances the way the rhythm works. Hebrew can hyphenate words, like English, with the result for the rhythm that two words count as one. This convention increases the number of Hebrew words in a line while not increasing the number of stresses. So *all her gateways* is hyphenated in Hebrew, as is *it's hard for her*; in each case three or four English words represent two Hebrew words but one stress. The pattern of stresses (the rhythm) in 1:4, for instance, is thus 3-3, 2-2, 2-2—though in terms of the number of words it is 3-3, 3-2, 2-3.

Lamentations' very first verse illustrates how more solemn poetry like that in these poems can work with slightly shorter lines than most First Testament poetry, with the second colon commonly having just two words or two stresses. In this case, v. 1 is 4-2, 2-2, 2-2. The opening line thus also illustrates how the shortness in the lines commonly results from the second colon being shorter than the first; it manifests "falling rhythm" as opposed to "rising rhythm" or "balanced rhythm."[26] It thus brings the reader up short.

Broadly, Lamentations' poetry (like that of Psalms, Proverbs, and Job) is more regular than that of the Prophets. Whereas prophets focus less on rhythmic considerations and may be more improvisational and less deliberate, in Lamentations, Psalms, Proverbs, and Job, liturgical, pedagogical, and poetic/literary considerations generate greater evenness. But I assume that any of this poetic material would be chanted, and such performance can cope with variety in the number of words in a line. One simply has to keep the rhythm going, as is the case with rap. In Lam 1 as a whole, a third of the

25. These two uncontroversial-appearing sentences actually conceal great complexities: see F. W. Dobbs-Allsopp, *On Biblical Poetry* (New York: Oxford University Press, 2015), 14–94.

26. See D. N. Freedman and J. C. Geoghegan, "Quantitative Measurement in Biblical Hebrew Poetry," in *Ki Baruch Hu: Ancient Near Eastern, Biblical, and Judaic Studies in Honor of Baruch A. Levine*, ed. R. Chazan, W. W. Hallo, and L. H. Schiffman (Winona Lake, IN: Eisenbrauns, 1999), 229–49; they argue that the poetry works on the basis of the number of syllables in a line rather than the number of stresses. See earlier D. N. Freedman and E. A. von Fange, "Metrics in Hebrew Poetry," *CTQ* 60 (1996): 279–305.

sixty-six lines are 3-2 and a third are 2-2. In Lam 2, half of the sixty-six lines are 3-2 and a quarter are 2-2. In Lam 3, about thirty of the sixty-six lines are 3-2 and about thirty divide fairly equally between 4-2, 3-3, and 2-2. In Lam 4, more than half the forty-four lines are 3-2 or 2-2. In Lam 5, in contrast, most of the twenty-two lines are 3-3. The qualifier "about" reflects how there is sometimes room for differences of opinion over the division between cola; further, throughout this discussion I am working with the way the Masoretes have punctuated the poetry (see "The Hebrew Text," p. 24).

Given the relative regularity of the rhythm, exceptionally short or exceptionally long cola or lines draw attention to themselves. The fourth colon in Lam 1:2, for instance, has only one stress, as does the second colon in 1:6. The poems include one tricolon, 4:15, and two four-line verses, 1:7 and 2:19.

C. THE RELATIONSHIP BETWEEN THE COLA

The opening verses of Lamentations illustrate another aspect of the way the poetry works: through the relationships between the two cola in a line. I refer to the verses and cola as 1a, 1b, 1c, 1d, and so on.

- In v. 1, each second colon contrasts with the preceding colon.
- In vv. 2a–b, 3a–b, 4c–f, the first colon makes a statement that the second colon re-expresses, sometimes in an intensified form; this complementing of cola is traditionally mislabeled "parallelism."
- In v. 4a–b, the first colon raises a question (Why are the people mourning?) that the second colon answers.
- In vv. 2c–d, 3c–f, the second colon simply completes the first. At one level, the division between cola is thus purely formal. But whereas parallelism slows the poetry down and facilitates reflection, this relationship between the cola drives the poetry forward.[27]

> In Lamentations the dominant texture of unbalanced lines effects a hypnotic limping beat (peculiarly appropriate for a dirge-like composition), while their propensity for enjambment effects a distinct feeling of forward movement as the syntax of the sentence carries over from one line to the next. Of course this tug of forward movement is almost immediately checked by the major pause at the end of the predominantly closed couplets. What results, then, are bursts of onward thrust alternating with moments of stasis. This stuttering movement complements the limping

27. F. W. Dobbs-Allsopp, "The Enjambing Line in Lamentations," *ZAW* 113 (2001): 371–73.

> rhythm established by the unbalanced lines, and together both counterpoint the regularity and evenness constructed by the stanzaic march of the acrostic and the sequence of closed couplets.[28]

(Note that in this quotation, "lines" are what I describe as "cola," and "enjambment" refers to relationships between cola as well as between bicola.)

Whole lines can also complement each other. In v. 1, all three are parallel. Most groups of three lines in Lam 1–3 and of two lines in Lam 4 are self-contained units that hold together; one could say that each stanza is a hexacolon or quadracolon. It is therefore appropriate to look for the links between lines within a stanza. On the other hand, one does not expect to find such links between stanzas, though they are sometimes there.

While the First Testament's poetry has rhythm, so does its prose, but the characteristic shortness of the sentences in poetry makes for a formal distinction between poetry and prose.[29] This distinction links with differences in grammar and syntax. Jer 52 includes many sentences linked by *waw*-consecutive verbs (a phenomenon that actually deconstructs the English notion of a sentence). In Lamentations, one self-contained sentence (one line) commonly follows another without such a link. Lam 1 has hardly any *waw*-consecutives; the first comes in v. 5, where alphabetical considerations require the verse to begin with *waw*. While there are lines in Lam 1 that are not self-contained and involve enjambment (vv. 7, 10, 11, 15, 16, 18, 22), most lines in the chapter comprise complete sentences; the next line then makes a new beginning. Likewise, when the two cola in a line are separate clauses, the second commonly follows the first asyndetically (and thus I translate them asyndetically, linking them simply with a comma or dash; e.g., 1:4c–d).

While the default word order in Lam 1–4 (though not Lam 5) corresponds to the regular Hebrew rule by placing the verb before the subject and object, the poetry can place the subject or object first and thus emphasize it. Further, sometimes asyndeton combines with a word order that places the object or subject before the verb, and I take that combination as commonly a sign that the clause with the non-standard word order is subordinate to the other clause (e.g., 1:2, 3). The question of word order in noun clauses is more complicated, and an adjectival predicate can precede its subject (thus 3:23 declares, "Your faithfulness is great," not, "Great is your faithfulness").[30]

28. Dobbs-Allsopp, *On Biblical Poetry*, 204.

29. D. R. Vance, *The Question of Meter in Biblical Hebrew Poetry* (Lewiston, NY: Edwin Mellen, 2000), 497.

30. See D. R. Hillers, "Observations on Syntax and Meter in Lamentations," in *A Light unto My Path: Old Testament Studies in Honour of Jacob M. Myers*, ed. H. N. Bream, R. D. Heim, and C. A. Moore (Philadelphia: Temple University Press, 1974), 266–67.

D. REPETITION, TERSENESS, IMAGERY, POINT OF VIEW, GENRE

The lines comprising 1:1–4 illustrate further formal features of Lamentations' poetry.

- It uses repetition, but repetition commonly combines with variation.[31] The first verse repeats a unique form of a word for *great*, used in two ways (with a construct and then a preposition). The second verse repeats the word for *cries* (infinitive then *yiqtol*).
- Yet the poetry is simultaneously succinct and terse; it is inclined to omit a number of the little words that aid communication. These include the object marker (which does come in, e.g., 1:9, 19; 2:1, 2), the relative particle (which does come in 1:7, 12, though the exceptions prove the rule), prepositions (e.g., 1:5e; contrast 1:18f), and the article (1:6, 7). It is a judgment call where translations need to recognize an unmarked relative clause, assume a preposition, or include "the" in English.
- The terseness includes the use of ellipsis, which can produce jerkiness: the poem may omit some part of speech or make a jump from one colon to the next and expect listeners to work out what the line means (e.g., 1:12; 2:18; 3:9). The way a bicolon may assume that a part of speech in one colon also applies in the other (e.g., 1:3a–b) is a recurrent example of this expectation.
- In addition, the poems make much use of hyperbole. Lam 1 uses the word *all* sixteen times.

Alongside the more formal features of the poems in Lamentations is their extensive use of imagery, which more profoundly differentiates poetry from prose. It makes these poems unlike the prayers in Ezra, Nehemiah, and Daniel but like the protest psalms in the Psalter. Poetry thus not only encourages structured thinking by means of the discipline required by poetic form but also facilitates depth of expression. In 1:1, each line involves a metaphor or simile. While the use of imagery is self-evident there, the poems commonly make statements that in other contexts could be literal but in this context are figurative. The man's description of his affliction in 3:1–24 is one example. The community's description of its experience in 5:2–18 is another. In poetry, there may be no one-to-one literal correspondence between the statements and the nature of events. We cannot reify the images in the poems. They function like metaphors even when they are not technically metaphors. This

31. See D. Marcus, "Non-recurring Doublets in Lamentations," *HAR* 10 (1986): 177–95.

aspect of Lamentations is one reason why the interpreter looking for historical data in the poems has a hard time finding them.

The poems work from more than one point of view. In Lam 1, there is the point of view of a witness who laments what has happened to the city but mostly speaks as if it happened to someone else and speaks somewhat objectively, and there is the point of view of the suffering city itself. The poem's own viewpoint embraces both. The two points of view make it possible to grieve over events from two angles—a more existential one and a more reflective one. Similar dynamics apply to each of the poems as they move between an implicit or explicit perspective of I, we, you, he/she, and they.

In reading the Psalms, an analysis of the genres that distinguishes between praise psalms, protest psalms, and testimony/thanksgiving psalms is key. Features of such psalms lie behind the poems in Lamentations, especially in Lam 5. Elsewhere the poems manifest features that characterize mourning songs that lament someone's death, and (as we have noted) laments at the destruction of a city. But as wholes, with the possible exception of Lam 5, the poems as such do not belong to such categories.[32] They are simply (alphabetical) poems. They do not belong to another genre.

III. AUTHORSHIP AND DATE

The five poems are anonymous. The similarities and differences between them may or may not indicate that they come from different poets.[33] Each might have issued from the individual reflection of a poet on his or her own or from a group of scribes or priests reflecting together. If they come from different poets, they have become part of a single collection in which they appear in a sequence that may be independent of any chronological implications; there is some indication of a concentric arrangement of the five poems.[34]

32. R. Albertz, *Israel in Exile: The History and Literature of the Sixth Century B.C.E.*, SBLStBL 3 (Atlanta: Society of Biblical Literature, 2003), 154; cf. C. R. Mandolfo's comments on genre in connection with Lamentations in *Daughter Zion Talks Back to the Prophets: A Dialogic Theology of the Book of Lamentations*, SemeiaSt 56 (Atlanta: Society of Biblical Literature, 2007), 55–77. Westermann's interpretation of the poems (*Lamentations*, 86–220) puts considerable emphasis on the way they combine elements from different genres, but the unity of the actual poems with their alphabetic form makes his approach implausible; the same applies to C. Houk's conclusion concerning "Multiple Poets in Lamentations," *JSOT* 30 (2005): 111–25.

33. On different approaches to this question, see R. B. Salters, "Searching for Pattern in Lamentations," *OTE* 11 (1998): 93–104; R. B. Salters, "The Unity of Lamentations," *IBS* 23 (2001): 101–10; E. Assis, "The Unity of the Book of Lamentations," *CBQ* 71 (2009): 306–29.

34. See especially J. Renkema, "The Literary Structure of Lamentations," in *The Structural Analysis of Biblical and Canaanite Poetry*, ed. W. van der Meer and J. C. de Moor, JSOTSup 74 (Sheffield: Sheffield Academic, 1988), 294–396.

LXX's preamble to its translation of Lamentations ascribes them to Jeremiah after the fall of Jerusalem (see the translation note on 1:1), but presumably this ascription comes from later guesswork or creative reflection.[35] It hardly indicates that an ascription to Jeremiah dropped out of the text or that a knowledge that Jeremiah composed the poems survived separately from the poems themselves. The attribution might have been inferred from the Jeremiah-like testimony in Lam 3 or the note about Jeremiah lamenting in 2 Chron 35:25. One can indeed imagine Jeremiah grieving in the manner of these poems after the disaster that overcame Jerusalem, and even though LXX's preamble has no historical value, the ascription to Jeremiah suggests several insights[36] without implying an identity of perspective.

- The poets compare with Jeremiah in their use of imagery and hyperbole, though in their use of the alphabetic form they have structured their work in a way that contrasts with Jeremiah.
- The poets are accomplished theologians like Jeremiah, familiar with and working with the theological perspectives expressed in Deuteronomy, 2 Kings, the psalms of protest, the Zion psalms, Proverbs, and Jeremiah itself (whether or not these scrolls as we know them existed in their day).
- Like Jeremiah, the poets thus combine a belief that Yahweh brings trouble to faithless people and that the fall of Jerusalem was an example of this principle with a recognition that this principle is not all that needs to be said about the way things work out for the people of God.
- The poets have a similar confidence to Jeremiah in protesting to Yahweh.
- The author of Lam 1 is someone who can imagine what it is like to be a woman, and the author of Lam 3 is someone who can imagine what it is like to be a man. In neither case does this fact establish the

35. A. Labahn considers the effect of this perspective within the LXX in "From Anonymity to Biography: Jeremiah as a Character Memorizing the Past in LamLXX," in *Reading Lamentations Intertextually*, ed. B. N. Melton and H. A. Thomas (London: T&T Clark, forthcoming 2021). J. Kalman ("If Jeremiah Wrote It, It Must Be OK: On the Attribution of Lamentations to Jeremiah," *AcT* 29 [2009]: 31–53) and L. Jonker ("The Jeremianic Connection: Chronicles and the Reception of Lamentations as Two Modes of Interacting with the Jeremianic Tradition?," *Scriptura* 110 [2012]: 176–89) consider more broadly the subsequent history of the making of this link.

36. N. C. Lee sees the poems as "a kind of 'extension' of the book of Jeremiah" (*The Singers of Lamentations: Cities Under Siege, from Ur to Jerusalem to Sarajevo*, BibInt 60 [Leiden: Brill, 2002], 130). P. R. House ("Lamentations," in D. Garrett and P. R. House, *Song of Songs, Lamentations*, WBC 23B [Nashville: Nelson, 2004], 285–87) seeks to leave the door open for the possibility of Jeremiah's authorship.

> author's gender. A woman's voice might speak naturally for a vulnerable and marginalized people.[37] The presumably androcentric and patriarchal structure of Israelite society was not incompatible with the prominence of women prophet-poets and musicians in the First Testament (e.g., Miriam, Deborah, Hannah), which makes it at least as likely that the authors of Lamentations were women as men.[38] Women are the lamenters in Israel,[39] as elsewhere,[40] and a Judahite might as likely assume female authorship as male authorship.[41]

The poems speak as though, like Jeremiah, the authors were personally acquainted with the devastation of the city, which was thus a recent event. Given that we know Jerusalem was devastated in 587 and that we know of no comparable later devastation, it seems logical to assume that the poems reflect this event, concerning which they convey a strong sense of actuality. Either the poets were involved in the situation or they were really good at imagining it. Thus "widespread, almost unanimous agreement, a remarkable feat in modern interpretation, holds that the biblical book of Lamentations stems from the land of Judah after the events of 587."[42] While the poems make virtually no reference to concrete people or events, they imply reference to the Babylonians, Nebuchadnezzar, and Zedekiah. They mention (among others) allies, babies, blind people, children, fathers, girls, kings, leaders, men, menstruants, mothers, mourners, old men, orphans, potters,

37. See B. N. Melton, "Conspicuous Females and Inconspicuous God: The Distinctive Characterization of Women and God in the *Megilloth*," in Melton and H. A. Thomas, *Reading Lamentations Intertextually*.

38. W. A. Bailey, "Lamentations," in W. A. Bailey and C. Bucher, *Lamentations, Song of Songs*, Believers Church Bible Commentary (Harrisonburg, VA: Herald, 2015), 23–24; see the nuanced discussion of the woman's voice in N. C. Lee, "Lamentations and Gender in Biblical Cultural Context," in *The Writings and Later Wisdom Books*, ed. C. M. Maier and N. Calduch-Benages, BW 1.3 (Atlanta: Society of Biblical Literature, 2014), 197–213; also C. Mandalfo, "Discourse of Resistance: Feminist Studies on the Psalter and Book of Lamentations," in *Feminist Interpretation of the Hebrew Bible in Retrospect*, ed. S. Scholz, vol. 1, Recent Research in Biblical Studies 5 (Sheffield: Sheffield Phoenix, 2013), 196–214; S. D. Goitein, "Women as Creators of Biblical Genres," *Prooftexts* 8 (1988): 1–33 (26–27 on Lamentations).

39. H. Cox and S. Paulsell, *Lamentations and the Song of Songs*, Belief: A Theological Commentary on the Bible (Louisville: Westminster John Knox, 2012), 21–23.

40. J. F. Hobbins, "Zion's Plea That God See Her as She Sees Herself," in *Daughter Zion: Her Portrait, Her Response*, ed. M. J. Boda, C. J. Dempsey, and L. S. Flesher, AIL 13 (Atlanta: Society of Biblical Literature, 2012), 167–72.

41. Contrast M. L. Conway, "Daughter Zion: Metaphor and Dialogue in the Book of Lamentations," in Boda, Dempsey, and Flesher, *Daughter Zion*, 104.

42. Middlemas, *Troubles of Templeless Judah*, 174.

priests, prisoners, prophets, royals, survivors, taboo people, victims, warriors, widows, women, and youths.[43] Such a list gives one an impression of the makeup of the city in a situation like that of the event they refer to, and it perhaps takes the reader inside the city in a way that names might not. The poems encourage a sense that they articulate a response to the situation in Jerusalem after 587. They hint at no reference to people or events beyond the catastrophe that came over Jerusalem and Judah at that time; the allusion to Edom in 4:21–22 tests and proves the rule. They speak in terms of the way one can imagine things being in that context and without indications that they presuppose a later situation (e.g., the time when city and temple have been rebuilt). Their language represents "transitional" Biblical Hebrew, having features in common with "Classical" or "Standard" Biblical Hebrew (the language characteristic of the period before the fall of Jerusalem) and also with Late Biblical Hebrew (the language characteristic of the Second Temple period) but far fewer of the latter than appear in Second Temple works such as Ecclesiastes, Esther, Ezra, Nehemiah, and Chronicles.[44]

Poets can, of course, write about an event centuries after it happened, projecting themselves into its time and writing (in this case) as if Jerusalem has not yet been rebuilt. And as a kind of thought exercise on our part, it is possible to picture a poet who lived a century or more after 587 seeking to imagine what it would be like to live in the aftermath of the fall of Jerusalem and what would be the appropriate response to it, and writing poems that expressed such an imaginative response.[45] The poems would then be a little like the story of Ruth, which is an imaginative telling of her story from some time after the period in which it is set. The book of Daniel includes a number of extensive passages that have the form of visions and predictions but are not actually predictive and may not be visionary. The form of a poem reacting to the fall of Jerusalem does not determine the poem's actual nature.

But it seems more plausible to follow the direction that the poems point in inviting us to think of the situation after 587 rather than starting from an

43. I adapt this list from A. Berlin, *Lamentations: A Commentary*, OTL (Louisville: Westminster John Knox, 2002), 13–14.

44. See F. W. Dobbs-Allsopp, "Linguistic Evidence for the Date of Lamentations," *Journal of the Ancient Near Eastern Society* 26 (1998): 1–36; cf. R. Hendel and J. Joosten, *How Old Is the Hebrew Bible? A Linguistic, Textual, and Historical Study* (New Haven: Yale University, 2018), 76.

45. Cf. T. Longman, *Jeremiah, Lamentations*, NIBCOT (Peabody, MA: Hendricksen, 2008), 330. C. Körting notes that the existence of a Lamentations-like work at Qumran, 4Q179, undermines the assumption that Lamentations must be a work reflecting mourning in the decades after 587 ("Lamentations: Time and Setting," in *Functions of Psalms and Prayers in the Late Second Temple Period*, ed. M. S. Pajunen and J. Penner, BZAW 486 [Berlin: de Gruyter, 2017], 137–52).

alternative subtlety. The poets were people who lived sometime between 587 and the 540s, which was also the period during which the Jeremiah scroll came into existence.[46]

IV. OCCASION, PLACE OF ORIGIN, AND DESTINATION

The impression one gets from 2 Kings and Jeremiah is that the city was indeed devastated by the Babylonians in 587. The walls were pulled down, the temple was wrecked, and the housing was burned down. The city was rendered virtually if not actually uninhabitable. The poems therefore hardly had their origin within the city.

On the other hand, there was an ongoing Judahite community elsewhere in Judah, and one can imagine the poems being composed and used by groups meeting for fasting and prayer in places such as Mizpah or Bethel on the kinds of occasions referred to in Zech 8:18–19.[47] (In this volume, at the end of the commentary on each chapter, I have tried to imagine how they might be responding.) The poems could then form "lessons" alongside possible readings from the Torah and the Prophets, in whatever form the Torah and the Prophets had at this point. But the poems give no direct information on the reasons they were written, how it was hoped or expected that they might be used, or how they actually were used. To judge from their content, one can imagine that the poets wrote them because

- they needed to think out their understanding of the 587 catastrophe;
- they wanted to help other Judahites think out their understanding;
- they wanted to encourage themselves in the context of their capital and country having been devastated and to encourage Judahites whose capital and country had been devastated;
- they needed to express their feelings about the catastrophe and to help other Judahites express their feelings ("With the collapse of the Jerusalem temple, these texts construct a rhetorical 'house for sorrow,' a shelter for mourning irretrievable losses"[48]);
- they wanted to help other people empathize with Jerusalem in its suffering; or
- they wanted to pray about the catastrophe and to help other Judahites pray.

46. See J. Goldingay, *The Book of Jeremiah*, New International Commentary on the Old Testament (Grand Rapids: Eerdmans, 2021).

47. See, e.g., Middlemas, *Troubles of Templeless Judah*, 122–70.

48. S. E. Balentine, "The Prose and Poetry of Exile," in Kelle, Ames, and J. L. Wright, *Interpreting Exile*, 352.

Their aims, then, were theological, educational, pastoral, cathartic, and religious. In these connections, Lamentations is unlike any other book in the Scriptures, though it resonates with a number of them.[49]

- It compares with Proverbs and the Song of Songs in comprising poetic reflection on human experience and God's involvement in it.
- It compares with Job and Ecclesiastes in raising questions and offering comfort and encouragement to people who are suffering and insight on God's involvement in suffering.
- It compares with Psalms in lamenting over things that God has done, protesting to God about it, and urging God to turn to his people.
- It compares with the narrative books and with Jeremiah in giving an account of a concrete event, the fall of Jerusalem.

Whom do the poems address, and whom do their different voices address? From time to time, they explicitly address Yahweh. From time to time, the voices address one another, though they are not exactly engaged in dialogue. They are more like voices comparing notes or voices that separately address whoever may be listening: the actual author who is engaged in reflection and grieving by composing a poem, the author's fellow theologians, the Judahite community that is also so engaged or needs to be, and God. The poems have had an established use in Jewish and Christian worship; they comprise "a liturgy of grief."[50] They are not like the average psalm of protest or praise in the sense of being mostly addressed to God. But they would not seem out of place alongside other psalms that are not addressed to God, such as Pss 1; 2; 49. It is difficult to imagine how these psalms were used in Israelite worship, though they seem more like texts that would be read for people to listen to, and so it is with the poems in Lamentations. "The poet wants to lead his congregation to prayer."[51] Indirectly, they could facilitate people's expressing to Yahweh their continuing grief over the state of city and community after 587. They could facilitate catharsis.[52]

49. See Melton and H. A. Thomas, *Reading Lamentations Intertextually*.

50. See L. C. Allen, *A Liturgy of Grief: A Pastoral Commentary on Lamentations* (Grand Rapids: Baker, 2011).

51. K. Koenen, *Klagelieder (Threni)*, BKAT 20 (Neukirchen: Neukirchener, 2015), 17. See further H. A. Thomas, "Relating Prayer and Pain: Psychological Analysis and Lamentations Research," *TynB* 61 (2010): 183–208; H. A. Thomas, "The Liturgical Function of the Book of Lamentations," in *Thinking Towards New Horizons: Collected Communications to the Nineteenth Congress of the International Organization for the Study of the Old Testament, Ljubljana 2007*, ed. M. Augustin and H. M. Niemann, BEATAJ 55 (Frankfurt: Lang, 2008), 137–47.

52. Koenen, *Klagelieder*, 92

V. CANONICITY

We know virtually nothing about the process whereby the Torah, the Prophets, and the Writings came to be the Scriptures for Jewish communities and thus for Christian communities, and scholarly opinions vary over the entire question.[53] We do know that by the time of Sirach (ben Sira or Ecclesiasticus), about 200 BC, "the Torah and the Prophets" had authoritative status, at least in his circles, but we do not know whether Lamentations counted as part of "the Prophets" or what otherwise was its position. We know there were copies of Lamentations among the Qumran documents[54] (along with some "remains of a text closely associated with the biblical Lamentations," 4Q179),[55] but in itself that fact need not mean it counted among the Scriptures. In *Against Apion* 1.8, Josephus refers to a twenty-two book list of the Scriptures. The number corresponds to the number of letters in the Hebrew alphabet, like the number of stanzas in each chapter of Lamentations, and the twenty-two may well coincide with the Torah, the Prophets, and the Writings as we know them, but Josephus does not provide a list of the twenty-two. In *Jewish Antiquities* 10.5.1, Josephus also comments that Jeremiah the Prophet composed an elegy to lament Josiah (to whom Tg takes Lam 4:20 to refer), which Josephus says was extant in his time. This comment supports the idea that Josephus includes Lamentations among the Scriptures.[56] The slightly later list in *b.* Baba Batra, which refers to Lamentations, lists twenty-

53. For what we know or may guess, see R. T. Beckwith, *The Old Testament Canon of the New Testament Church and Its Background in Early Judaism* (Grand Rapids: Eerdmans, 1985).

54. See F. M. Cross, "4QLam," in E. C. Ulrich et al., *Qumran Cave 4: XI: Psalms to Chronicles*, DJD 16 (Oxford: Clarendon, 2000), 229–37; J. T. Milik, "Lamentations," in *Les "Petites Grottes" de Qumrân: Exploration de la Falaise: Les grottes 2Q, 3Q, 5Q, 6Q, 7Q à 10Q, le rouleau de cuivre*, ed. M. Baillet, J. T. Milik, and R. de Vaux, DJD 3 (Oxford: Clarendon, 1962), 174–78; G. R. Kotzé, *The Qumran Manuscripts of Lamentations: A Text-Critical Study*, SSN 61 (Leiden: Brill, 2013).

55. T. Ilan, "Canonization and Gender in Qumran," in *The Dead Sea Scrolls and Contemporary Culture: Proceedings of the International Conference Held at the Israel Museum, Jerusalem (July 6–8, 2008)*, ed. A. I. Roitmans, L. H. Schiffman, and S. Tzoref (Leiden: Brill, 2011), 515. See J. M. Allegro with A. A. Anderson, *Qumrân Cave 4.I (4Q158–4Q186)*, DJD 5 (Oxford: Clarendon, 1968), 75–77 (cf. *DSS* 1:368–71); see further, T. Ilan, "Gender and Lamentations: 4Q179 and the Canonization of. the Book of Lamentations," *Lectio Difficilior: European Electronic Journal for Feminist Exegesis* (2008): 1–16; also G. R. Kotzé, "Lamentations at Qumran," in Melton and H. A. Thomas, *Reading Lamentations Intertextually*.

56. Lamentations influenced Josephus's account of the fall of Jerusalem in his day; see H. H. Chapman, "'Let Us Test and Examine Our Ways and Return to the Lord': Josephus' Interpretation of Lamentations," in Melton and H. A. Thomas, *Reading Lamentations Intertextually*.

four books, but counting Lamentations with Jeremiah (for instance) would make it possible to think of them as twenty-two, in correspondence with the number of letters in the alphabet.

The LXX translation of the Scriptures into Greek includes Lamentations, but it also includes Baruch between Jeremiah and Lamentations and the Letter of Jeremiah between Lamentations and Ezekiel. On the other hand, Jerome's translation into Latin, which came to be known as the Vulgate, includes only the Torah, the Prophets, and the Writings on the basis of their being the Scriptures recognized by the Jewish community as he knew it. And as far as we know, Baruch and the Letter of Jeremiah, along with the other works that came to be termed the Apocrypha or Deuterocanonical Writings, never counted among the Scriptures for the Jewish community.

While we have so little information on the question of how Lamentations came to be in the Scriptures, we know of no controversy about its status there. Unlike books such as Daniel, there is only one form of the book. Unlike Esther, it features among the Qumran documents. Unlike books such as Wisdom, it was written in Hebrew and appears in the Hebrew Scriptures as well as in LXX. Unlike Ecclesiastes and Ezekiel, no questions were raised about it by rabbinic discussions after the fall of Jerusalem in AD 70.

A. THE CANONICAL PROCESS

My working assumption is that the question of who decided which books should be in the canon has no answer, in the sense that they did not become canonical because there was a body that decided they should be. The development of the canon just happened, even if eventually a body affirmed them. The development will have been analogous to the process whereby things become "canonical" in Western culture—documents such as the United States Constitution and the Westminster Confession, novels such as *The Scarlet Letter* and *To Kill a Mocking Bird*, or musical works such as *Rhapsody in Blue* or "Strange Fruit." The process involves at least three factors, whose interaction may vary. But one way or another

- something commends itself to influencers within the community on the basis of the bells it rings, the questions to which it provides satisfying answers, the way it moves people;
- partly under the influence of the influencers, it commends itself to ordinary people; and
- it later receives official status by authoritative political or ecclesial or cultural bodies.

So one or more poets (who might have been people such as Levites with authoritative status in the community, or their wives) wrote the individual poems that we now call Lamentations 1, 2, 3, 4, and 5. These commended themselves to influencers and ordinary people by facilitating their response to the fall of Jerusalem, as different psalms commended themselves to people's praise and prayer and gained a place in their worship and spirituality. Thus "Lamentations would have become part of Israel's sacred writings in the same way the Psalms did."[57] A context for Lamentations doing so would be worship gatherings in places such as Mizpah and Bethel, to which we have referred. Authoritative figures such as Levites in these circles perhaps concluded that these five poems should form a collection, and the collection perhaps came to be used more systematically in worship gatherings. It thus gained a semi-official place in the community's worship resources.

The assumption of such a process would fit with the role that Lamentations plays as background to Isa 40–55[58] and to Zech 1–8.[59] To put it another

57. H. L. Ellison, "Lamentations," in *The Expositor's Bible Commentary*, ed. F. E. Gaebelein, vol. 6 (Grand Rapids: Zondervan, 1986), 699.

58. On this relationship, see B. D. Sommer, *A Prophet Reads Scripture: Allusion in Isaiah 40–66*, Contraversions: Jews and Other Differences (Stanford: Stanford University Press, 1998), 127–30; N. K. Gottwald, *Studies in the Book of Lamentations*, SBT 14 (London: SCM, 1954), 44–46; C. A. Newsom, "Response to Norman K. Gottwald, 'Social Class and Ideology in Isaiah 40–55,'" *Semeia* 59 (1992): 75–77; P. T. Willey, *Remember the Former Things: The Recollection of Previous Texts in Second Isaiah*, SBLDS 161 (Atlanta: Scholars, 1997); T. Linafelt, *Surviving Lamentations: Catastrophe, Lament and Protest in the Afterlife of a Biblical Book* (Chicago: University of Chicago Press, 2000), 62–79; K. M. O'Connor, *Lamentations and the Tears of the World*, Catholicity in an Evolving Universe Series (Maryknoll, NY: Orbis, 2002), 139–47; L.-S. Tiemeyer, "Geography and Textual Allusions: Interpreting Isaiah 40–55 and Lamentations as Judahite Texts," *VT* 57 (2006): 367–85; R. A. Parry, "Prolegomena to Christian Theological Interpretations of Lamentations," in *Canon and Biblical Interpretation*, ed. C. G. Bartholomew et al., Scripture and Hermeneutics 7 (Grand Rapids: Zondervan, 2006), 400–406; L.-S. Tiemeyer, "Two Prophets, Two Laments and Two Ways of Dealing with Earlier Texts," in *Die Textualisierung der Religion*, ed. J. Schaper, FAT 62 (Tübingen: Mohr, 2009), 185–202; L.-S. Tiemeyer, "Lamentations in Isaiah 40–55," in Parry and H. A. Thomas, *Great Is Thy Faithfulness?*, 55–63; K. M. Heffelfinger, "'I am He, Your Comforter': Second Isaiah's Pervasive Divine Voice as Intertextual 'Answer' to Lamentations' Divine Silence," in Melton and H. A. Thomas, *Reading Lamentations Intertextually*. If Lam 3 comes from the Persian period, the movement would be the opposite: see J. Middlemas, "Did Second Isaiah Write Lamentations iii?" *VT* 56 (2006): 511–14.

59. On this relationship, see M. R. Stead, "Sustained Allusion in Zechariah 1–2," in *Tradition in Transition: Haggai and Zechariah 1–8 in the Trajectory of Hebrew Theology*, ed. M. J. Boda and M. H. Floyd, LHBOTS 475 (London: T&T Clark, 2008), 144–70; also M. R. Stead, "Zechariah's Intertextual Reversal of Lamentations," in Melton and H. A. Thomas, *Reading Lamentations Intertextually*. Here the implication sometimes is that Lamentations' questions still need asking (e.g., Zech 1:12).

way, whereas the people's laments and protests in these poems meet with no response within the poems (they are, after all, laments and protests, like many psalms that do not incorporate a response from God), Isa 40–55 documents the response within the First Testament,[60] and so do Matthew and Luke within the Scriptures as a whole.[61]

In substance, Lamentations sits between the Psalms on one hand and Isa 40–55 and Zechariah on the other. Both the independence of Lamentations and its association with those responses are important. To leap too quickly from the questions in Lamentations to the answer short-circuits the nature of the relationship between God and his people. Never to take into account that answer terminates the relationship. Somehow Lamentations' gaining the status of a proper response to the circumstances of Judah after 587 survived the process whereby city and temple came to be rebuilt and the grieving, protests, and prayers came not to be needed in the same way they originally were. Yet "the literature of survival works to keep *alive* the memory of *death*."[62] It also works to provide the words with which people could respond to later calamities, perhaps smaller scale and affecting only individuals, to judge from the way it has been used in recent years. Its other ongoing function is not merely to enable the afflicted to voice their suffering but "to discomfort the ungrieving."[63] To put that point another way, the location of Lamentations within the Torah, the Prophets, and the Writings implies paradoxically that the poems themselves become part of God's speaking, like the Psalms. This inference certainly holds for the New Testament, to judge from 2 Tim 3:16.

B. THE BOUNDS AND THE ORDER OF THE CANON

The question of the distinctive canonicity of the Scriptures is largely a Christian one. It was within a Christian context, some while after New Testament

60. See T. Linafelt, "Surviving Lamentations (One More Time)," in *Lamentations in Ancient and Contemporary Cultural Contexts*, ed. N. C. Lee and C. Mandolfo, SymS 43 (Atlanta: Society of Biblical Literature, 2008), 57–58; earlier, T. Linafelt, "Surviving Lamentations," *HBT* 17 (1995): 56; T. Linafelt, "The Impossibility of Mourning: Lamentations after the Holocaust," in *God in the Fray: A Tribute to Walter Brueggemann*, ed. T. Linafelt and T. K. Beal (Minneapolis: Fortress, 1998), 280–83. C. R. Mandolfo (*Daughter Zion Talks Back*, 117) critiques the "controlling" nature of Yahweh's responsive discourse; but contrast also Heffelfinger, "'I am He, Your Comforter'."

61. S. Kang and P. M. Venter, "A Canonical-Literary Reading of Lamentations 5," *HvTSt* 65 (2009): 257–63.

62. Linafelt, *Surviving Lamentations: Catastrophe, Lament and Protest*, 21.

63. P. Bowers, "Acquainted with Grief: The Special Contribution of the Book of Lamentations," *Africa Journal of Evangelical Theology* 9/2 (1990): 38.

times, that the question of a canon or "rule" and its limits became important. And in modern times, both Christians and Jews have to live with the fact that the contents of the Scriptures were established a couple of thousand years ago and that we are not in a position to trace the process whereby it happened or to decide whether the decisions were right. As Luther's convictions made him question whether Esther or James should really be in the canon, so the convictions of some modern scholars have made them ask questions about Lamentations.[64] And in theory, the Jewish community or the Christian community could reopen the question and make some new decisions about the bounds of the Scriptures or about whether to have Scriptures, as the Christian community could reopen the question whether the doctrine of the Trinity is true. Good luck with that venture if you would like to try.

Christians can console themselves with the consideration that if we were able to ask Jesus or Paul what count as "the Scriptures," they would quite likely answer that they comprise what we know as the Torah, the Prophets, and the Writings, and they would thus include Lamentations. But it is at most "quite likely." Theologically and religiously, we might add that it would have been odd for God to let his people come to the wrong conclusion about the question and that we might be safer assuming that they got it right than assuming that we could do better. One of the points about Lamentations, as about other books, is that in some ways it immediately commends itself to us and we can see why it is in the Scriptures, and in some ways we do not like it and we can see that it offers to deliver us from the limitations of our current likes and dislikes.

Within the order of the Scriptures that were eventually preserved in the Greek and Hebrew Scriptures, Lamentations appears in two different places, and the two locations offer different pointers to the poems' significance. Placing Lamentations after Jeremiah might draw more attention to the strand in Lamentations that sees the fall of Jerusalem as a consequence of Judahite waywardness, or it might imply a protest against such a reading.[65] A difference between Lamentations and Jeremiah is Lamentations' reduced stress on Judah's waywardness as the cause of the fall of Jerusalem, along with a more positive view of Zion as a place of worship and a place that was precious to its people.[66] The later medieval placing of Lamentations among the Five Scrolls within the Writings puts these works together as texts used on one worship occasion each year—Pesah, Shavuot, Tisha B'Av, Sukkot, and Ha-

64. See D. Guest, "Hiding behind the Naked Women in Lamentations: A Recriminative Response," *BibInt* 7 (1999): 439.

65. See the discussion in G. Goswell, "Assigning the Book of Lamentations a Place in the Canon," *Journal for the Evangelical Study of the Old Testament* 4 (2015): 1–19.

66. See Mandolfo, *Daughter Zion Talks Back*, 79–102.

nukkah (though they do not come in this calendrical order in MT^L or MT^A).[67] In synagogue worship, the Five Scrolls are read in the manner of canticles in Christian worship (one example is the Magnificat, Luke 1:46–55), especially in places where the choir plays a key role. As Lamentations is chanted by a worship leader, with the congregation joining in under their breath, this use in worship may contribute to an understanding of the text itself.[68]

VI. THE HEBREW TEXT

The translation in this commentary follows the Masoretic Text—the version of the Torah, the Prophets, and the Writings that appears in the Leningrad Codex from AD 1000 (MT^L). It is unlikely that this text exactly corresponds to the text of the poems as they might have been known in, say, Mizpah or Bethel in 550 BC, though it is also unlikely that it is very different. The fragments of a version of Lamentations from Qumran (4QLam and 5QLam) from about 100 BC are very slightly different,[69] and other different versions will underlie the Septuagint Greek translation, the other Greek versions (known as Aquila, Theodotion, and Symmachus), the Latin Vulgate, the Aramaic Targum, and the Syriac Peshiṭta.[70] In the notes in this commentary, I record many of the differences possibly implied by these translations. In addition, modern scholars have made many suggestions regarding what might have been an earlier form of the text that has not survived, either in the Hebrew texts we have or in the old translations.

The standard twentieth-century critical edition of the Torah, the Prophets, and the Writings, *Biblia Hebraica Stuttgartensia* (for which T. H. Robinson covered Lamentations), provides many examples of differences in Hebrew manuscripts from the Masoretic version (nearly all being later than its time) and of differences implied by the ancient translations, along with examples of scholarly suggestions for emending the text. The more recent *Biblia Hebraica Quinta* (for which R. Schäfer covered Lamentations) includes much more such information and is able to include reference to the Qumran scrolls, but in accordance with changed scholarly inclination, it is less inclined to

67. See, e.g., J. A. Gladson, *The Five Exotic Scrolls of the Hebrew Bible: The Prominence, Literary Structure, and Liturgical Significance of the Megilloth* (Lewiston, NY: Edwin Mellen, 2009), 13–14; A. Erickson, "Recent Research on the Megilloth," *CBR* 14 (2016): 298–318.

68. See P. M. Joyce, "Sitting Loose to History: Reading the Book of Lamentations without Primary Reference to Its Original Historical Setting," in *In Search of True Wisdom: Essays in Old Testament Interpretation in Honour of Ronald E. Clements*, ed. E. Ball, JSOTSup 300 (Sheffield: Sheffield Academic, 1999), 248–50.

69. See Milik, "Lamentations"; Cross, "4QLam."

70. See H. van Rooy, "The Ancient Versions of Lamentations," *Scriptura* 110 (2012): 227–36.

propose emendations to the text. In contrast, *The Hebrew Bible: A Critical Edition* is a text-critical project that seeks to construct an eclectic text on the basis of the various manuscripts and the ancient translations rather than reproducing MT; it hopes to be closer (in the case of Lamentations) to the form of the poems as they would have been known in 550 BC.

Very occasionally I may be inclined to follow scholarly suggestions regarding the emending of MT in this way, but my general view is that while our emending the text may produce an older version at some points, it probably will not at others, and that it is not clear that overall we end up with something preferable to MT. "The ambiguity of MT is often preferable to some scholars' conjectures."[71] The old translations into Greek, Latin, Aramaic, and Syriac do have significance in another direction. Insofar as the translators were working with a text more or less identical with MT, they inform us how they were interpreting this text, and their interpretive work is thus both interesting in its own right and instructive for us. This significance is a further reason for my incorporating notes of their renderings.

Another aspect of MT is intriguing. While it does not lay out the text in poetic lines, printing the text in poetic lines on the basis of its text is rarely controversial. But rhythmically, the layout implied by MT can be surprising. We have noted that sometimes MT implies second cola that comprise only one word, through its hyphenating two words in a colon.[72] As is the case with the vowels in MT, which were an addition to the original consonantal text, we do not know how old is the reading tradition that the Masoretes' work preserves. Where MT implies one-stress cola, I am tempted to think that the poet might have composed them as two words so that they had two beats: in other words, the author composed a poem characterized by more even prosody, and the lines have become more uneven in MT. It does not make a difference to the translation, but it makes a difference to the way the poet or another reader would chant the verse. But we cannot know whether the Masoretes have lost track of the original version of the prosody, and my attempts to guess at an older version, again, might not take me nearer the original version.

71. R. B. Salters, *Lamentations: A Critical and Exegetical Commentary*, ICC (London: T&T Clark, 2010), 315.

72. R. de Hoop notes that MT's practice undermines modern assumptions about matters such as the prevalence of bicola in Lamentations ("Lamentations: The Qinah-Metre Questioned," in *Delimitation Criticism: A New Tool in Biblical Scholarship*, ed. M. C. A. Korpel and J. M. Oesch, Pericope: Scripture as Written and Read in Antiquity 1 [Assen: Van Gorcum, 2000], 80–104). On the other hand, W. L. Holladay argues, against MT, that *all* in, e.g., 1:2 and 6 should count as a word and not lose its stress to the next word, which eliminates two one-stress cola ("*Hebrew Verse Structure* Revisited," *JBL* 118 [1999]: 26; following M. P. O'Connor, *Hebrew Verse Structure* [Winona Lake, IN: Eisenbrauns, 1980]).

VII. THEOLOGY

The two central themes of the theology of the First Testament are Yahweh as the God of Israel and Israel as the people of Yahweh. Lamentations offers a distinctive take on this twofold theme.

In Lamentations, the dominant characteristics of Yahweh are his active sovereignty and his blazing anger. There is no doubt that he is Lord—Lam 3 is particularly fond of referring to Yahweh by that word, and it appears in some lines that especially focus on his sovereignty.

> Who is it who said and it happened,
> when the Lord did not order it?
> From the mouth of the One On High there does not go out
> dire things and a good thing? (3:37–38)

By "sovereignty," Christians can mean that nothing happens that God does not permit and that everything eventually serves his purposes. Lamentations also believes in a more active sovereignty. God is directly responsible for the things that happen in Israel's experience. Christians may seek to safeguard the possible negative implications of that fact by attributing events to human decision-making or to the acts of other supernatural powers or to chance—not everything has to be deliberately caused by some personal entity. Likewise, other city laments have the option of attributing events to different deities. Lamentations assumes that the one God is unequivocally responsible for what happens in his world.[73] This conviction implies the good news that the world is under control even if the one who has control does some odd things.

Lamentations focuses further on the fact that in God's exercising his sovereignty, blazing anger has been his defining characteristic in his people's recent experience. "There is no other book of the Hebrew Bible where the wrath and the violence of Jhwh are depicted in such gloomy colors."[74]

> How the Lord with his anger was beclouding
> Ms. Zion! . . .
> He was not mindful of his footstool

73. E. L. Greenstein, "The Wrath at God in the Book of Lamentations," in *The Problem of Evil and Its Symbols in Jewish and Christian Tradition*, ed. H. G. Reventlow and Y. Hoffman, JSOTSup 366 (London: T&T Clark, 2004), 41–42; though Greenstein does not draw any comforting implications.

74. U. Berges, "The Violence of God in the Book of Lamentations," in *One Text, A Thousand Methods: Studies in Memory of Sjef van Tilborg*, ed. P. C. Counet and U. Berges (Leiden: Brill, 2005), 34.

> on the day of his anger. . . .
> He tore down in his fury
> Ms. Judah's strongholds. (2:1–2)

One can compare the way Lamentations talks about Yahweh's anger with the way Paul talks about God's wrath. On one hand, it is more an indication of the nature of his action than of his feelings. On the other, recognizing that Yahweh was expressing anger also affirms that he is a real, full, fully-orbed person with the range of feelings that a person has—he has what one might see as the negative feelings as well as the positive ones. The problem in Lamentations is not the absence of God.[75] It is the presence of God.

Just once Lamentations also talks about the positive feelings. Its comment is then of profound significance.

> Even if he makes sorrowful, he has compassion,
> in accordance with the vastness of his acts of commitment.
> Because he did not humble from his heart
> and make human beings sorrowful. (3:32–33)

Notwithstanding the grimness of God's actions, Lamentations recognizes that he has key First Testament qualities such as compassion (the word can suggest the feelings a mother has for her baby) and commitment (the self-giving that happens without there being any prior obligation and continues when the other party has forfeited any right to its doing so). And it recognizes that these qualities are more central to Yahweh's nature than the wrathful attitude that Judah has recently experienced. They belong in his heart, as wrath does not.

A first striking feature of Israel as the people of Yahweh in Lamentations is that Israel means Judah. There is a practical reason for this narrowing. A century and a half have passed since Ephraim went out of existence. But whereas Jeremiah and Ezekiel have a vision for Yahweh's restoring of Ephraim as well as Judah (Jeremiah's vision perhaps partly for family reasons, Ezekiel's simply for theological reasons), Lamentations has none.

It would be an oversimplification to say that a second feature of Israel or Judah as the people of Yahweh is that Judah means Jerusalem, but not much of an oversimplification. There are also practical reasons for this narrowing. By the time of the Babylonian siege, Judah has already shrunk to little more than Jerusalem. There is also the theological consideration that David and Solomon had made Jerusalem and in particular Mount Zion central to Israel, and Yahweh had gone along with that move. The city and the temple were

75. Though E. Boase takes absence as one of Lamentations' defining divine characteristics ("The Characterisation of God in Lamentations," *ABR* 56 [2008]: 32–44).

integral to what Israel was. The city was Yahweh's footstool, his appointed place, the place they used to call "totality of beauty, joy to all the earth" (2:1, 6, 15). The temple was Yahweh's house, the sanctuary, the place for observing appointed times and Sabbaths, the place where the altar was (2:6–7).

The trouble is that neither people nor city had lived in a way appropriate to their being Yahweh's people and to Mount Zion being the location of Yahweh's sanctuary. In one sense, they can therefore hardly complain at the way Yahweh's anger has burst over them, though it has been overwhelming. "What could the 'bad figs' say for themselves?"[76] Yet the extraordinary freedom with which they do protest at Yahweh's treatment of them (and protest before and to Yahweh) implicitly presupposes that other fact: that commitment and compassion are more central to Yahweh than wrath, and that they are indeed Yahweh's people talking to Israel's God. "In the book of Lamentations, God's mercy is expressed through the lament of the people."[77]

VIII. MAIN THEMES AND THEIR IMPLICATIONS

Lamentations comprises a multi-faceted response to the events of 587 that embraces grief, explanation, protest, confession, and appeal. An appreciation of Lamentations' aim and significance thus depends upon recognizing that it holds together in an unstable unity a variety of theological themes and convictions. There is not one main theological perspective lying behind it.[78] It has been said that "Lamentations . . . is built on contradiction, not consistency."[79] There can be no "systematizing" of Lamentations. It is a whirlwind.[80] After all, people going through personal loss are entitled to speak in confused fashion as they are "casting around for some meaning in the darkness."[81] And a focus on theological analysis may be a way of avoiding facing the pain that the poems express. "Lamentations . . . is more about the *expression* of suffer-

76. W. J. Fuerst, *The Books of Ruth, Esther, Ecclesiastes, The Song of Songs, Lamentations*, Cambridge Bible Commentaries on the Old Testament (Cambridge: Cambridge University Press, 1975), 261.

77. F. Villanueva, "Is There Mercy in the Book of Lamentations?," *Journal of Asian Evangelical Theology* 21 (2017): 47.

78. As M. S. Moore rightly argued long ago in "Human Suffering in Lamentations," *RB* 90 (1983): 534–55.

79. M. J. Bier, *"Perhaps There Is Hope": Reading Lamentations as a Polyphony of Pain, Penitence, and Protest*, LHBOTS 603 (London: T&T Clark, 2015), 120.

80. J. Middlemas, "The Violent Storm in Lamentations," *JSOT* 29 (2004): 94.

81. P. M. Joyce, "Lamentations and the Grief Process," *BibInt* 1 (1993): 312; see further P. M. Joyce, "Psychological Approaches to Lamentations," in Parry and H. A. Thomas, *Great Is Thy Faithfulness?*, 161–65.

ing than the meaning behind it."[82] Its aim is to "give grief a chance."[83] But theological implications are present in the expression of pain.

We can reflect on the multiplicity of Lamentations' theological convictions and motifs by considering its links with other streams of First Testament thinking. Both illumination and muddying issue from considering Lamentations in light of Deuteronomistic, wisdom, prophetic and Zion theology. The problem with these scholarly constructs is that they are scholarly constructs, whose meaning may be taken as self-evident but may not be defined. In addition, these constructs do not cover the full range of streams of thinking that lie behind Lamentations,[84] and other streams do not have convenient parallel names. I therefore rather think in terms of Scriptures that are influential on Lamentations and with which it engages in dialogue, which include

- Deuteronomy, 2 Kings, and Jeremiah, which stress the way wrongdoing will issue in trouble;[85]
- Proverbs and some psalms, which urge trust in Yahweh and promise Yahweh's faithfulness;
- those psalms that encourage protest in light of trouble; and
- those psalms and prophets that affirm Yahweh's commitment to David and to Zion.

An aspect of the genius of Lamentations is to assume that all these insights have something to teach. But a problem that issues from its being not so much a "theology in shreds"[86] as an irreducibly polyphonic text[87] is that both scholarly and popular interpretation can easily focus on one set of convictions and sideline others, partly on the basis of personal, contextual, and cultural preference. Something similar is true about Lamentations Rabbah, which emphasizes that the fall of Jerusalem was a response to Israel's waywardness, though it begins from God's involvement in mourning for the city.[88]

82. T. Linafelt, "Zion's Cause," in *Strange Fire: Reading the Bible after the Holocaust*, ed. T. Linafelt, BibSem 71 (Sheffield: Sheffield Academic, 2000), 279.

83. K. Queen-Sutherland, "Teaching/Preaching the Theology of Lamentations," *Int* 67 (2013): 189.

84. Cf. F. W. Dobbs-Allsopp, "Tragedy, Tradition, and Theology in the Book of Lamentations," *JSOT* 74 (1997): 45–46.

85. E. Boase brings out the tension in "Chaos and Order: Lamentations and Deuteronomy as Responses to Destruction and Exile," in Melton and H. A. Thomas, *Reading Lamentations Intertextually*.

86. I. G. P. Gous, "A Survey of Research on the Book of Lamentations," *OTE* 5 (1992): 200; it is not his own view.

87. See Bier, *"Perhaps There Is Hope"*, 192–216.

88. H. A. Thomas, "The Rabbis Talk Back through the Prophets: Intertextuality, Lam-

A. THE EXPLOSION OF INTEREST

Whereas it might once have seemed that Lamentations received little scholarly or critical attention,[89] in the 1990s there developed "an explosion of interest in the book of Lamentations"[90]—an explosion that grew further over the subsequent decade.[91] In that context, it has also been said that

> a significant change occurred in Lamentations scholarship after 1990 when the traditional themes of suffering as punishment and the need for repentance began to be disputed. Ideological criticism became prominent, and resulted in either a rejection of that content and message or its significant reinterpretation in light of current social and political values.[92]

The implication is not that the scholarly world totally abandoned the idea that Lamentations emphasized Judah's responsibility for what happened to it.[93] But paradoxically, the application of feminist and postcolonial approaches to interpretation contributes to enabling Lamentations to have its voice while also aiming "to contribute to the dethroning of biblical authority as it is now construed. . . . Biblical authority, rather, should inhere in the recognition that biblical discourse is a projection of a never-ending cosmic dialogue." Such interpretation will, for instance, "challenge the Bible's bias against 'pagan' religions."[94] Yet such a postmodern ideology involves one in a "strong misreading" of Lamentations, which robs Ms. Zion of her voice even while paying lip service to caring about it.[95]

---

entations, and Divine Mourning," in Melton and H. A. Thomas, *Reading Lamentations Intertextually*.

89. House, *Lamentations*, 278.

90. C. W. Miller, "The Book of Lamentations in Recent Research," *CBR* 1 (2002): 9.

91. H. A. Thomas, "A Survey of Research on Lamentations (2002–2012)," *CBR* 12 (2013): 8–38.

92. Conway, "Daughter Zion," 101. The year 1990 was the date of the German original of Westermann's *Lamentations*, which breathes a different atmosphere from the works to which Conway refers.

93. See J. Renkema, "Theodicy in Lamentations?," in *Theodicy in the World of the Bible: The Goodness of God and the Problem of Evil*, ed. A. Laato and J. C. de Moor (Leiden: Brill, 2003), 410–28. R. Williamson also concludes this is finally the dominant view in Lamentations ("Taking Root in the Rubble: Trauma and Moral Subjectivity in the Book of Lamentations," *JSOT* 40 [2015]: 7–23).

94. Mandolfo, *Daughter Zion Talks Back*, 3, 5, 6, 77; this work was the background to Boda, Dempsey, and Flesher, *Daughter Zion*.

95. Hobbins, "Zion's Plea," 149; the quoted phrase comes from H. Bloom, *The Anxiety of Influence* (New York: Oxford University Press, 1973), 141, quoted in Mandolfo, *Daughter Zion Talks Back*, 28.

While ideological criticism may imply looking for the ideology expressed in the text, it may thus imply evaluating the text on the basis of one's own ideology. And while one ideological reading might thus question Lamentations' references to waywardness and punishment, another ideological reading might stress the challenge issued by that motif. Jerusalem might stand for other guilty cities—for one's own guilty city.[96] We might prefer to sidestep the idea that our waywardness issues in God's rejection of us. And whereas Lamentations had been read in one unbalanced direction, it came to be read in another unbalanced direction that was prepared to see the poems' admissions of wrongdoing as not seriously meant or as "perfunctory."[97] While Lamentations is not just about retribution, neither is it just an expression of protest.[98] "Yhwh is in the right, according to Zion, in the following sense. She defied his word. Zion does not defy her Lord yet again by invoking privilege or pretending otherwise. Her punishment is nonetheless unbearable, and she will not cease in her protest to that effect."[99]

Nor is the theme of punishment and the need for repentance only a traditional perspective, if "traditional" implies that people thought this way in the past but have now grown out of it.[100] People continue to ask what they did to earn what has happened, and they continue to protest about it. Not only was this reaction a feature of response to disaster in the past; it continues to be a feature, as reactions to twenty-first-century disasters in New Orleans and in the Philippines indicate.[101] And people may sometimes be right to ask that question. At the same time, protesting and asking questions is also a longstanding feature of response to disaster:[102] Lamentations is "a mandate to question."[103]

96. See D. Berrigan, *Lamentations: From New York to Kabul and Beyond* (Lanham, MD: Sheed and Ward, 2002).

97. A. Cooper, "The Message of Lamentations," *JANESCU* 28 (2001): 4. Salters (*Lamentations*, 313) in balanced fashion comments that "this link between sin and punishment, while not overplayed, is clearly drawn in all the poems of Lamentations"; cf. M. J. Boda's comments in "The Priceless Gain of Penitence," in Lee and Mandolfo, *Lamentations in Ancient and Contemporary Cultural Contexts*, 98–101. Middlemas (*Troubles of Templeless Judah*, 171–218) treats sin as one of the themes of Lamentations, though she also describes it as "downplayed."

98. C. J. H. Wright, "Lamentations," *International Bulletin of Missionary Research* 39/2 (2015): 60.

99. Hobbins, "Zion's Plea," 157.

100. It is an aspect of A. Henderson's study of Lamentations in "When Tragedy Strikes," *ResQ* 37 (1995): 97–101.

101. M. M. Homan, "Rebuilding That Wicked City," in Kelle, Ames, and J. L. Wright, *Interpreting Exile*, 209–11; F. Villanueva, *Lamentations: A Pastoral and Contextual Commentary* (Carlisle: Langham, 2016), 73.

102. See classically J. L. Crenshaw, "Popular Questioning of the Justice of God in Ancient Israel," *ZAW* 82 (1970): 380–95.

103. H. Gossai, "Reading Lamentations after the *Shoah*: A Mandate to Question," in Melton and H. A. Thomas, *Reading Lamentations Intertextually*.

B. THEODICY AND ANTITHEODICY

Another way to make this point would be to note how the word *theodicy* recurs in discussions of Lamentations.[104] Lamentations, 2 Kings, and Jeremiah sit alongside each other as scrolls that belong in the aftermath of the 587 catastrophe. Whereas 2 Kings has been described as an act of praise at the justice of the judgment of God,[105] more recently it has been described as an exercise in theodicy.[106] Jeremiah has been seen the same way.[107] The word *theodicy*, devised by Gottfried Leibniz in the eighteenth century, etymologically suggests the justice of God or the justification of God, and discussion of theodicy involves the attempt to handle the question how one can believe in the goodness and the power of God given the existence of evil in the world. "Divine justice and divine omnipotence appear to be constantly on trial."[108] For modern biblical scholars, theodicy is thus an important subject, though it is hardly true that "theodicy is the ultimate, inescapable problem of the Old Testament."[109] But with a narrower focus, it is a significant question in 2 Kings, Jeremiah, and Lamentations, which are concerned with understanding one particular catastrophe. Neither 2 Kings nor Jeremiah thinks that task is very difficult. The fall of Jerusalem happened because of Judah's waywardness; it was Yahweh's response to that waywardness. The aim of the Lamentations Targum, too, might be described as "vindicating God."[110] And the classic Christian response to the problem of evil involves emphasizing humanity's freedom to decide to do wrong and seeing trouble as the consequences of that wrongdoing. If "the theme of Lamentations" is "an exploration of the traumatized relations between Israel and God in the immediate aftermath of the Destruction,"[111] then "the attribution of responsibility is identified as one of the critical representations necessary in the creation of a compelling trauma narrative."[112]

104. See the survey in Bier, *"Perhaps There Is Hope"*, 12–32.

105. G. von Rad, *Old Testament Theology*, vol. 1 (New York: Harper, 1962), 357–58.

106. E.g., M. A. Sweeney, *I and II Kings* (Louisville: Westminster John Knox, 2007), 3.

107. E.g., A. R. P. Diamond, "Jeremiah," in *Eerdmans Commentary on the Bible*, ed. J. D. G. Dunn and J. W. Rogerson (Grand Rapids: Eerdmans, 2003), 543–622.

108. D. Bergant, *Lamentations*, AOTC (Nashville: Abingdon, 2003), 71.

109. So W. Brueggemann, "Some Aspects of Theodicy in Old Testament Faith," *Perspectives in Religious Studies* 26 (1999): 253; cf. D. Rom-Shiloni, "Theodical Discourse: Theodicy and Protest in Sixth Century BCE Hebrew Bible Theology," in *Theodicy and Protest: Jewish and Christian Perspectives*, ed. A. Deeg et al., Studien zu Kirche und Israel: Neue Folge 7 (Leipzig: Evangelische, 2018), 55.

110. The subtitle of C. M. M. Brady's study, *The Rabbinic Targum of Lamentations: Vindicating God*, Studies in the Aramaic Interpretation of Scripture 3 (Leiden: Brill, 2003).

111. A. Mintz, *Ḥurban: Responses to Catastrophe in Hebrew Literature* (New York: Columbia University Press, 1984), 26; cf. A. Mintz, "The Rhetoric of Lamentations and the Representation of Catastrophe," *Prooftexts* 2 (1982): 4.

112. Boase, "Fragmented Voices," 60.

In Lamentations, however, "complaints, protests, and confessions . . . spread blame around."[113] Lamentations plays "the blame game: You did it. She did it. God did it."[114] In 1998, but in light of the Holocaust, Zachary Braiterman devised the term *antitheodicy* to denote responses to the problem of evil that comprised more protest than explanation.[115] And Lamentations "blames God, yells at God to pay attention, and then seeks to make reparation for any harm done by claiming God's goodness and steadfast love."[116] Lamentations comprises neither theodicy nor antitheodicy—or rather, it works with both.[117] Like a child needing to come to terms with both the "good" and the "bad" side to its mother, Lamentations implies the need to come to terms with both sides of its position, not just to affirm one. We need more than one perspective.[118] "The central dilemma of the book" is that it simply juxtaposes the acknowledgment of wrongdoing and the descriptions of misery so that "parataxis works to establish not connections but dissonances."[119] In Lamentations "we are invited into the tensive interplay of unresolvable and open dialog."[120] The question is "essentially a matter of the way in which the past is made present; whether one remains at the level of reproach or whether one withstands the horror by having the strength to comprehend even the incomprehensible."[121]

If there is to be a way of living with the unresolvable, it lies outside Lamentations. It lies in recalling what Yahweh has done in the past, as recounted in the story told in Exodus and Joshua that provides the basis for holding onto Yahweh when everything has collapsed. It lies more overtly in paying attention to Yahweh's response to Lamentations in Isa 40–55. The New Testament confirms these two angles in inviting people who are suffering and who believe in Jesus to look to the story told in the Gospels and to look to the promise of what God is going to do in Revelation.

113. Boase, "Fragmented Voices," 61.

114. Queen-Sutherland, "Teaching/Preaching the Theology of Lamentations," 185.

115. Z. Braiterman, *(God) After Auschwitz* (Princeton: Princeton University, 1998), 37.

116. T. Houck-Loomis, "Good God?!? Lamentations as a Model for Mourning the Loss of the Good God," *Journal of Religion and Health* 51 (2012): 703.

117. As E. Boase almost concludes in "Constructing Meaning in the Face of Suffering: Theodicy in Lamentations," *VT* 58 (2008): 449–68.

118. Villanueva, *Lamentations*, 73.

119. Landy, "Lamentations," 330.

120. C. J. Sharp, "Sites of Conflict: Textual Engagements of Dislocation and Diaspora in the Hebrew Bible," in Kelle, Ames, and J. L. Wright, *Interpreting Exile*, 372.

121. T. W. Adorno, "The Meaning of Working through the Past," in *Can One Live After Auschwitz?* (Stanford: Stanford University Press, 2003), 15; cf. V. J. Seidler, "'Their Hearts Melted and Became as Water.' Lamentations: Ethics after Auschwitz," *European Judaism* 44 (2011): 103.

IX. ANALYSIS OF CONTENTS

- Lam 1: A voice grieves over the invasion, emptying, grief, and humiliation of Ms. Zion as a result of her waywardness, and Ms. Zion herself pleads to be seen, voices her pain and loneliness, acknowledges her rebellion, and pleads for Yahweh to deal with her attackers.
- Lam 2: A voice recounts how Yahweh in his burning anger has overwhelmed Ms. Zion with great destruction, pictures this destruction more concretely, grieves over her suffering, and urges her to add her own voice to this cry of protest, which she does.
- Lam 3: A voice gives an anti-testimony to having been attacked but then signifies a commitment to keep trusting Yahweh; another voice confirms this statement of faith and invites the community to turn to Yahweh; the first voice recalls Yahweh's earlier deliverance and urges him to deliver again.
- Lam 4: In a shorter poem, a voice recalls the story of events before and at the fall of Jerusalem, notes the wrongdoing of priests and prophets, adds implicit theological comments, including reference to the capture of Yahweh's anointed, and declares that Yahweh will bring redress on Edom.
- Lam 5: In the shortest poem and the only one that does not work alphabetically, a voice describes a series of concrete examples of the people's suffering and sets that description in the context of pleas for Yahweh to take note and restore the people; the poem ends on a down note.

The Book of
LAMENTATIONS

Text and Commentary

LAMENTATIONS 1: "IS THERE PAIN LIKE MY PAIN?"

The first poem grieves over the destruction of Jerusalem by the city's adversaries and by Yahweh, laments over the ongoing anguish of people who identify with the city, recognizes that the city's rebellion justified Yahweh's action, but pleads with Yahweh to look at its suffering and finally to take action against its devastators. It thus does not complain about Yahweh's action, though it does begrudge the action of its human devastators, nor does it imply that the calamity was excessive. The description "lament" is more appropriate for Lam 1 than it is for the other poems and for most of the so-called "lament psalms," which are characterized more by protest than lament. But accepting the propriety of Yahweh's action does not rule out pleading with Yahweh to take a different sort of action.

Through the poem, the city is personified as an individual, and specifically as a woman. It is a key image in Lam 1, as it will be in Lam 2 and 4.[1] If "pain can only be experienced by individuals," then speaking of the city's pain as if it is the experience of an individual makes it possible to communicate that pain, and the personification also makes it possible for the city to become an interlocutor.[2] "The female personification of Jerusalem allows envisioning a relationship between the city, its inhabitants, and god."[3] Two voices engage

1. See E. Boase, *The Fulfilment of Doom? The Dialogic Interaction between the Book of Lamentations and the Pre-exilic/Early Exilic Prophetic Literature*, LHBOTS 437 (London: T&T Clark, 2006), 83–101.

2. K. M. Heim, "The Personification of Jerusalem and the Drama of Her Bereavement in Lamentations," in *Zion, City of Our God*, ed. R. S. Hess and G. J. Wenham (Grand Rapids: Eerdmans, 1999), 130, 131, 144.

3. C. M. Maier, "Body Space as Public Space," in *Constructions of Space II: The Biblical City and Other Imagined Spaces*, ed. J. L. Berquist and C. V. Camp, LHBOTS 481 (London: T&T Clark, 2008), 134.

in the grieving. Initially, the lamenting voice is that of a witness who narrates events in the third person. It represents the perspective of someone looking on at what goes on between the city and Yahweh.[4] The equivalent voice in the second poem will actually use the verb "witness." Then in due course, the poem reports how the city addresses Yahweh; the woman speaks for herself. The two voices are not exactly in dialogue in that they do not address one another, though they are in reaction to one another, and they express similar overlapping grief over what has happened to the city. The reporting voice speaks in support of the suffering voice.

While the poem comprises twenty-two verses beginning with the successive letters of the alphabet, it is only "rather unobtrusively" alphabetical,[5] as there are three lines to each verse (four to v. 7). Each line comprises two cola. Thus the poem encompasses

- the witness's descriptions of the event: vv. 1, 2e–f, 3, 5, 6, 7, 8, 9a–d, 10a–d, 11a–d, 17;
- the witness's descriptions of the ongoing situation: vv. 2a–d, 4;
- the witness's implicit appeal to Yahweh: v. 10e–f;
- the city's appeals to Yahweh and to other people: vv. 9e–f, 11e–f, 18c–d, 20a–b, 21f, 22a–b;
- the city's descriptions of the event: vv. 12–13, 14, 15, 16c–f, 18a–b, 18e–f, 19, 20c–f, 21c–e, 22c–d;
- and the city's descriptions of the ongoing situation: v. 16a–b, 22e–f.

At each point the poem's perspective and spirituality correspond to those of Jeremiah; the people who came to attribute the poem to Jeremiah were not being dim-witted.

Broadly speaking, each verse in the poem is self-contained; there is no continuity from one verse to the next. The fragmentation of the poem[6] and the jerkiness of the transitions between the verses correspond to the community's situation.[7] The main principle of formal structure in the poem is thus the alphabetical one, though the distinction between the two voices broadly divides it into two halves. Verses 1–11 mostly speak about Zion in the third person. But within this first half of the chapter, there is some movement

4. See further W. F. Lanahan, "The Speaking Voice in the Book of Lamentations," *JBL* 93 (1974): 41–49.

5. E. S. Gerstenberger, *Psalms, Part 2, and Lamentations*, FOTL 15 (Grand Rapids: Eerdmans, 2001), 477.

6. F. W. Dobbs-Allsopp, *Lamentations*, IBC (Louisville: Westminster John Knox, 2001), 58.

7. Koenen, *Klagelieder*, 20.

from mostly factual description to more giving some account of the city's feelings, which thus leads into two brief quotations from her words to Yahweh in vv. 9e–f and 11e–f. This development prepares the way for the focus on her words in vv. 12–22, the second half of the poem. Here Ms. Zion speaks in the first person, except in vv. 15e–f and 17. In vv. 21–22, Ms. Zion closes the chapter with a prayer for Yahweh to take action against her attackers; the verb *deal* acts as a bracket around vv. 12–22.[8] But the themes of the two halves are the same, and with the exception of the way the prayer closes the chapter, the verses could be shuffled into a different order without loss.

In substance the two voices do not express two points of view; they look at events and situations in the same way. But they do present two angles on what has happened—the angle of a witness who speaks about Zion and the angle of someone who reports or imagines what Zion says. They agree that Zion has gone through a terrible experience, that she is alone and abandoned by her allies, that she cries and has no comforter, that she is humiliated, that people starved, that Yahweh put her down because of her rebellions. The difference is that the first voice speaks more about the objective nature of the event and its consequences—about the fate of the city's leaders and their helplessness, about the feelings of priests and young people, about the inability of refugees to find somewhere to settle, about the invasion of the sanctuary, and about the loss of treasures. The first-person report focuses more on Ms. Zion's own feelings of grief, speaks more of Yahweh's responsibility for what happened (he is the subject of many active and forceful verbs) while acknowledging that he was in the right, and relates her appeals to people and to Yahweh to look and for Yahweh to act against her attackers.[9] Naturally the first voice speaks in terms of what the person can see, the woman-city in terms of what she experiences and feels.[10] But the overlap of the two voices, whereby Zion speaks in vv. 9 and 11 and the witness speaks in vv. 15 and 17, signals the identity of their perspective. In some ways, the poem might parallel (say) a Brit composing a poem about 9/11 or about Hurricane Katrina that seeks to enter into the experience and the aftermath of the event. Speaking in the third person as the poem does is not an indication that the witness does not identify with the city; it can make it possible to articulate

8. J. A. Berman notes many other verbal links in the poem in "Criteria for Establishing Chiastic Structure: Lamentations 1 and 2 as Test Cases," *Maarav* 21 (2014): 57–69. W. D. Reyburn suggests a division into strophes in "Anatomy of a Poem: Lamentations 1," in *Discourse Perspectives on Hebrew Poetry in the Scriptures*, ed. E. R. Wendland (Reading, UK: United Bible Societies, 1994), 147–69. R. B. Salters discusses approaches to the structure in "Structure and Implication in Lamentations 1?," *SJOT* 14 (2000): 293–300.

9. C. W. Miller emphasizes the differences in "Reading Voices: Personification, Dialogism, and the Reader of Lamentations 1," *BibInt* 9 (2001): 393–408.

10. Lanahan, "Speaking Voice in the Book of Lamentations," 42–44.

things in a more objective way. Both voices presuppose that Yahweh is the real God (e.g., vv. 17–18) and both address Yahweh (e.g., vv. 9, 10, 11). And the poem is not about a foreign town with which the poet does not identify, like the prophecies about other towns and nations in Jer 46–51. The poet is a Judahite, Jerusalem is the poet's city, and the Judahites are the poet's people. The poem as a whole could have expressed itself much more briefly. But "when we wish to penetrate into the hearts of those whose sorrow we desire to alleviate, it is necessary that they should understand that we sympathize with them."[11]

Intermingling the voices of witness and woman-city thus contributes to a combining of distance, objectivity, and factuality with involvement, subjectivity, and emotion. Intermingling factual and down-to-earth with figurative and metaphorical also contributes to the combining. The implication is not that the witness's voice simply has the one and the woman-city has the other. The difference does not mean that the witness is detached or indifferent or that the woman-city is irrational or immoderate—neither of which would be true. It is the woman-city who refers to the breaking of young men, to people going into captivity, and to priests and elders perishing, while also speaking as a groaning mother whose insides churn. It is the witness's voice that does much of the portraying of the city as a woman, a widow, a princess, and someone crying uncontrollably in her grief, as well as speaking of exile, invasion, hunger, and the loss of the city's treasures. Such more objective portrayal can function like a photomontage,[12] and we know that "when properly used, photography, including TV, can also nourish empathy."[13] Both voices also refer to the wrongdoing that properly issued in the trouble that Yahweh brought about.

This common perspective also finds expression in the way the broad formal distinction between the two halves of the poem is qualified by some overlap. The woman-city already speaks in the last line of v. 9 and the last line of v. 11. Conversely, unless the last line of v. 10 also comes from the lips of Jerusalem, there in the first half the witness personally addresses Yahweh. Other lines in vv. 1–11 also suggest the witness looking at things from the perspective of the woman-city: "Yahweh, he made her sorrowful" (v. 5); "there was no one comforting for her" (v. 9). Here and throughout, there is another sense in which the witness identifies with the city in its suffering. It

11. J. Calvin, *Commentaries on the Book of the Prophet Jeremiah and the Lamentations*, trans. J. Owen, 5 vols. (repr. Grand Rapids: Christian Classics Ethereal Library), 5:356.

12. R. A. Parry, *Lamentations*, The Two Horizons Old Testament Commentary (Grand Rapids: Eerdmans, 2010), 41; cf. B. Morse, "The Lamentations Project: Biblical Mourning through Modern Montage," *JSOT* 28 (2003): 113–27.

13. Cox and Paulsell, *Lamentations and the Song of Songs*, 19.

compares with the book of Job setting its discussion among non-Israelites yet having them work with a perspective that reflects the author's living within the framework of commitment to Yahweh. Likewise, in Lam 1 the poet or the implied author of the poem is someone who identifies with Jerusalem and speaks both via the voice of the city and via the voice of the witness. The poem enables its author to express a personal reaction to the city's devastation in the words of the witness and also in the words of the woman-city. And the acceptance of the poem within the Judahite community suggests that it enabled other people to do so, too. It legitimates the expression of grief, embodies and stimulates reflection, presupposes acceptance of responsibility, and draws people into prayer of confession and of pleading for Yahweh to take action against the human perpetrators of the catastrophe.

One aspect of the poem's figurative form of expression is its use of hyperbole, neatly exemplified by its use of the word *all* sixteen times:[14] all her friends, all her neighbors, all her pursuers, all her gateways, all her glory, all her treasures, all who honored her, all her treasures, all her people, all who pass, all the time, all my sturdy men, all you peoples, all my enemies, all their dire fate, all my rebellions. The witness and the woman-city agree on the all-consuming nature of the catastrophe. The poem incorporates many other repeated uses of words, sometimes with variation or paronomasia, as well as examples of the juxtaposing of similar words that suggest paronomasia. In addition to emphasizing and underlining, the repetition has a number of other effects.

- *sat down . . . among the nations*, vv. 1a–d, 3c: the city and its inhabitants who left had the same experience
- *great*, vv. 1b, 1d (the only times this form of the word comes), with related expressions in vv. 3b, 5d: the former significance of the city is similarly paralleled by the servitude people experienced before they left, but also by the rebellions that issued in the disaster
- doubling of the verb "cry," v. 2a
- *for her/me there is/was no one comforting*, vv. 2c, 9d, 17b, 21b (see also v. 16c)
- *her friends*, v. 2d; *her great friends*, v. 19a: the move from *qal* to *piel* enhances the expression's irony
- *enemies/enemy*, vv. 2f, 5b, 9f, 16f, 21c
- *humbling*, vv. 3a, 7b, 9e: the term suggests a consistency in people's experience before the catastrophe, during it, and on an ongoing basis

14. C. J. H. Wright, *The Message of Lamentations*, The Bible Speaks Today: Old Testament (Nottingham: Inter-Varsity, 2015), 58.

- *pursuer*, vv. 3e, 6f
- *assembly*, vv. 4b, 15d: the repetition ironically applies first to the gathering of the people in Jerusalem, then to the mustering of an enemy army (though either or both occurrences may refer to the festival occasion for which people assembled)
- *desolate*, vv. 4c, 13e, 16e: the term applies to the gateways, to the woman-city herself, and to her children
- *her/my priests*, 4d, 19c: the first time they are alive but crying out, the second time they have breathed their last
- *cry out*, vv. 4d, 8e, 11a, 21a (the related noun occurs in v. 22e): the priests, the woman-city (three times), her people
- *girls*, vv. 4e, 18e: sorrowful the first time, gone into captivity the second time
- *sorrowful*, vv. 4e, 5c, 12e: first the girls are sorrowful, then Yahweh has made the city so
- *hard* (*mar*), v. 4f; cf. *defied* (*mārâ*), vv. 18b, 20d (which LXX takes as from *mārar*): the paronomasia suggests a link between the hard time the city is having and the defiance she acknowledges
- *adversary/adversaries/pressure*, vv. 5a, 5f, 7e, 7g, 10a, 17d, 20a; cf. *narrows*, v. 3f, from this root
- *rebellions*, vv. 5d, 14a, 22d
- *went as captives/into captivity*, vv. 5e, 18f
- *was mindful*, vv. 7a, 9b: she thought about her suffering but not about her future
- *the things she/they valued*, vv. 7c, 10b, 11c (with two different spellings): twice referring to objects in the temple, but in v. 11c to family possessions
- *hand of*, vv. 7d, 10a, 14b, 14e: the last two occurrences juxtapose the activity of Yahweh's hand and the enemy's hand
- *did wrong, wrong*, v. 8a
- *something for shaking one's head at* (*nîdâ*), v. 8b; cf. *something taboo* (*niddâ*), v. 17f: the paronomasia suggests a link between the two
- *despised/despicable*, vv. 8c, 11f: people came to despise the woman-city; she came to despise herself
- *turned back*, vv. 8f, 13d: she turned back in light of people's despising; Yahweh turned her back before her adversary
- *[bread/food to] bring back [my/their] life*, vv. 11b–d, 16d, 19f: the first and last occurrences relate to the need during the siege to eat rather than starve, while the middle occurrence relates to the present need for another kind of reviving
- *look*, vv. 11e, 12b, 18d, 20a: the bidding addresses God, people, God, people

- *take note*, vv. 11e, 12b: the bidding addresses God, then people
- *pain*, vv. 12c (with doubling of the noun), 18d
- *deal [out]*, vv. 12d, 22b, 22c: what Yahweh has done to Judah shapes the plea for what he should do to the woman-city's adversary
- *go down*, vv. 13b, 16b: there is a parallel between the fire and the tears
- *summoned*, vv. 15c, 19a, 21e: Yahweh summoned attackers (successfully), the woman-city summoned helpers (unsuccessfully), Yahweh summoned the day of catastrophe (successfully)
- *young men*, vv. 15d, 18e
- *my eye, my eye*, v. 16a–b
- *defied*, vv. 18b, 20d (with doubling of the verb): see the comment on *hard*, v. 4f
- *listen*, vv. 18c, 21a, 21c: an appeal to listen meets with something worse than a negative response
- *dire fate*, vv. 21c, 22a (the second occurrence may denote dire behavior)

At other points the poem achieves its effect by using different words to refer to the same object or related objects:

- widow, Ms. Zion, exposed, taboo
- slavery, without rest, something for shaking one's head, despised, humbled, hunger, pain
- cries, tears
- comforter, helper
- broke faith, became the head, laughed, magnified himself, spread his hand, came to the sanctuary, deceived, listened, celebrated
- friends, neighbors
- enemies, adversaries, pursuers
- paths, gateways
- mourning, desolate, crying out, sorrowful, it's hard, faint, tired, churning
- priests, girls, officials, elders
- rebellion, wrongdoing, uncleanness, unmindfulness, defiance
- little ones, children, my girls and my young men
- look, take note, listen, spread hands

The poem has a wide-ranging theological background (see "Main Themes and Their Implications," pp. 27–32).[15]

15. Cf. Koenen, *Klagelieder*, 31–34.

- It presupposes the assumptions underlying many psalms concerning the significance of Jerusalem for theology and spirituality. Jerusalem was a city destined to be of paramount honor among the nations; the poem's grief at the city's suffering accepts rather than questions that significance. It presupposes the importance of the Jerusalem temple as a sacred place that should not be trampled by heathen people who are heedless of its sanctity and of the majesty of its God. It assumes the importance of Zion's festivals, priests, and singers, and the importance of the valuable accoutrements of its worship.
- It presupposes the assumptions underlying the Torah and many prophetic books concerning the vulnerability of the city to attacks from Yahweh if it ignores Yahweh's expectations for its life. It knows that Yahweh is powerful and tough and can be a God of blazing anger, and it knows that Yahweh's Day is a prospect about which to be apprehensive in present history. It is not very specific about the nature of Yahweh's expectations, though it speaks as prophets do of wrongdoing, rebellion, defiance, and uncleanness, and it hints at Jeremiah's emphasis that Judah needs to trust in Yahweh rather than in alliances with its neighbors. The chapter melds a prophetic perspective with its lyric poetry.[16]
- It shares with both the Psalms and Jeremiah the assumption that the relationship between Judah and Yahweh includes a freedom to lament one's experiences of suffering, even when these issue from one's wrongdoing, to urge Yahweh to pay attention to one's suffering, and to pray for him to take action against his own human agents who brought about one's calamity. It is not afraid of hutzpah.[17] Like protest psalms, it speaks in first person, second person, and third person, though it contains no statement of trust or promise of praise or anticipatory praise. It differs both from psalms that protest at trouble on the basis of having been faithful to Yahweh and from psalms and prose confessions that focus on acknowledging guilt; it compares more with psalms that recognize wrongdoing but focus on prayer.[18]

16. H.-J. Kraus, *Klagelieder*, 2nd ed., BKAT 20 (Neukirchen: Neukirchener, 2015), 35.

17. M. Leaman, "Love's Angry Lament: Confronting Our Anger with God: Based on Lamentations 1–3," *Journal of Pastoral Care and Counseling* 63/5 (2009): 1–11.

18. See further J. Goldingay, "Models for Prayer in Lamentations and Psalms," in Melton and H. A. Thomas, *Reading Lamentations Intertextually*.

In expounding the significance of these theological perspectives, the poem also takes for granted the image in Hosea and Jeremiah of Jerusalem as a woman, though it uses that image in a different way. Here "Daughter Zion . . . presents an alternative figure to the representations of her by the prophets."[19] In Lam 1, the image facilitates a grieved portrayal of the city's suffering. The city is like a princess who has been deposed, a wife who has been widowed, a flirt who has been let down, a mother who has lost her children, a daughter who has lost her honor, a girl who has been exposed, a menstruant who has failed to take responsibility for her bleeding.[20] Further, "the introduction of Zion as a speaker is a means by which the poet expresses the central tragedy of the situation. It is not only the disaster of a nation that has fallen, nor is it the distress of an individual community; it is a greater person who is in anguish, Zion, the city of God . . . , not identical with those alive at any one time."[21]

In form, the poem overlaps with funeral laments and with city laments known from elsewhere in the ancient Near East (see "Background," pp. 2–4). Like city laments, it personifies the city, grieves over its destruction by God, and prays that calamity may come on its destroyers. It does not have God weeping over its destroyed sanctuary like the Sumerian Ningal or abandoning the city or returning, nor does it picture the city being rebuilt or give praise for that restoration in prospect.

At various points the poem makes one think of different Babylonian attacks on Jerusalem:

- 601 fits the reminiscence of Deut 23:3(4) in v. 10
- 597 fits the reference to deportation, specifically of king and officials, but the continuing presence of priests implies sacrilege rather than destruction
- 587 fits the references to hunger and fire

Likewise it is possible to identify within the poem figures from the events to which it refers—for instance, peoples such as Babylon and Moab, Ammon, and Edom. It is also possible to identify events such as the Babylonian pursuit

19. J. Middlemas, "Speaking of Speaking," in Boda, Dempsey, and Flesher, *Daughter Zion*, 46.

20. C. M. Maier constructs her "biography" beyond her suffering, into Isa 40–66 ("Die Biographie der heiligen Stadt: Jerusalem im Wandel der alttestamentlichen Überlieferung," *EvT* 70 [2010]: 164–78).

21. S. P. Re'emi, "Lamentations," in *Amos and Lamentations: God's People in Crisis*, by R. Martin-Achard and S. P. Re'emi, ITC (Edinburgh: Handsel, 1984), 83; cf. Hillers, *Lamentations*, 79–80.

and capture of Zedekiah and his troops. But such possible references come at random points and in random connections, and for the most part they share in the poem's figurative portrayal. Pursuit, for instance, is a down-to-earth reality that has become a figure. The implication is that the poem does not relate to one moment in Jerusalem's story and does not invite readers to relate it to one moment and one set of references.[22]

Among approaches to making links with actual readers' own time and situation are these four.

(1) Jewish communities read Lamentations on Tisha B'Av (see the opening paragraphs of this commentary, and "Canonicity," pp. 18–23). Reading the poem after the restoration of city and temple would prohibit the community from forgetting their devastation, would encourage lament and prayer in a context like that of the 160s, and would encourage it again after AD 70. It has facilitated Jewish grieving over subsequent calamities, especially following the Holocaust. It encourages Christians to join in that grieving. A midrash says that the Messiah will be born on Tisha B'Av, "but I fear this is only because grief, if deep enough, will reach out to anything."[23] It is said that some Jews in Poland in the 1930s would burn the Tisha B'Av liturgy after the Tisha B'Av commemoration because surely the Messiah would come before that occasion next year.[24]

(2) On the basis of v. 12 in the KJV, an appreciation of Lam 1 can naturally start from Jesus's suffering.[25] Since the ninth century AD, churches have read from Lam 1 on Maundy Thursday. In the sixteenth century, Giovanni Pierluigi da Palestrina (Palestrina is the name of his city) set parts of Lam 1 to music for the Tenebrae services,[26] and in the eighteenth century George Frideric Handel included words from v. 12 in *The Messiah*. The KJV's rendering of v. 12, "Is it nothing to you, all ye that pass by," goes back to the Great Bible of 1549, although already in 1546 Johannes Bugenhagen had commented acerbically, "Nothing is said here concerning the pas-

22. I. W. Provan, "Reading Texts against an Historical Background: The Case of Lamentations 1," *SJOT* 4 (1990): 130–43.

23. Slavitt, *Lamentations*, 4.

24. P. M. Joyce and D. Lipton, *Lamentations through the Centuries*, Blackwell Bible Commentaries (Chichester: Wiley, 2013), 163.

25. E. F. Davis, "Building Hope," in *Preaching the Luminous Word: Biblical Sermons and Homiletical Essays* (Grand Rapids: Eerdmans, 2016), 221. See the papers in Parry and H. A. Thomas, *Great Is Thy Faithfulness?*, esp. 101–41, 175–97.

26. Joyce and Lipton, *Lamentations*, 42.

sion of Christ," as people claim who "certainly have no faculty of comprehension for the holy Scriptures." And the verses are in the order they are just for the sake of an alphabetical order, not one that "pertains to something else."[27]

(3) A focus in the Western world on questions of sex and sexual abuse in the late twentieth century suggests another context. In Lam 1, a kaleidoscope of images turns quickly from a lonely widow, to a degraded princess, to a whore, to a rape victim, to a betrayed lover, to an abandoned wife.[28] The portrayal of Zion as a woman might imply blaming women for the fate of the community. "Despite claims that this metaphor was meant to humiliate the male community and stimulate repentance, the female figure provides an easy scapegoat behind which the male community may hide."[29] Does it encourage "dehumanization"?[30] Or does the focus on women and the adopting of the image of the city as a suffering woman reflect the female authorship of the poems?

(4) More generally among Western Christians in the late twentieth century, Lamentations came to be newly appreciated in the context of awareness of suffering—both individual suffering and (perhaps more aptly) the suffering of communities. If one asks the question "Whose text is this?" one answer is, it belongs to the people of God as a whole and to other suffering cities and communities.[31] It could make one think about Germany and England after the

27. Bugenhagen, "Threni Ieremiae," in *In Ieremiam Prophetam Commentarium* (Wittenberg: Seitz, 1546), 546–47; cf. J. J. Tyler, ed., *Jeremiah, Lamentations*, Reformation Commentary on Scripture (Downers Grove, IL: InterVarsity, 2018), 456.

28. Berlin, *Lamentations*, 47; but see C. Frevel's critique of interpretation that inflates the theme of sexual violence in Lam 1 ("Von fremden Händen und bloßgestellten Frauen: Ein Zwischenruf zur Inflation sexueller Gewalt in der Deutung von Klagelieder 1," in *Im Lesen Verstehen: Studien zu Theologie und Exegese*, BZAW 482 [Berlin: de Gruyter, 2017], 255–74).

29. Guest, "Hiding behind the Naked Women," 425, 445.

30. L. J. Claassens, "A True Disgrace?," in *Fragile Dignity: Intercontextual Conversations on Scriptures, Family, and Violence*, ed. L. J. Claassens and K. Spronk, SemeiaSt 72 (Atlanta: Society of Biblical Literature, 2013), 73–90; but see the "Response" by D. Erbele-Küster on pp. 91–100.

31. See Cox and Paulsell, *Lamentations and the Song of Songs*; O'Connor, *Lamentations and the Tears of the World*; Lee and Mandolfo, *Lamentations in Ancient and Contemporary Cultural Contexts*, SymS 43 (Atlanta: Society of Biblical Literature, 2008), which includes comparisons and contrasts with Chinese, Jewish, African American, Balkan, Iraqi, South African, and New Orleans laments.

Second World War, about 9/11,[32] about Gaza and Beirut,[33] about the Balkans,[34] about China,[35] about Syria,[36] about Iraq,[37] about the Philippines,[38] about Vietnam,[39] about the Dalits,[40] about the Turks,[41] about African Americans,[42] about women and children in Auschwitz.[43] "Lamentations hardly needs interpretation for peoples who live in the ruins of destroyed cities, whose societies are decimated by genocide, or who barely subsist in the face of famine and poverty."[44] Nevertheless, as is the case with Jewish reading of Lamentations, while it is possible to invite people to voice their suffering in the way Lam 1 does,[45] it is also problematic insofar as this invitation may encourage people to take for granted the implication that their sufferings must be God's punishment for their waywardness.

32. Cox and Paulsell, *Lamentations and the Song of Songs*, 6–14.

33. Parry, *Lamentations*, 179.

34. Lee, *Singers of Lamentations.*

35. A. C. C. Lee, "Engaging Lamentations and *The Lament for the South*," in *Distant Voices Drawing Near: Essays in Honor of Antoinette Clark Wire*, ed. H. E. Hearon (Collegeville: Liturgical, 2004), 173–87; cf. also A. C. C. Lee, "Mothers Bewailing: Reading Lamentations," in *Her Master's Tools? Feminist and Postcolonial Engagements of Historical-Critical Discourse*, ed. C. Vander Stichele and T. Penner, GPBS 9 (Atlanta: Society of Biblical Literature, 2005), 195–210; A. C. C. Lee, "Reading Daughter Zion and Lady Meng," in *The Five Scrolls*, ed. A. Brenner-Idan, Gale A. Yee, and A. C. C. Lee, Texts@Contexts (London: T&T Clark, 2018), 159–73.

36. N. C. Lee, "Lamentations and Polemic: The Rejection/Reception History of Women's Lament . . . and Syria," *Int* 67 (2013): 155–83.

37. N. Sarras, "Daughter Zion Identifies with Syrian and Iraqi Women: A Reading in the Book of Lamentations," *Word & World* 37 (2017): 84–92.

38. Villanueva, *Lamentations.*

39. K. L. Nguyen, *Chorus in the Dark: The Voices of the Book of Lamentations*, HBM 54 (Sheffield: Sheffield Phoenix, 2013).

40. C. Motupalli, "Beyond Boundaries: Exploring the Interconnections of Lamentations and Dalit Poetry," *Bangalore Theological Forum* 44/2 (2012): 92–108.

41. D. Shute, "Interpreting Lamentations: Theodicy and the Turks," in *A Companion to Peter Martyr Vermigli*, ed. T. Kirby, E. Campi, and F. A. James, Brill's Companions to the Christian Tradition (Leiden: Brill, 2009), 267–82.

42. S.-C. Rah, "Truth Be Told: A Necessary Funeral Dirge in the Middle of Our Conversation," *ExAud* 31 (2015): 200–205.

43. K. M. Wilson, "Daughter Zion Speaks in Auschwitz: A Post-Holocaust Reading of Lamentations," *JSOT* 37 (2012): 93–108.

44. K. M. O'Connor, *Lamentations and the Tears of the World*, xiv.

45. C. Cavazos Renken, "Lamentations 1," *Int* 67 (2013): 194–95; A. Smith, "'Look and See If There Is Any Sorrow Like My Sorrow': Systemic Metaphors for Pastoral Theology and Care," *Word & World* 21 (2001): 5–15; D. Guest, "Lamentations" (reading the scroll on behalf of LGBTQ people).

1:1 "Is There Pain Like My Pain?"

Grant, Almighty God, that as the deformity of thy Church at this day is sufficient to dishearten us all, we may learn to look to thine hand, and know that the reward of our sins is rendered to us, and that we may not doubt but that thou wilt be our physician to heal our wound, provided we flee to thy mercy; and do thou so retain us in the assurance of thy goodness and paternal care, that we may not hesitate, even in extreme evils, to call on thee in the name of thine only-begotten Son, until we shall find by experience that never in vain are the prayers of those, who, relying on thy promises, patiently look for a remedy from thee alone, even in extreme evils, and also in death itself.—Amen.[46]

aleph[a] [1]*How the city sat down*[b] *alone,*[c]
one that was great[d] *with a people.*
She became like a widow,[e]
one that was great among the nations.
Princess among the provinces,
she came into slavery.[f]

a. LXX precedes v. 1 with "After Israel was taken captive and Jerusalem was laid waste, Jeremiah sat crying and uttered this lament about Jerusalem, and said"; various MSS of Vg have something similar. The tradition may build on 2 Chr 35:25, though that note refers to the death of Josiah. Tg has a different introduction in which Jeremiah asks why Jerusalem's destruction happened; what follows in Lam 1 is then God's reply.

b. I follow LXX, Syr, Vg in translating the *qatal* verb as past. Contrast the *yiqtol* in 3:28.

c. "How lonely sits" (cf. NRSV, NIV) is misleading; "how" does not qualify *alone*, which is actually a noun, meaning "[in] isolation." BHS, *NJPS*, taking *'êkâ* to mean "alas," print it outside the line as an anacrusis (cf. Kraus, *Klagelieder*, 36). But as the *aleph* word it is unlikely to be extra-metrical; and Lam 1; 2; 3; and 5 all begin with a four-stress colon. (Lam 4 begins with a 3-3 line, which carries comparable weight.)

d. *Rabbātî* is either an archaic construct form or simply has a linking *î* (GK 90kl; *IBHS* 8.2) that "serve[s] only a decorative purpose" (DG 27). On the construct expression, see DG 35d.

e. Whereas in Lam 1–2 MT generally locates the *athnah* accent (signifying the major midpoint pause in a verse) after the first line or after the second line, in v. 1 it has the *athnah* here, which suggests reading the verse as a double tricolon.

f. For *mas*, LXX, Vg have "tribute," the meaning in later Hebrew (BDB). The third line in v. 1 reverses the order of cola compared with the first two; v. 1e–f thus forms an a-b-b'-a' sequence with v. 1c–d and brings the opening verse to a marked close.

1 "Lamentations opens upon a universe of sorrow."[47] The poem begins by plunging headlong into a pronouncement, like the book of Psalms but other-

46. Calvin, *Jeremiah and Lamentations*, 5:363.

47. K. M. O'Connor, *Lamentations and the Tears of the World*, 17.

wise more or less uniquely in the First Testament; it lacks both any narrative framework and any indication of a figure who lies behind it in some way. "A man were never able to expresse how effectuall and proper, upon the sudden and first entrance, these exclamations are."[48] Like most narratives and other poetic books, it also lacks any indication of an addressee.[49] *How* (*'êkâ*) is not inherently an expression of horror or grief, "a gasp of desperation,"[50] but an expression of astonishment.[51] The fact that it begins with aleph is a major reason for its being the first word in the poem (as in 2:1; 4:1), but it recurs (4:2) when there is no such need, which suggests that its meaning as a pointer to bewilderment does count. Nor is there anything inherently bad about sitting alone (Num 23:9; Deut 33:28; Jer 49:31), which can suggest "solitary security."[52] Thus *how the city sat down alone* need not signal something undesirable. But soon, "its uniqueness turns into its nemesis."[53] The force of the *how* carries over into the second and third lines of v. 1, and what follows in vv. 2–4 will further bring out the negative implications of the city's being alone (but see also 3:28). The horrified potential of the word *'êkâ* thus emerges in the nature of what it refers to; "there is no question here of a sort of amorphous grief."[54] Taking the *how* as a question, Tg imagines Yahweh mourning with a similar "how" when he threw Adam and Eve from the garden, hinting at a link with the "where are you?" (*'ayyekâ*) of Gen 3:9.[55] Isa 1:21 also utters a horrified "how" at the sight of the city, but it is an exclamation at its faithlessness. Nearer home, this *how* follows on the occurrences of the word in Jer 48:39; 51:41, which from a Judahite angle might be expressions of satisfaction,[56] but only because from a Moabite or Babylonian angle it is an expression of horror.

"Tragic reversal" is a prominent motif in Lam 1,[57] and v. 1 expounds it in three ways. "A series of tragic reversals"[58] came to the city; its fate is expressed in disturbing language and imagery.[59] The verse's three lines are par-

48. D. Toussaine, *The Lamentations and Holy Mourninges of the Prophet Ieremiah* (London: Bate, ca. 1587), 3.

49. Thomas, "Poetry and Theology," 127.

50. D. Bergant, "*'êkāh:* A Gasp of Desperation (Lamentations 1:1)," *Int* 67 (2013): 144–54.

51. See BDB.

52. Hillers, *Lamentations,* 64.

53. Landy, "Lamentations," 330.

54. J. Renkema, *Lamentations,* HCOT (Leuven: Peeters, 1998), 94.

55. P. S. Alexander, *The Targum of Lamentations: Translated, with a Critical Introduction, Apparatus, and Notes,* ArBib 17B (Collegeville, MN: Liturgical, 2007), 125.

56. Again, see BDB.

57. House, "Lamentations," 338.

58. L. Rong, *Forgotten and Forsaken by God (Lam 5:19–20): The Community in Pain in Lamentations and Related Old Testament Texts* (Eugene, OR: Pickwick, 2013), 65.

59. Guest, "Hiding behind the Naked Women," 415.

allel, each drawing a contrast between what Jerusalem had been and what has happened to it. Lamentations has in common with 1 and 2 Kings the triad of kingship, city, and temple,[60] but for Lamentations it is the city that most counts. *City* is a feminine word, which facilitates the personifying of a city as a woman. The semi-identification of a city with a goddess (notably, Athena) may be part of the background to the usage,[61] but the more immediate background is the picturing of a city and a people as a woman in the Prophets, sometimes with positive but sometimes with negative implications (see "Main Themes and Their Implications," pp. 27–32, with the references). This city had been *great with a people*, a city that was home to a numerous people. It was not big by some standards, but it had that distinction within Judah, at least. It had been *great among the nations*: again, the description depends on what one compares it with and on when one does the comparison. Perhaps the verse refers back to Israel's heyday under David. Likewise, the woman-city was a *princess among provinces*. Presumably these are the provinces of the Babylonian Empire (cf. Ezek 19:8), though becoming a marginalized jurisdiction as a mere province of an empire will be more literally true when Persia has replaced Babylon.[62]

Within each line, the point then lies in the contrast between the impressive description (*great, great, princess*) and the present reality of what has happened to Jerusalem. When a city falls, *una dies interest inter magnam civitatem et nullam*—"There is but one day between a great city and no city."[63] Isaiah 47:1, 5 will three times anticipate the moment when Yahweh tells Babylon to sit down in the sense of descending from her throne and sitting on the ground to get on with some work. Babylon's sitting will be a reversal of the one that she imposed on Jerusalem. Jerusalem is now alone in the sense of being empty. Its people are all gone. If it has been abandoned and it has no inhabitants, one might ask whether it is really a city at all.[64] But the poem continues to work with the personification. While one way of personifying a

60. J. A. Dearman, "Out of Sight but Not out of Mind (2 Kings 23:27): Reading 1–2 Kings with Lamentations," in Melton and H. A. Thomas, *Reading Lamentations Intertextually*.

61. Cf. E. R. Follis, "The Holy City as Daughter," in *Directions in Biblical Hebrew Poetry*, ed. E. R. Follis, JSOTSup 40 (Sheffield: Sheffield Academic, 1987), 173–84.

62. C. Mitchell, "'How Lonely Sits the City': Identity and the Creation of History," in *Approaching Yehud: New Approaches to the Study of the Persian Period*, ed. J. Berquist, SemeiaSt 50 (Atlanta: Society of Biblical Literature, 2007), 71–83; she goes on to ask how Jerusalem copes with being alone, widowed, and marginalized, and she answers: by writing history.

63. The saying is attributed to Seneca by J. Trapp (*A Commentary or Exposition upon These Following Books of Holy Scripture: Proverbs of Solomon, Ecclesiastes, the Song of Songs, Isaiah, Jeremiah, Lamentations, Ezekiel and Daniel* [Kidderminster: Simmons, 1660]). But I have not been able to locate it.

64. Peter Martyr Vermigli, *Commentary on the Lamentations of the Prophet Jeremiah* (Kirksville, MO: Truman State University, 2002), 11.

city lets the city stand for its people, here the city that is empty of people retains a person-like nature; distinguishing city from people makes it possible to imagine how the city looks from a less anthropocentric angle.[65] Whereas the idea that the exile turned Judah into an empty land is a myth, the idea of Jerusalem being turned into an empty city is not so misleading. The destruction wrought by the Babylonians (Jer 52:12–14) made it more or less uninhabitable (see the comments on ongoing life in Judah under "Occasion, Place of Origin, and Destination," pp. 16–17). The next verse will further explain the city's aloneness. Within v. 1, meanwhile, only in the middle line does it become explicit that the poem is talking about a woman, and then in shocking fashion it jumps straight to her being *a widow*. "In the midst of life we are in death," I say each time I minister at a funeral. Here, the question is whether in the midst of death we can be in life.[66] Although the idea is not that the woman-city is dead, this poem does have parallels with a dirge mourning a death, like Amos 5:2.[67] Has her husband died, then? Is her God dead?[68] The poem implies rather that her husband has abandoned her. She is only *like* a widow.[69] We should not press the imagery. There is an analogy with the way the First Testament elsewhere can imply both that she has been divorced and that she has not. What, then, is the significance of being a widow and being alone? It has been said that "widows are among our country's most oppressed minorities."[70] Being a widow is not merely to have lost the love of your life; it is to be without resources or support and to be seriously vulnerable.[71] "For all time this is my place to sit down/settle," Yahweh had said (Ps 132:14).[72] But he has gone. When Isa 47:8 imagines Babylon confident that she will never sit as a widow, it is again envisaging a reversal of the fate imposed on Jerusalem. The third line further pictures Jerusalem as having found herself not merely doing menial housework for herself and not merely joining another family as something

65. P. Trudinger, "How Lonely Sits the City: Reading Lamentations as City and Land," in *Exploring Ecological Hermeneutics*, ed. N. C. Habel and P. Trudinger, SymS 46 (Atlanta: Society of Biblical Literature, 2008), 41–52.

66. Cf. Linafelt, *Surviving Lamentations: Catastrophe, Lament and Protest*, 35.

67. X. H. T. Pham (*Mourning in the Ancient Near East and the Hebrew Bible*, LHBOTS 302 [Sheffield: Sheffield Academic, 1999], 37–95) emphasizes the significance of mourning as a key to understanding Lam 1, which paints a portrait of people mourning the "death" of their city.

68. M. L. Mitchell, "A Reading of the Imagery of Lamentations" (PhD diss. McGill University, 2004), 34.

69. Cf. *b.* Sanhedrin 104a.

70. J. Brothers, *Widowed: A Guide to Living after Loss* (New York: Ballantine, 1990), 81; quoted in Allen, *Liturgy of Grief*, 36.

71. See further Bailey, "Lamentations," 28–29. *B.* Ketubbot 103a contains interesting material on the rights of a widow.

72. Calvin, *Jeremiah and Lamentations*, 5:354.

like a bondservant but as conscripted into actual servitude to some family, into something worse than bond service. "Loneliness and powerlessness" will be recurrent themes through Lamentations.[73]

bet [2]*She cries, cries*[a] *in the night,*
so her tears are on her cheek.
For her, there is no one comforting
from all her friends.
As all her neighbors broke faith with her,[b]
to her they became enemies.[c]

a. The infinitive absolute precedes the finite verb, conveying a highlighting effect.

b. The word order (subject before verb) and the asyndeton suggest that this clause is subordinate to the next one.

c. The last words of v. 2c–d and v. 2e–f, *her friends* and *enemies*, are participles from similar verbs (*'āhēb* and *'āyab*) with opposite meanings. And *all her neighbors* and *to her enemies* come at the extremities of v. 2e–f, bookending the line and marking the contrast.

2 Crying is Zion's first action in Lamentations.[74] And nighttime is when one may be especially overcome with grief (cf. Pss 6:6[7]; 77:6[7]; 119:55), though the parallelism in the first line might take for granted an implicit reference to daytime in the second colon, when tears are ever-present on the city's cheeks. She has lots of reasons to cry. What in particular applies here?

In the parallelism between the lines, the second and third give the answer. *Comforting* (*nāḥam piel* participle) is a key word in the chapter (vv. 9, 16, 17, 21); the verb will also recur in 2:13. It makes for another anticipatory link with Isa 40–55 (40:1; 49:13; 51:3, 12, 19; 52:9; 54:11), where it also recurs from Jer 31:13, though in Isaiah and Jeremiah Yahweh is the comforter. The exposition of the comfort theme in these passages informs Paul's disquisition on comfort in 2 Cor 7:5–13.[75] The context in those different passages indicates that comfort is both affective and practical. Here, following on the first line with all that crying, it initially suggests the affective. When a person loses someone dear to them, it is to be expected that people will come to comfort them; "all mourners ought to have comforters, and to be without a comforter is a particularly grievous thing."[76] Leading into the

73. J. Hunter, *Faces of a Lamenting City: The Development and Coherence of the Book of Lamentations*, BEATAJ (Frankfurt: Lang, 1996), 96.

74. K. M. O'Connor, "Lamentations," in *The New Interpreter's Bible*, ed. L. E. Keck, vol. 6 (Nashville: Abingdon, 2001), on the passage.

75. J. Kaplan, "Comfort, O Comfort, Corinth: Grief and Comfort in 2 Corinthians 7:5–13a," *HTR* 104 (2011): 433–45.

76. S. M. Olyan, *Biblical Mourning: Ritual and Social Dimensions* (Oxford: Oxford University Press, 2004), 46.

last line, comfort also suggests the practical. Jerusalem's *friends*, specifically her *neighbors*, are people such as Moab, Edom, and Ammon, with whom Judah had been involved in conversations about joint action only a decade before the city's fall (see Jer 27). *Friends* does not in itself carry negative connotations,[77] as if to imply that the city is a "loose woman."[78] But read in light of Jeremiah, the words *friends* and *neighbors* gain a snide overtone: they suggest lovers with whom Judah was involved in illicit relationships (Jer 3:1, 20; 5:8; 6:21; 22:20, 22).

Whether or not the snide tone obtains, there is no doubt that these associates let Jerusalem down; *broke faith* is another Jeremiah verb (Jer 3:8, 11, 20; 5:11). If Lamentations implies that Jerusalem broke faith with Yahweh and entered into illicit relationships with other peoples, then it is with poetic justice that those other peoples broke faith with Judah. They not only let her down; they *became enemies to her.* The verse evokes both sympathy and accusation.[79]

gimel [3]*Judah went into exile*[a] *away from*[b] *humbling,*
away from greatness of servitude.[c]
Though she sat down among the nations,[d]
she did not find rest.
All her pursuers, they caught up with her
among the narrows.[e]

a. The verb *gālətâ* is feminine; *Judah* can be feminine when it denotes the country and its people. Vg nicely renders "migravit" (see the commentary).

b. For *min* here and in the next colon, Vg, Tg have "on account of," which is quite appropriate.

c. Tg refers the line to the humbling and servitude people imposed on each other, alluding to the story in Jer 34.

d. The asyndeton and the word order (subject before verb—the pronoun *hî'* being semantically unnecessary) again suggest that this clause is subordinate to the next one.

e. *Məṣārîm* are thus distressing or narrow places (Vg, Tg) rather than oppressors or adversaries (LXX). An abstract meaning such as "distress" (NRSV, NIV) is unlikely in the context. The word might remind people of *miṣrayim* (Egypt); it is as if people found themselves back in a metaphorical Egypt when they sought refuge somewhere (for some people it was the literal Egypt; see Jer 43).

77. I. W. Provan, *Lamentations*, NCB (London: Marshall, 1991), 36.

78. K. M. O'Connor, "Lamentations," in *Women's Bible Commentary*, ed. C. A. Newsom, Sharon H. Ringe, and Jacqueline E. Lapsley, rev. ed. (London: SPCK, 2014), 280.

79. Hillers, *Lamentations*, 81.

3 The fall of Jerusalem was just the last stage of a bad experience. To judge from the second and third lines, the exile to which the first line refers is not the Babylonians herding Judahites off but the self-imposed exile of Judahites who sought refuge *among the nations* during the years leading up to the city's fall and afterwards, when people took themselves off to somewhere such as Ammon or Egypt.[80] In Lamentations, there is actually little focus on exile from the land or on the land itself,[81] which fits with the poems having their origin in Judah rather than (for example) Babylon. In referring to Judah, the poem moves the focus for a moment from the city to the people of the city and the country, but with an implication of solidarity between the people who left the city in various directions and the people who stayed behind until the end.[82] The country's history of subservience, the series of invasions, and the protracted final campaign by the Babylonians had been an experience of *humbling* (*'ōnî*), of being put down and afflicted and made to suffer (1:7, 9; 3:1, 19, 33; 5:11), so that for practical purposes people had long been in *servitude* to the Babylonians; in effect the two expressions may form a hendiadys. They recall the Israelites' original experience of humbling and servitude in Egypt (e.g., Gen 15:13; Deut 26:6). So Judah's subjection to Babylon in the years running up to the city's fall had led many Judahites to get out so as to settle elsewhere.

The verb for this settling (*yāšab*) is the same verb as in v. 1: as the city now *sat down* alone in its place, the Judahites had *sat down* in their places of refuge, perhaps breathing a sigh of relief. But they *did not find rest*. The experience fits the warning in Deut 28:65; the parallel is the first of a number of allusions in the poems to Yahweh's threats in Deut 28–32 and Lev 26, which have been fulfilled and more than fulfilled.[83]

Why did the city's people not find rest? The last line apparently explains, though it is a little enigmatic. Pursuing and catching up recalls the story of Zedekiah's flight, where the two words come together (e.g., Jer 52:8). The description of Zedekiah's fate in the Arabah becomes a description of or a metaphor for the fate of other Judahites. In Lamentations, it is the first of many examples of turning concrete events into figures of speech in this way.

80. See R. B. Salters, "Lamentations 1:3: Light from the History of Exegesis," in *A Word in Season: Essays in Honour of William McKane*, ed. P. R. Davies and J. D. Martin, JSOTSup 42 (Sheffield: JSOT Press, 1986), 73–89.

81. J. L. Helberg, "Land in the Book of Lamentations," *ZAW* 102 (1990): 372–85.

82. Koenen, *Klagelieder*, 43.

83. D. C. Flanders, "The Covenant Curses Transposed: Allusions in Lamentations to Deuteronomy 28–32 and Leviticus 26," in *Megilloth Studies*, ed. B. Embry, HBM 78 (Sheffield: Sheffield Phoenix, 2016), 96–109.

dalet 4*The paths to Zion*[a] *are mourning*
for lack of people coming to an assembly.[b]
All her gateways are desolate,
her priests are crying out.
Her girls[c] *are sorrowful,*[d]
and she herself, it's hard for her.[e]

a. Lit. "paths of Zion"; LXX, Vg, Tg translate literally and may imply streets *in* the city.

b. LXX, Syr, Vg take *mô'ēd* to denote "festival," which will be the implication; people are gathering for a festival. But etymologically the word denotes something that has been officially set—an occasion, event, time, or meeting (it recurs in 2:6, 7, 22). Here, *assembly* is more likely following *coming [to]*, and the word has this meaning in v. 15d.

c. *Bətûlâ* (like Greek *parthenos* and Latin *virgo*) means a teenage girl, a girl of marriageable age. She would be charitably assumed to be a virgin, but the word does not exactly have that actual meaning—hence the addition in some passages of a phrase such as "who had not had sex with a man" or "with whom no one had had sex" (Gen 24:16; Judg 11:24, 39). Over against *na'ărâ* or *yaldâ* or *'almâ*, it might suggests vulnerability; it denotes a girl under the care and protection of her family. But those other words do not come in Lamentations, and *bətûlâ* is simply the female correlative to *bāḥûr* (1:18; 2:21).

d. LXX "being led off" (cf. Aq, Sym) apparently takes *nûgôt* not as *niphal* from *yāgâ* but as *qal* passive from *nāhag*; and from *yāgâ* one would actually expect *nôgôt*. MT might be a composite form (G. R. Driver, "Hebrew Notes on 'Song of Songs' and 'Lamentations,'" in *Festschrift Alfred Bertholet zum 80. Geburtstag*, ed. W. Baumgartner et al. [Tübingen: Mohr, 1950], 136).

e. In form, *mar* might be a noun or an adjective, but the construction matches 2 Kgs 4:27, which suggests a (stative) verb.

4 The poem returns to the fate of Jerusalem in light of that flight and the city's final fall, though it speaks of *Zion* rather than Jerusalem. Both names come three times in the chapter; Zion comes more frequently in Lam 2–4. Insofar as the implications of the two names can be distinguished, Zion refers especially to the city as the place to which Yahweh is committed, where he dwells, and where festivals happen. Verse 4 incorporates a sequence of nonverbal clauses (omitting *are* each time helps one to get the impression) that describe the ongoing nature of life in the city. Three times a year, the *paths to Zion* from north, east, south, and west would normally throng with people coming for the *assembly* on occasions such as Pesah, Shavuot, and Sukkot. But the roads are empty and quiet instead of being noisy and joyful; it is as if the paths themselves are sad (cf. Jer 14:2).[84]

The *gateways* to which the paths lead are the entrances to the city or to the temple area, and normally they would also be places of joy and praise

84. Cf. D. R. Hillers, "'The Roads to Zion Mourn' (Lam 1:4)," *Perspective* 12 (1971): 126; he also notes broader parallels with Joel 1:1–20.

because of where they lead (Pss 9:14[15]; 100:4). But it follows that they are *desolate*—which can denote physical ruin but in this context suggests a continuation of the idea of mourning. They are grieving over the absence of people going through them for the festival. And obviously the *priests are crying out* in grief over this lack—or they would be if they had not fled, been taken off into exile, or been killed. The description may thus seem surreal.[85] Would there be priests there who had not been Jerusalem-based or who had joined other people in going off to take refuge elsewhere and have come back? Perhaps the poem is simply imagining priests there and grieving.

Likewise, the city's *girls* would be sorrowful (if they were there) instead of being able to lead processions with dancing and playing (Tg; cf. Exod 15:20–21; Jer 31:13). If worship has stopped, there is neither joy nor life, only grief and death; the verse speaks of the end of all life.[86] To sum it up: yes, *it is hard for her*, for Zion; the verse comes to a climax with a verbal expression to close—the only verb in the verse.

he [5]*Her adversaries became the head*
though her enemies were relaxed.[a]
Because Yahweh, he made her sorrowful[b]
on account of the greatness of her rebellions.
Her little ones, they went as captives[c]
before the adversary.

a. LXX renders *šālû* from the rare verb *šālâ* ("flourished"); cf. Vg "got rich" (see BDB). The word order (subject before verb) combined with the asyndesis here suggests that this second clause is subordinate to the first clause.

b. Vg, Aq "said" derives *hôgāh* from *hāgâ* rather than *yāgâ*; Sym "led" again derives it from *nāhag* (see the translation note on v. 4).

c. LXX, Tg "in captivity" translates as if the text said *baššəbî* (cf. v. 18).

5 The poem goes back to the event of the city's fall, how it happened, and what followed. For *adversaries* to become *the head* recalls the threat in Deut 28:44, and in this further allusion to such threats, it gives another hint about where the poem will need to go in acknowledging why things happened as they did. It was not *her enemies* who were supposed to be *relaxed* and at ease (Ps 122:6–7), but they were able to be so in taking control and then in exercising it. Prosaically put, the adversaries/enemies found it easy to take Jerusalem (though the time and effort involved in doing so suggests that they might not have seen it that way).

85. Dobbs-Allsopp, *Lamentations*, 60.

86. Koenen, *Klagelieder*, 46.

Thus *Yahweh, he made her sorrowful* (like the girls of v. 4). The first line's allusion to the threat in Deut 28:44 has hinted whose intention might have been fulfilled in what happened, and this line makes the point more explicit. Here for the first time the poem is "introducing Yahweh"[87] and emphasizing its point by putting him before the verb. Is this declaration about his involvement an observation that readers should welcome?[88] Its implication is that at least this city destruction was not random and meaningless, nor was it simply caused by the willfulness of an enemy, nor did it happen because Yahweh was incapable of stopping it or not interested in doing so. Nor was it a random act on Yahweh's part: he undertook it *because of the greatness of her rebellions*. In this sense, the calamity that overcame Jerusalem is one she has to accept responsibility for. She had engaged in insurrection; it was "not simply a mistake or a violation of social or ritual prescription."[89] It involved flouting the authority of its King. The reference to Zion's wrongdoing arrives quite casually, like the reference to Yahweh's involvement. Both thus indicate assumptions that the poem simply takes for granted. It does not feel the need to argue the points. The incidental nature of the references to Zion's wrongdoing does not give the impression that "the theological intent of chapter one of Lamentations is to justify God's destruction of the Temple in Jerusalem as punishment for sin."[90] Theodicy is not a focus of the poem. Lamentations 1 does illustrate how "the problem of evil is contemplated in Lamentations from the perspective of human suffering rather than human sin"[91]—or at least more from that perspective. Yet for all its protests and remonstrations at Yahweh's action and subsequent inaction, evidently Lamentations is not against the idea that guilt can issue in retribution and that in her experience it has done so. There is risk involved in making this principle work backward, so as to provide a retrospective explanation of an event, as Job's friends do.[92] But Lamentations is not simply working retrospectively; it has lots of concrete prophetic warnings to back up its assessment.[93] Nor is the poem critiquing the city in the way, say, a Brit might criticize the United States for its approach to gun control or an American might critique Britain for its imperial past. It more resembles people in the United States or in Brit-

87. House, "Lamentations," 350.

88. See D. J. A. Clines, "Lamentations," in *Eerdmans Commentary on the Bible*, ed. J. D. G. Dunn and J. W. Rogerson (Grand Rapids: Eerdmans, 2003), 618.

89. D. Bergant, "The Challenge of Hermeneutics: Lamentations 1:1–11: A Test Case," *CBQ* 64 (2002): 11.

90. N. Graetz, *Unlocking the Garden: A Feminist Jewish Look at the Bible, Midrash, and God* (Piscataway, NJ: Gorgia, 2005), 115.

91. Dobbs-Allsopp, "Tragedy, Tradition, and Theology," 55.

92. U. Berges, *Klagelieder*, HThKAT (Freiburg: Herder, 2002), 103.

93. See further v. 8 and the commentary on it.

ain grieving over their own country's difficulty in dealing with such issues. But the poem does not yet make explicit that Zion herself acknowledges her rebellions; it is the commentator on the situation who refers to them as explaining the disaster and the sorrow it brought.

As the first line raises a question about why it happened and the second answers it, the second line raises a question about the nature of this sorrow and the third answers it. The sorrow consisted in the exiling of the city's *little ones*, driven before their captors like cattle. While the *little ones* might be literal children, the fact that it follows the previous two lines suggests that the expression more likely refers to the people in general. It is another expression of pathos. The word commonly appears in contexts that suggest vulnerability.[94]

waw [6]*So from Ms. Zion*[a] *went away*
all her majesty.
Her officials became like deer[b]
that did not find pasture.
They went without energy
before the pursuer.

a. In the construct expression *bat-ṣiyyôn*, traditionally "daughter of Zion," the "of" would be similar to the "of" in phrases such as "land of Egypt" (see, e.g., JM 129f); it is an appositional or defining genitive. See the commentary.

b. LXX, Vg "rams" implies *'êlîm* for MT *'ayyālîm*; it makes good sense as a metaphor for officials but poor sense in connection with the reference to looking for pasture.

6 The poetic expression *Ms. Zion*, more literally "daughter Zion,"[95] recurs in Isaiah and Jeremiah as well as being frequent in Lam 2 (see the commentary there). In the background may again be the idea of a city having a patron goddess and of a city as a god's wife. It is one of the ways of spelling out the conventional picture of the city as a woman. But the First Testament background of the expression also makes Ms. Zion a symbol of praise and joy (e.g., Pss 9:14[15]; 48:2[3], 11[12]). In light of those associations, the statement that her *majesty* (*hādār*) has gone away is especially disturbing,[96] though in due course Yahweh will promise to restore her image (see Isa 52:1–2; 62:11).

94. M. L. Mitchell, "Reading of the Imagery of Lamentations," 43.

95. See J. A. Dearman, "Daughter Zion and Her Place in God's Household," *HBT* 31 (2009): 144–59; Dearman is responding to M. H. Floyd ("Welcome Back, Daughter of Zion!" *CBQ* 70 [2008]: 484–504), who replies in "The Daughter of Zion Goes Fishing in Heaven," in Boda, Dempsey, and Flesher, *Daughter Zion*, 177–200.

96. Cf. A. Labahn, "Metaphor and Intertextuality: 'Daughter of Zion' as a Test Case," *SJOT* 17 (2003): 58–67.

The similar phrases "daughter Judah" (1:15; 2:2, 4) and "daughter my people" (2:11; 3:48; 4:3, 6, 10) indicate that the expression's application is not confined to cities, and parallel phrases such as "daughter Edom," "daughter Babylon," and "daughter Egypt" (e.g., 4:21–22; Jer 46:11; 51:33) indicate that there is nothing inherently endearing about the expression. Nevertheless, Zion's being designated a widow, a mother, and now a daughter heightens the emotion of the poetry.[97] More specifically, her being a daughter and someone therefore owed protection by her father will add to the force of what follows in vv. 7–8.[98]

Once more the first line has raised a question that the next line clarifies: What is this majesty? It was not only the children or the people in general who went into exile from the city (v. 5). *Majesty* is especially an attribute of a king (Pss 21:5[6]; 45:3–4[5–6]; see also Isa 5:14; 53:2; Prov 14:28; Dan 11:20) and of Yahweh as King (Pss 96:6; 104:1; 111:3; 145:5). And from Jerusalem the king indeed went away (two of them, in fact: Jehoiachin and Zedekiah) along with the rest of the majesty of the palace and the city's *officials*.

Yet again, the middle line, too, raises a question as well as answering one. How were the officials like *deer that did not find pasture*? The last line suggests that they resemble the deer in Ps 42:1(2). The phrase might refer to the vain seeking of refuge of which v. 3a–d spoke. Or it might refer to their exhaustion by the time the city fell, when they could not think of anywhere to go and were easily captured, like the king recalled by v. 3e–f. Or it might bring to mind again the driving like animals at which v. 5 hinted. Or it might bring to mind deer seeking to evade capture, who in that situation can get paralyzed by fear. The simile anyway suggests that they were easily taken and slaughtered.

zayin 7 *Jerusalem was mindful*[a]
of the days[b] *of her humbling and her being put down,*[c]
Of all the things she valued,[d]
those that were[e] *from days of old,*
When her people fell into the adversary's hand,
and there was no helper for her.[f]
The adversaries looked at her—
they laughed over her ceasing.[g]

a. For *zākərâ yərûšālim*, 4QLam reads *zkwrh yhwh* ("be mindful, Yahweh"). On the 4QLam readings in v. 7, see G. Kotzé, "A Text-Critical Analysis of Lamentations 1:7 in

97. D. A. Bosworth, "Daughter Zion and Weeping in Lamentations 1–2," *JSOT* 38 (2013): 226.

98. Cf. C. M. Maier, *Daughter Zion, Mother Zion: Gender, Space, and the Sacred in Ancient Israel* (Minneapolis: Fortress, 2008), 74.

4QLam and the Masoretic Text," *OTE* 24 (2011): 590–611; cf. Kotzé, *Qumran Manuscripts of Lamentations*, 41–52.

b. NRSV, NIV, NJPS have "in the days," which would be accusative of time, but other examples of accusative of time (GK 118i) are more punctiliar, and syntactically it is more natural to take the phrases as the object of the verb (so LXX, Vg, Tg).

c. *Mərûdîm* looks like a passive participle from *mārad* ("rebel"), and an active form of that verb would fit (cf. Vg, Aq), but the passive makes poor sense. BDB, *HALOT*, *DCH* rather take it as a noun from *rûd* ("wander"), which would involve a metonymy; Jerusalem herself does not wander. But on all three occurrences (cf. 3:19; Isa 58:7), the word pairs with *ʿānî* or *ʿŏnî*, which suggests that the noun derives from *rādad* or *rādâ*, or a byform (Tg; also LXX, "rejections").

d. For *maḥămudêkā*, 4QLam has *mkʾwbnw* ("our pain"; see note a).

e. Vg "that she had." The *ʾăšer* would usually not appear in poetry; I take it as introducing an independent relative clause (GK 138e).

f. Whereas all eighteen lines so far have been syntactically self-contained, here the first three lines link by enjambment; neither v. 7c–d nor v. 7e–f can stand on its own.

g. LXX, Aq "settling" (in exile) derives *mišbattekā* from *yāšab* (cf. vv. 1a, 3c). One could reduce the verse to the usual three lines, taking the last two lines as a conflate text, or one could rework the first two lines (see, e.g., R. Schäfer, "Der ursprüngliche Text und die poetische Struktur des ersten Klageliedes," in *Sôfer mahîr: Essays in Honour of Adrian Schenker Offered by the Editors of Biblia Hebraica Quinta*, ed. Y. Goldman, A. van der Kooij, and R. D. Weis [Leiden: Brill, 2006], 239–49).

7 "Memory is a bitter herb . . . ; sharp on the tongue, in the mind, memory heals, it confers the will to endure."[99] Paradoxically, memory is both Judah's great curse and its vital resource. People's shared memory holds them together as a community, but remembering is at the same time a devastatingly painful business. In this connection, for the first time the poem speaks of *Jerusalem* (cf. vv. 8, 17; 2:10, 13, 15; 4:12) as opposed to Zion (see the commentary on v. 4). Jerusalem refers to the city as the nation's capital and as a place where people live, the location of the palace and of people's homes and businesses. One would often have a hard time pressing this difference (see v. 17), but here *the days of her humbling and her being put down* sounds like an allusion to what happened to the city as capital. While the events of 587 will be especially in mind, the plural *days* and the plural word for *being put down* suggest a reference to the city's broader experiences, including those of 601 and 597, like the reference to humbling and the departure of Judahites in v. 3.

The verse makes a subtle move in combining reference to thinking about humbling/being put down and thinking about *all the things she valued, those that were from days of old*; the line really refers to thinking about the loss of these things. The valuable things (*maḥămuddîm*) might naturally include

99. Berrigan, *Lamentations*, 15–16.

objects from the temple (cf. Joel 3:5 [4:5]), which was plundered in 597 and in 587, but those objects are usually referred to as "treasures" (*ʾôṣərôt*; 2 Kgs 24:13). "Valuable things" more often denotes things that could be destroyed (cf. 2 Chr 36:19; Isa 64:11[10]), so the reference could cover cutting up the gold objects in the temple and breaking up its pillars (2 Kgs 24:13; 25:13). It adds to the indications that the verse refers to more than the events of 587, given that many if not most of the valuable things actually went in 597 and others were destroyed then. The naming of Jerusalem as opposed to Zion also points to the broader destruction of impressive buildings in the city—but including the devastation of the temple itself, which is otherwise oddly unmentioned.

The city's fall meant that its people as well all these things *fell into the adversary's* hand, as 2 Kgs 24 and 25 describes. *There was no helper for her* corresponds to the formulation in 2 Kgs 14:26, when Yahweh acted to "help" Ephraim in a way it did not deserve; there was no such mercy here.

The unexpected fourth line adds insult to injury with the comment about Jerusalem's consequent *ceasing* (*mišbāt*), its life effectively coming to an end. The verb "cease" (*šābat*) refers to what people do (or rather do not do) on the ceasing day each week and in the ceasing year (*šabbāt*; Vg translates "Sabbaths" here). Readers might then perceive an irony in this comment (see 2 Chr 36:21).

khet [8]*When Jerusalem did wrong, wrong,*[a]
that's how she became something for shaking one's head at.[b]
All who had honored her, they despised her,[c]
because they saw her nakedness.
Yes, she—she cried out,
and turned away.

a. Lit. "wronged a wrong," with the noun before the verb, which (combined with the asyndesis) suggests that the clause is subordinate to the one that follows. 4QLam has infinitive absolute *ḥṭwʾ* instead of the noun *ḥēṭʾ*.

b. *Nîdâ* from *nûd* (cf. LXX, Vg; also 4QLam *lnwd*); Tg "wandering" assumes another aspect of the meaning of *nûd*. Admittedly, for shaking the head, one would expect "the head" to be explicit, as in Ps 44:14[15] (B. Albrektson, *Studies in the Text and Theology of the Book of Lamentations with a Critical Edition of the Peshitta Text*, Studia Theologica Lundensia 21 [Lund: CWK Gleerup, 1963], 63–64). Verse 17 has *niddâ* ("taboo") from *nâdad* (cf. Aq), and perhaps we are to assume both connotations (Lee, *Singers of Lamentations*, 103–6). See further G. R. Kotzé, "Lamentations 1:8a in the Wordings of the Masoretic Text and 4QLam," *Scriptura* 110 (2012): 190–207; cf. Kotzé, *Qumran Manuscripts of Lamentations*, 52–59.

c. GK 67y calls *hizzîlûhā* an Aramaizing form from *zālal* (v. 11).

8 As in v. 5, the poem refers incidentally to the background of Jerusalem's trouble in its wrongdoing without feeling any need to argue this link. But the "incidental" reference is underlined by the particular formulation, which combines verb and noun for *wrong*. Whereas rebellion (v. 5) suggests Yahweh as king and the city as ignoring his authority, wrong suggests failing someone who might be a peer or failing to reach a standard, offending against a person or against standards. The unique doubling of the word suggests no small-scale culpable failure, though the poem provides no specifics. "You know what they are." But once more, the stress lies on the affliction that the offenses explain. The argument corresponds to that in the Prophets (e.g., the "that's how . . ." [*ʿal-kēn*] in Jer 5:6; 10:21; 44:23), in which they are moving not from offense to threat but from affliction to cause. *Shaking one's head* at something is a sign of dismay or horror (cf. *mānôd* in Ps 44:14[15]; but see the translation note).

With some hyperbole, the poem pictures there being many people who had *honored* and admired Jerusalem, but now their estimate goes in reverse. Whereas they had made something of her, now they insult her; the second line continues from the first line's reference to shaking the head. While vv. 6–7 hinted at the theme of honor and shame, it now becomes explicit: "The book of Lamentations as a whole is not simply a memoir of loss but a cry over the loss of honor."[100] The reason is that she is like a woman who has had her clothes torn off; *nakedness* (*ʿerwâ*) is regularly a word for someone's private parts. In a traditional society, as in a modern one, one may choose to share one's nakedness with one's lover, but the imposition of nakedness is another matter, and it is something that makes one (perhaps irrationally) feel shamed. The city has been dishonored and shamed by what has happened to it in the way a woman is dishonored and shamed by having her clothes torn off. In the background is the more concrete way in which men commonly assault women sexually when they attack a city (cf. 2:11). The concrete act done to individual women becomes an image for the metaphorical assault on the corporate woman-city. There is no suggestion here that the woman is a whore and that the poem is expressing disgust with her for that reason.[101] The comparison and contrast with Isa 1:21 is significant: perhaps either Lam 1:1, 8 are reworking the comment in Isaiah or Isa 1:21 is reworking the comment in Lamentations. And Isa 47:1–5 again promises a reversal of what Babylon did to Jerusalem.[102]

A woman treated thus would indeed cry out (*zāʿaq*), like Tamar (2 Sam 13:19). The reference to sexual violence appears in the poem not to

100. B. Savarikannu, "Expressions of Honor and Shame in Lamentations 1," *Asia Journal of Pentecostal Studies* 21 (2018): 87.

101. M. Hausl, "Lamentations: Zion's Cry in Affliction," in *Feminist Biblical Interpretation: A Compendium of Critical Commentary on the Books of the Bible and Related Literature*, ed. L. Schottroff and M.-T. Wacker (Grand Rapids: Eerdmans, 2012), 343.

102. Bergant, *Lamentations*, 41.

degrade its victim but to communicate the horror of it from the victim's angle.[103] More literally, Judah cried out (Isa 35:10; 51:11) and also turned back when faced by the foe (Pss 9:3[4]; 44:10[11]; 56:9[10]). This woman would indeed be unable to face anyone. She would share that sense that she had been shamed. So she *turned away*.

> The image of the city-woman in her abject state elicits both revulsion and pity. As we watch her, and the poet forces us to watch her, we are torn by ambivalent urges: we cannot bear to look but we cannot turn our eyes away. The more we look, the more we shame her by seeing that which should not be seen. But we must look, for the poet calls upon us to see what has happened to the city and to partake in her suffering. We become actors in the "drama" of this chapter.[104]

tet [9]*Though her pollution was in her hems,*[a]
she was not mindful of her future.
And she went down in extraordinary ways—
there was no one comforting for her.
Look at my humbling, Yahweh,
because the enemy made big.

a. LXX, Vg "feet" is not inappropriate in that *šûlîm* denotes the bottom of a robe that stretches down to the feet.

9 The development within v. 9 is similar to that in v. 8: once again a matter-of-fact recognition of wrongdoing is the background to a more extensive depiction of what followed from it. *Pollution,* contamination or stain (*ṭum'â*), implies being involved with or in contact with something that is incompatible with who Yahweh is. Such involvement or contact means that one therefore cannot come into Yahweh's presence. The cause of the pollution may be something morally neutral (such as a genital emission), something unethical (such as extortion or assault), or something religiously improper (such as serving other gods). Certainly the ethically and religiously improper had contributed to the fall of Jerusalem. Tg assumes that this pollution is the kind that issues from menstruation, which means a woman has to avoid contact with anything sacred as long as her menstruation lasts, though it is odd that it is associated here with *her hems,* the bottom part of a garment, which sounds more like the result of walking through something filthy. Perhaps the idea is that she was not bothering about her menstrual blood flowing right

103. Maier, *Daughter Zion, Mother Zion,* 147.
104. Berlin, *Lamentations,* 48.

down, which provides a metaphor for the city not bothering to conceal the ethical and religious wrongdoing that defiled it. Jerusalem had behaved like a woman who didn't bother. Anyway, it meant *she was not mindful of her future*, or of her end, or of her posterity.[105] That word (*ʾaḥărît*) can simply denote what or who will come after, or it can denote the final outcome of something,[106] which in this context will mean the final "No" of God.[107] Any of these significances might apply to Jerusalem in this connection; whichever exactly applies, the idea is that she just did not care about the implications of her behavior. (Isaiah 47:7 perhaps suggests that Babylon failed to learn from Zion's mistake.[108])

And so *she went down* (the verb from which came the noun in v. 7b). She sank, she went under, and she found herself afflicted and suffering, *in extraordinary ways*. This last term (*peleʾ*) is horrifyingly ironic. Everywhere else it denotes something that is extraordinary in a positive way, beginning in Exod 15:11. The comment about a comforter then repeats the words of v. 2c with the same implications, though in a different order and here with reference to the past event of the city's fall.

Humbling, too, picks up from v. 7b, but this last line in the verse brings a change, as Jerusalem herself now speaks for the first time in the poem, and in her words Yahweh is addressed for the first time. So she interrupts to interpolate a plea in the midst of the onlooker's report.[109] There is no implication that she is averse to what the witness has been saying. The opening lines have made clear this onlooker's sympathy for Jerusalem;[110] if anything, that report has given Ms. Zion permission and encouragement to speak for herself in the way she now does. People who speak about their pain "seek not only to describe but to persuade." Here the poet comes clean with the fact that all the way along the poem was seeking to persuade, and perhaps implies that all the way along the person it was seeking to persuade was God.[111] But whereas the witness has been speaking *about* Yahweh, Ms. Zion now speaks *to* Yahweh,[112] appealing over the witness's head to God himself.[113] She thus assumes that the implicit critique in the first line of this verse does not preclude her

105. R. Gordis, *The Song of Songs and Lamentations: A Study, Modern Translation and Commentary*, Texts and Studies of the Jewish Theological Seminary of America (New York: Ktav, 1974), 155–56.

106. See H. Seebass, "אַחֲרִית, *ʾaḥărît*," *TDOT* 1:207–12.

107. Kraus, *Klagelieder*, 34.

108. Koenen, *Klagelieder*, 58.

109. Middlemas, "Speaking of Speaking," 46.

110. Cf. Conway, "Daughter Zion," 105.

111. Linafelt, *Surviving Lamentations: Catastrophe, Lament and Protest*, 49.

112. Linafelt, "Surviving Lamentations," *HBT* 17 (1995): 46.

113. C. J. H. Wright, *Lamentations*, 65.

praying; the authority of the witness's report may be one important thing, but the plea of its subject also matters. Although appeal to God has less focus here than it will have later in Lamentations, appeal to God thus does have a place in the poems from more or less the beginning. It makes for a contrast with Ecclesiastes. In both these scrolls God is silent, but Ecclesiastes does not address God and does not suggest any assumptions about God's listening to the questions raised in the scroll. Lamentations does.[114] What is the one thing or the first thing that Ms. Zion wants? Her plea is that "God see her as she sees herself."[115] The appeal to Yahweh to look is "a core expression" in Lamentations.[116] If the first part of Lam 1 took the form of a funeral lament, "the report of her death has been greatly exaggerated and she cries out."[117] The content of her plea recalls a lament psalm: *Look at my humbling* (cf. Pss 9:13[14]; 25:18). Her boldness about praying even though she comes to Yahweh as a person guilty of faithlessness parallels other psalms and prayers that neither deny great faithlessness nor focus on it (e.g., Pss 38; 39). In such psalms, people pray as moral or religious failures, but they pray anyway. Here, the implication of the plea *to look at my humbling* will emerge only in the last lines of the poem. In v. 9 the poem simply provides a rationale for the plea (which will also be relevant there). "I may have been faithless, but what about the wrongdoing of the one whom you used to attack me?" This enemy *made big*: It is a standard formulation for wrongdoing as involving willful self-assertion. Usually passages indicate who is the victim of the self-assertion (e.g., Jer 48:26, 42; Zeph 2:8, 10); here the previous colon implies the victim's identity.

yod [10]*His own hand the adversary spread*
over all the things she valued,[a]
Because she saw nations
that came to her sanctuary,
Ones that you commanded should not come
into the congregation that belongs to you.[b]

a. In v. 7 *maḥmōd,* here *maḥmad,* apparently without difference in meaning.

b. The periphrastic expression conveys some emphasis over against the simple "your congregation" with suffix (DG 36 remark 3). The last two lines in this verse involve further enjambment; indeed, I take all three lines as one sentence.

114. B. N. Melton, *Where Is God in the Megilloth? A Dialogue on the Ambiguity of Divine Presence and Absence,* OTS 73 (Leiden: Brill, 2019), 176–77.

115. Hobbins, "Zion's Plea That God See Her as She Sees Herself," 150.

116. Cf. Renkema, *Lamentations,* 139.

117. J. Middlemas, "War, Comfort, and Compassion in Lamentations," *ExpT* 130 (2018–19): 354.

10 The poem returns to third-person speech. Not only did the people fall into the adversary's hand (v. 7d). This fate overcame *all the things she valued* (v. 7b). *His own hand* and *the things she valued* (more literally, "his hand" and "her valuables") come at either end of the line, framing it by means of the disagreeable contrast. The hand could have been both destroying the big things and appropriating the portable things.

Then, in the middle of the line, the mention of the sanctuary more or less makes explicit that the things she valued are things associated with the temple, not just with the city in general. But the mention of the sanctuary relates to a scandal that is perhaps worse. The destroying and plundering meant that *nations came to her sanctuary* and must have come inside it. Only in v. 10 in the First Testament is the temple described as *her* sanctuary, Ms. Zion's sanctuary.[118] "Jackboots have marched in the temple where barbarous hands have besmirched the sacred objects and fouled the holy places where fear and respect should have kept them away."[119]

In addition, in the third line, the verb "come into," which often denotes sex, joins other hints in the poem that the fall of Zion was the rape of Zion.[120] "Ammonite and Moabite does not come into Yahweh's congregation" (Deut 23:3 [23:4]): Lamentations uses overlapping words in reporting that *nations came into the congregation that belongs to you*. Moabites and Ammonites indeed appear (along with Chaldeans and Arameans) in connection with the beginning of the end for Jerusalem in 2 Kgs 24:2. To judge from the story in the First Testament of Ruth the Moabite, as well as the stories involving people such as Uriah the Hittite and Ebed-melech the Sudanese, there would be no objection to foreigners coming to worship in the sanctuary and joining the congregation in that connection. But destroyers and plunderers, "infidels,"[121] trampling it is a different matter. A Sumerian city lament protests:

> That enemy entered my dwelling-place wearing (his) shoes
> That enemy laid his unwashed hands on me
> He laid his hands on me, he frightened me
> That enemy laid his hands on me, he prostrated me with fright
> I was afraid, he was not afraid (of me)
> He tore my garments off me, he dressed his wife (in them)
> That enemy cut off my lapis-lazuli, he placed it on his daughter.[122]

118. Berges, *Klagelieder*, 108.

119. Slavitt's paraphrase (*Lamentations*, 63).

120. See F. W. Dobbs-Allsopp and T. Linafelt, "The Rape of Zion in Thr 1,10," *ZAW* 113 (2001): 77–81.

121. Renkema, *Lamentations*, 143.

122. Dobbs-Allsopp, *Weep, O Daughter of Zion*, 48.

In this third line of v. 10, the witness interrupts his or her own description of events and follows Ms. Zion in addressing Yahweh,[123] or perhaps Ms. Zion herself interrupts as she did in v. 9. Either way, the line reaffirms an awareness that, while description of what happened is important, so is talking to God.

kaph [11]*Her entire people were crying out,*
looking for bread.[a]
They would have given over[b] *the things they valued*[c] *for food*
to bring back life.
Look, Yahweh, and take note,
because I became despicable.[d]

a. While in isolation the participial clauses could be taken to have present reference, the link of substance with the previous verse and with the next line suggests that these participles, too, have past references.

b. I take the *qatal* verb to refer to an action "whose accomplishment in the past is to be represented, not as actual, but only as possible" (GK106p).

c. The *ketiv* has *maḥmōd* as in v. 7; the *qere* has *maḥmad* as in v. 10. 4QLam, LXX have "the things she valued," assimilating to those earlier occurrences.

d. 4QLam has masculine *zwll,* apparently making the witness the subject. Tg renders "gluttonous" (cf. BDB, 272), which ill-fits the context, while V. A. Hurowitz, on the basis of an Akkadian word, suggests "beggar" ("*zwllh* = Peddler/Tramp/Vagabond/Beggar: Lamentations i 11 in Light of Akkadian zilulû," *VT* 49 [1999]: 542–44), and H. A. Thomas suggests "thoughtless" ("The Meaning of *zōlēlâ* (Lam 1:11) One More Time," *VT* 61 [2011]: 489–98). Qara, in the Breslau version of his commentary (Anderson, "Medieval Jewish Exegesis of the Book of Lamentations" [PhD diss., University of St. Andrews, 2004], 69–70), has "cheap" as an alternative to "worthless."

11 The poem moves to speak more concretely about the city's people and about something that is more down-to-earth but was a matter of life and death during the siege of Jerusalem, when the city ran out of grain and therefore of their food staple (see Jer 37:21; 38:9; 52:6). Actually the word for bread (*leḥem*) can denote food more generally, which certainly the next (parallel) line refers to. "Hunger" is a standard element in Jeremiah's threats against Judah and Jerusalem; the vast majority of occurrences of the word in the First Testament come in Jeremiah and Ezekiel, and in Lamentations (2:19; 4:9; 5:10).

The desperate nature of the people's situation is indicated by the willingness they would have shown to trade *the things they valued* for food. Here the things are family belongings, or even their children (cf. Hos 9:16). If the line alludes to actual trading, it can hardly refer to the circumstances before the

123. C. W. Miller, "Reading Voices," 398.

city's fall, when there was no bread to trade for; after the fall, the Babylonian army presumably had food for which one might be able to barter. More likely the line indicates the trading they would have been prepared to do if there had been any food to trade for. On either interpretation, the point is that they desperately needed to get food somehow, so as *to bring back life*. They were almost in Sheol; they would have starved to death, as people no doubt did. In the down-to-earth significance attaching to the phrase *bring back life* here, it is almost distinctive to Lam 1 (cf. vv. 16, 19; cf. Ps 35:17; Job 33:30); it has possibly less down-to-earth meaning elsewhere (Ruth 4:15; Ps 19:7[8]; Prov 25:13; cf. Ps 23:3, which has a similar expression with a *polel* rather than a *hiphil* verb).

After that dramatic recollection, the poem returns to put words on the lips of the city; the first half of the chapter thus ends with this appeal to Yahweh.[124] The woman-city's speaking will dominate the second half of the poem. Again she interrupts the witness's description of events; again she appeals to Yahweh to *look*. She will have assumed that Yahweh is omniscient or all-seeing, but she wants Yahweh not merely to see but to look and pay attention and therefore act on what he sees: hence the addition of *take note*. Her sense that she *became despicable* might indicate that she had internalized the perspective of people who viewed her that way (v. 8), but following v. 11a–d, the words more directly suggest an objective point about her situation.

lamed[12] *Though it's not yours,*[a] *all who pass on the way,*
take note and look.
Is there pain like my pain,
that which was dealt out to me,
That with which[b] *Yahweh made me sorrowful*[c]
on the day of his angry blazing?

a. While the elliptical expression *lôʾ ʾălêkem* ("not for you") might be a question (Is it nothing to you?) or an exclamation (It is nothing to you!) or a wish (May it be nothing to you!), the least speculation is involved if we take it as a statement of fact, which links with the following phrase. In light of the asyndeton, I then take the colon as concessive.

b. For *ʾăšer*, Vg has "because"; but for both occurrences in v. 12, see the translation note on v. 7.

c. As in v. 5, Vg (and Sym) derives the verb from *hāgâ* rather than *yāgâ* (LXX has a double translation); 4QLam has *hwgiʾny* which might suggest *hwgiʿny* ("wearied me"; D. C. Flanders, "What Did YHWH Do in Lam 1:12? Correcting a Misreading in the DJD Edition of 4QLam," *VT* 66 [2016]: 513–23).

12 Having "interrupted" in v. 11e–f, Ms. Zion continues to speak. Yet instead of continuing to plead with Yahweh to look at what other people have done to

124. Hunter, *Faces of a Lamenting City*, 131.

her, as in a psalm, the city pleads with other people to look at what Yahweh has done to her.[125] But the notional appeal to passersby also implicitly reinforces the appeal to Yahweh. Jerusalem wants to be seen and recognized. She uses the same verbs she used toward Yahweh in v. 11, though in reverse order. Here she is not asking for any action on anyone's part; she simply needs to be noticed. The motif of people passing by a ruined city with horror recurs as an aspect of prophetic threat or anticipation (Jer 18:16; 19:8; 22:8; 49:17; 50:13). Zephaniah 2:15 imagines passersby whistling and shaking a fist when Assyria falls. And actually, no one much passed by Jerusalem; it was not on a main road. The image of passersby recognizing the city's pain externalizes the reaction of its own people, which is one reason why Zion turns from appealing to Yahweh to appealing to passersby. There is another sense in which the appeal might seem puzzling. Zion has just described herself as having become despicable. Surely she does not want to be looked at? Yet at the same time she does. "The personified city both disclaims and demands the observers' gaze."[126] In suffering, one does long to be seen and recognized by other people, so that conversely, comfort means sharing in mourning with the mourner.[127]

The poem underscores its appeal by making explicit a conviction that the passersby had not experienced anything of the kind they can see has happened here. Is the woman-city's question "self-serving"? Is she so unique?[128] Human nature may demand that the uniqueness of one's suffering be recognized.[129] Actually, the city's "claim" to uniqueness is not much of an exaggeration; Jerusalem had been devastated with distinctive thoroughness. Passersby might be tempted to avoid looking, because looking can make one feel anxious, lest one has the same experience. The experience was a pain when it happened, and it is the kind of pain that then continues. The city still sits devastated and pathetic, aware of having been assaulted and invaded, with that awareness still a reality even if the attacking army has gone.

Whereas the middle line uses a passive verb and indicates no agent, and thus leaves open the possibility that the dealing out was done by the invaders, the third line excludes any simple understanding along those lines. Behind the action of the invaders was the action of Yahweh. While the verse thus continues to voice the words of the city, it speaks about Yahweh to the passersby, and it will continue to speak *about* rather than *to* Yahweh through

125. Berges, *Klagelieder*, 110.

126. M. L. Mitchell, "Reading of the Imagery of Lamentations," 55.

127. Berlin, *Lamentations*, 48; referring to G. A. Anderson, *A Time to Mourn, A Time to Dance*, 84.

128. House, *Lamentations*, 357.

129. Bailey, "Lamentations," 33.

vv. 13–18. Its thus speaking about Yahweh points to another consideration lying behind its not continuing to address Yahweh. As the poem will assume that Yahweh sees everything, so it explicitly declares that Yahweh is responsible for the catastrophic event on which it focuses. *Yahweh made me sorrowful* (cf. vv. 4, 5). It was *the day* that prophets had threatened (e.g., Jer 17:16, 17, 18; 18:17; Zeph 1:7, 8, 9), the day of Yahweh, the day *of his angry blazing* (Jer 4:8, 26; 12:13; 30:24; Zeph 2:2). The phrase suggests the expression not of a spontaneous or irrational emotion but of a considered divine response to wrongdoing.[130]

mem [13]*From on high he sent fire into my bones*[a]
and made it go down.[b]
He spread a net for my feet,
he turned me back.
He made me a desolation,
faint all the time.

a. Tg understands the bones to refer to Judah's fortified cities.

b. While *wayyirdennâ* looks like a form from *rādâ,* which would mean "he/it won over them" (cf. Vg "instructed/chastised"?), LXX rather suggests it comes from a byform of *yārad*; cf. v. 7b and the translation note, and v. 9c.

13 Yahweh is *on high,* in the heavens, which ought to be a reason for encouragement; the one who is on high is on his people's side and can rescue and put down threats (Pss 18:16[17]; 92:8[9]; 93:4; 144:7). But now "the wrath of God is revealed from heaven" (Rom 1:18).[131] Yahweh becomes the subject of five tough statements. First, *he sent fire.* While the previous verse referred to the fierceness of his wrath, this verse refers to a burning supernatural fire in a more down-to-earth way (Pss 11:4–6; 18:8–13[9–14]) or to the literal fire that consumed the city as a result of its fall (Jer 38:17–18; 39:8). The fire raged within the physical city and thus within the bodily person of the personified city. The one-word second colon underlines the point. The attributions of responsibility to Yahweh become more trenchant as the poem spells out the implications of Yahweh bringing about his day.[132] Indeed, in "Zion's lament over Yahweh as enemy and aggressor"[133] in vv. 12–21 as a whole, "the presentation of God's actions . . . is unusually dark."[134] The passage justifies the com-

130. Koenen, *Klagelieder,* 69.
131. Vermigli, *Lamentations,* 41.
132. Koenen, *Klagelieder,* 69.
133. Berges, *Klagelieder,* 109.
134. Dobbs-Allsopp, *Lamentations,* 72.

ment that "this book may well be called, The Lamentations of Lamentations; like as Solomon's Song is called for its excellence, The Song of Songs."[135]

To speak metaphorically, Yahweh the hunter set a net before Ms. Jerusalem as if she were a bird or an animal, again taking the kind of action that human adversaries sometimes took, of which Israel spoke in its prayers (Pss 10:9; 57:6[7]). It was a net she could not evade; it overturned her or turned her back (cf. v. 8). As the enemy spread his hand (v. 10), so Yahweh spread a net.

He thus made her *a desolation*: the city was physically so, but in v. 4 the related adjective referred to the desolation of grief, and the second colon confirms this connotation here. *Faint* (*dāwâ*) can refer to a woman when she is "unwell" during menstruation, so the idea might be that Ms. Zion is that way all through the month. Further, the noun for faintness is another element in the threats in Deuteronomy (28:60). "As a survivor of trauma, there is no aspect of her body, spirit, or her environment unaffected by the catastrophe."[136]

nun [14]*The yoke of my rebellions bound itself on,*[a]
as by his hand they were interweaving.[b]
They went up[c] *on my neck,*
it made my energy collapse.
The Lord[d] *gave me*
into hands[e] *against which I cannot stand.*

a. The verb *śāqad* (*niphal*) is a *hapax legomenon*; the translation is a guess from the context. LXX, Vg "watched" implies a form from *šāqad*. 4QLam implies *niqšrh* ("bound am I"?); see the discussion in Kotzé, *Qumran Manuscripts of Lamentations*, 86–89.

b. The asyndeton and word order with the verb coming second suggest that this clause is subordinate to the one that precedes it.

c. For *'ālû*, 4QLam, Sym imply *'ullô*, "his yoke."

d. 4QLam has *yhwh*; MT might be assimilating to v. 15 or to the later relinquishment of uttering the name.

e. The construct *bîdê* governs the unmarked relative clause (see GK 130d); I take the line as 2-3 (cf. v. 7h) rather than locating the transition between cola after the construct noun.

14 The poem takes up and develops yet a further familiar metaphor. A yoke need not be a bad thing; it harnesses the ox to the task it needs to undertake, and a wise farmer ensures that it fits comfortably. But an iron yoke was another threat in Deuteronomy (28:48). The parallel colon hints at the

135. Paschasius Radbertus, *In Threnos sive Lamentationes Jeremiae Libri Quinque*, PL 120:1061; cf. E. Ann Matter, "The Lamentations Commentaries of Hrabanus Maurus and Paschasius Radbertus," *Traditio* 38 (1982): 150.

136. K. M. O'Connor, *Lamentations and the Tears of the World*, 29.

profound idea that the yoke did not merely issue from the city's rebellions; the rebellions became the yoke—the yoke consisted in the rebelliousness. But the verse's direct point is more prosaic. It implies a metonymy: the rebellions generated sanctions, and Yahweh made sure they combined so as to impose themselves on the city as if they were the ropes of a yoke and the city were an ox. It was Yahweh's *hand* that made it happen. In a "confluence of YHWH's actions, Zion's sin, and enemy agency,"[137] Yahweh's hand worked hand in hand with the adversaries' hand(s) (vv. 7, 10).[138]

And the yoke was so heavy that it sapped the animal's energy. The first two lines of the verse combine the emphases of the chapter as a whole: while the woman-city's confession would function to "clear away every vestige of self-righteousness,"[139] with some pathos she also laments her helplessness.

The third line then builds on the image from the second. Yahweh followed up the imposition of the energy-sapping yoke by bringing attackers that the animal/city had lost the capacity to resist. The poem here (and twice in v. 15) speaks of *the Lord* rather than Yahweh; the expression suggests his sovereignty. The respective number of occurrences in the chapter (three and seven) matches the ratio in Lamentations as a whole, where "the Lord" is an alternative to Yahweh in the way that other texts use the word "God" (which comes in Lamentations only at 3:41).

samek [15]*He heaped up*[a] *all my sturdy men,*
the Lord in my midst.
He summoned against me an assembly[b]
to break my young men,
When the Lord trod a press[c]
for young Ms. Judah.[d]

a. Other occurrences of the rare verb *sālâ* suggest having a low opinion of something or throwing it aside. But Tg "tread down" points to a meaning that one might associate with *sālal*, which fits with the subsequent lines (cf. Hillers, *Lamentations*, 74).

b. In LXX, Syr, Vg, Tg, Yahweh "proclaimed [*qārā'*] a set time/festival," which was the significance of *mô'ēd* in v. 4 (such proclaiming is the responsibility of the Israelites in Lev 23:4, 37), which makes good if harrowing sense and fits the idea of Yahweh viewing a battle as a kind of sacrifice. But issuing a proclamation and thus summoning an assembly *against me* rather suggests commissioning attackers (cf. 2:22).

c. The asyndetic clause with the object before the verb is subordinate to the previous clause. I follow LXX, Vg in taking *press* as the verb's object (cf. Neh 13:15). For "as in a wine

137. M. J. Bier, *"Perhaps There Is Hope"*, LHBOTS 603 (London: T&T Clark, 2015), 61.

138. Koenen, *Klagelieder*, 73.

139. J. A. Dearman, *Jeremiah and Lamentations*, NIV Application Commentary (Grand Rapids: Zondervan, 2002), on the chapter.

press" (e.g., NRSV), one would expect a preposition (as in Judg 6:11; Isa 63:2); in addition, this understanding involves taking *lə* in the parallel colon as the object marker, which would be unusual.

d. *Bətûlat bat-yəhûdâ* is literally "girl daughter Judah," a construct chain; on *bətûlâ*, see the translation note on v. 4, and on *bat* and the construct, see the translation note and comment on v. 6.

15 Zion continues to make Yahweh the subject of troublesome verbs; "the main actor of all cruel acts is the Lord."[140] She now restates the point in v. 14 in terms of two or three different metaphors. The first line sets two or three ideas in tension. While it is in keeping with Hebrew grammar for a sentence to begin with its verb, one would then expect the subject to follow, but here the word order delays the subject and generates the collocation of a dismissive verb with a significant object. The object is the city's *sturdy men* (*'abbîr*), its strong and forceful warriors—the word can refer to bulls. But they are being heaped up like grain at harvest (Jer 50:26).[141] And the one who is effortlessly and thoughtlessly making a pile of them does so as *the Lord* who thus acted *in my midst*. The Lord acting in the midst of the city should surely be good news (Ps 46:5[6]; Isa 12:6; Joel 2:27), but references to God in the midst of the city often carry some irony or threat (Jer 14:9; Amos 5:17; Mic 3:11). Indeed, "the entire verse . . . turns Israel's traditional language upside down."[142]

The middle line thus has Yahweh tossing the warriors aside by summoning *an assembly*: such is Zion's image for Yahweh's arousing an invading army to *break* those sturdy fighters, who are now called her *young men*. Sturdy warriors do have the vigor of youth; but etymologically the young men (*baḥûrîm*) are the elite.

The verse closes with an even more brutal version of how "traditional harvest language has been transformed into gruesome war imagery."[143] Zion speaks of *young Ms. Judah* herself in a way that suggests her vulnerability and then goes on to picture her as a harvest of grapes that are put into the press for treading (see the translation note). There Yahweh does the trampling for her (that is, against her; cf. *for Jacob* in v. 17). The image recurs in Isa 63:3; Joel 3:13 [4:13], but in those passages, the victims are the nations. Tg has the nations defiling the girls of Judah until their blood flows like the wine in a press. It is indeed a bloodbath.[144]

140. Berges, *Klagelieder*, 116.
141. Thomas, "Poetry and Theology," 152.*
142. Salters, *Lamentations*, 80.
143. Thomas, "Poetry and Theology," 152.
144. Koenen, *Lamentations*, 77.

ayin[a] [16]*As I was weeping over these with my eye,*
my eye[b] *was running down with water,*[c]
Because one comforting went far away from me,
one bringing back my life.
My children became desolate
because the enemy was strong.

a. Whereas MT has vv. 16 and 17 in an order that corresponds to the later regular alphabet, 4QLam has the order *pe* then *ayin*, as do Lam 2–4. "It is hardly possible to decide which sequence is the original one" (R. Schäfer, "Lamentations," in *General Introduction and Megilloth*, ed. A. Schenker et al., *BHQ* 18 [Stuttgart: Deutsche Gesellschaft, 2004], 118*).

b. 4QLam has only one *'ênî*, as do LXX, Syr, Vg, which looks like a simplification. Tg takes *my eye, my eye* to denote "my two eyes," but there is no parallel for such usage. The usage rather compares with *šālôm šālôm* in Isa 26:3, where the first occurrence closes one colon and the second opens the next. The line then works 4-3, which is more plausible than 5-2 or 3-4 or 3-2-2. Normally it is plural eyes that weep, but Jer 13:17; Ps 88:9[10] parallel the singular, and "my eye" recurs in 3:48, 49, 51. Cf. F. M. Cross, "Studies in the Structure of Hebrew Verse," in *The Word of the Lord Shall Go Forth: Essays in Honor of David Noel Freedman in Celebration of His Sixtieth Birthday*, ed. C. L. Meyers and M. P. O'Connor (Winona Lake, IN: Eisenbrauns, 1983), 148–49; Schäfer, "Lamentations," 119*.

c. As in v. 11, the participles take their tense reference from the line that follows.

16 As she was being overwhelmed by the invader, Zion was weeping *over these*—over the young men to whom she referred in v. 15. In *running down* (cf. Jer 14:17) *with water*, her eye was like a fountain of tears (Jer 9:1 [8:23]). Her crying never stopped (cf. v. 2). It is the longest line in the poem, its length corresponding to the unending nature of the weeping.

Back then as now, the reason was that *one comforting went far away from me.* If that expression means something more specific than that she had no comforter (cf. vv. 2, 9), then the comforter who had gone far away was perhaps the Egyptian army. Whoever it was might have been able to save me, *bringing back my life* (cf. v. 11), rescuing me from Sheol, from the clutches of death that were about to enfold me (cf. this phrase in Ps 35:17). *B.* Sanhedrin 98b derives from this verse a name for the Messiah as "the comforter," who may be far away at the moment, but who will come.

But at that moment (again to rephrase what has preceded), actually Ms. Jerusalem's *children* (that is, the city's inhabitants) *became desolate* (in both the physical and the emotional sense) *because the enemy was strong* and they lacked the energy to resist.[145]

145. G. Brunet thinks of an internal enemy (*Les Lamentations contre Jérémie: Réinterpretation des quatre premières Lamentations*, BEHER 75 [Paris: Presses Universitaires de France, 1968], 1–27).

pe [17]*Zion spread out her hands*[a]*—*
there was no one comforting for her.
Yahweh commanded[b] *for Jacob*
his adversaries around him.
Jerusalem became
something taboo[c] *among them.*

a. Lit. "spread out with her hands," a "peculiar" usage (GK 119q), though JM 125m gives a number of examples.

b. For MT *ṣiwwâ*, 4QLam has *ṣph* ("kept watch").

c. *Niddâ*; see the translation note on v. 8. Vg has "polluted by menstruation."

17 For one verse, the poem reverts to third-person speech about Zion/Jacob/Jerusalem. Spreading one's empty hands is a regular posture for prayer, but it is a natural pose in pleading with a human being. Does the verse have in mind both an appeal to Yahweh and an appeal to possible human comforters? In relation to Yahweh, Solomon's reference to hand-spreading in connection with the aftermath of Yahweh's giving his people over to an enemy (1 Kgs 8:38) is especially telling in this context. Following on that first colon, the fact that *there was no one comforting* for Zion implicitly points to the content of the plea.

Horrifically, Yahweh's response is the opposite. He could have *commanded* comforters or helpers *for Jacob* (cf. Ps 91:11). Instead, he summoned *adversaries* for him (that is, against him; cf. v. 15f) by summoning them *around him.* "Jacob" here appears for the first time in Lamentations (cf. 2:2–3) as an alternative way of referring to Judah and thus to the people for whom Jerusalem is capital.

The closing description of the city indicates the estimation Jerusalem gained *among them*—among its attackers. The picture is thus of the adversaries siding with Yahweh in his assessment of the city. If the hands were spread out to the passersby/neighbors/adversaries as well as to Yahweh, then this closing line is their response.[146] The implication may be that Jacob had not recognized how it had done wrong and had thereby made the city unclean (cf. v. 9). But whereas the woman-city's own words on either side of this verse twice refer to her rebellions and twice to her defiance of Yahweh, the witness's voice here rather underlines the suffering, not the sin.[147] And there is no inherent link between being *taboo* and being sinful, just as is the case with most terms that are translated by words such as uncleanness, defilement, and impurity. The word for taboo (*niddâ*) refers especially to the need for a menstruant woman to stay separate from things that are sacred

146. Salters, *Lamentations*, 89.

147. Bier, *"Perhaps There Is Hope"*, 63.

and from people who might themselves be affected by her taboo; it is only if she fails to maintain that separation from the sacred that questions about sin arise. So the poem here likely refers only to the adversaries viewing the city as something to avoid contact with. It is a burden that the onlooker recognizes she bears.

tsade [18]*Yahweh is in the right,*
because I defied[a] *his bidding.*
Listen, please, all you peoples,
and look at my pain,
When my girls and my young men
went into captivity.[b]

a. LXX "embittered" derives the verb from *mārar* rather than *mārâ* (so also in v. 20).

b. The asyndeton and word order (subjects before verb) suggest that this third line is subordinate to the second.

18 If the onlooker downplayed any reference to the city's wrongdoing in v. 17, in the first line of v. 18 the city itself now makes the poem's most explicit confession of guilt and acceptance of responsibility. While its acknowledgment of the righteousness of God is hardly the highpoint of the poem,[148] it is a significant affirmation. It corresponds closely to Jer 12:1, where literally Jeremiah says, "Yahweh, you in the right"; here Zion says, "Yahweh, he in the right." But there, Jeremiah goes on implicitly to question the link between Yahweh's action (or inaction) and his being in the right; here, the poem accepts it, as Dan 9 later "expresseth this whole sentence"[149] at much greater length (cf. Neh 9:33). There is nothing ironic or sarcastic about the confession,[150] though its lack of specificity contrasts markedly with the description of the woman-city's denigration and agony.[151] Perhaps the implication is that Yahweh has answered Jeremiah's plea; in acting against Jerusalem, he has done the right thing.[152] *In the right* (*ṣaddîq*) denotes faithfulness and truthfulness in one's relationships with people, so that here the acknowledgment indicates that Yahweh has not been unfaithful in doing what he did. The bicolon provides a classic example of the sort of parallelism where the first

148. Kraus, *Klagelieder*, 33.

149. H. Broughton, *The Lamentations of Ieremy* (Amsterdam [?]: 1608), on the verse.

150. Contrast Lee, *Singers of Lamentations*, 123–24.

151. G. Hens-Piazza, *Lamentations*, Wisdom Commentary (Collegeville, MN: Liturgical, 2017), 17.

152. B. Gosse, "Les 'Confessions' de Jérémie, la vengeance contre Jérusalem à l'image de celle contre Babylone et les nations, et Lamentations 1," *ZAW* 111 (1999): 58–67.

colon raises a question that the second answers. How could it be the case that Yahweh is in the right in the suffering he has brought to Jerusalem? The second colon gives the answer. *His bidding* (the word literally means "his mouth") could suggest both the Torah and the prophetic word.

Whereas in other verses, the link between lines is easy to see, here the link between the first and second lines is less obvious. But first, a serious confession that someone is in the right, of the kind that came in the first line, needs to be public, and Zion invites *all you peoples* to listen as witnesses to her confession (cf. Yahweh's own appeal to "peoples, all of them" in Mic 1:2). The rest of the second and third lines then spells out the action Yahweh took as an expression of being in the right, taking up motifs from earlier verses: *girls* and *young men* (vv. 4, 15), *went into captivity* (v. 5; on the difference in formulation, see the translation note there), and *look* and *pain* (v. 12). Ms. Zion thus repeats their "wild appeal."[153]

qoph [19]*I summoned my great friends*[a]*—*
those people, they deceived me.
My priests and my elders—
they breathed their last in the city,
As they searched for food for themselves
so they might bring back their life.

a. The participle was *qal* in v. 2; here it is *piel*—hence the translation *great friends*. It also has both the article and a pronominal suffix.

19 Zion here gives her own version of the point about her *great friends* that the onlooker made in v. 2. She implies some irony, as her summons compares and contrasts with Yahweh's (v. 15), and inevitably his won. Whereas Judah had been in alliance with its neighbors, the way things turned out involved the neighbors joining with the Babylonians against Judah.

Although v. 4 expressed some sympathy for the *priests*, elsewhere Lamentations shares Jeremiah's perspective that neither priests nor *elders* deserve sympathy; the two stances come close together in 4:13, 16. The Jerusalem elders would be the heads of households and other senior lay figures who had escaped the deportation in 597. Being a priest or elder evidently did not mean you were less likely to die of starvation than other people (see v. 11).

resh [20]*Look, Yahweh, because it was distressing for me,*[a]
as my insides churned.[b]
My heart turned over within me,

153. Allen, *Liturgy of Grief*, 59.

because I defied and defied.[c]
Outside, the sword bereaved,
at home, very death.[d]

a. With *ṣar-lî,* cf. *mar-lāh* in v. 4f; here, too, I take *ṣar* as a verb rather than a noun or adjective (with *HALOT*, 1058). The time reference of the noun clause is suggested by the next colon.

b. The asyndeton combined with the placing of the subject before the verb suggests that this clause is subordinate to the preceding one.

c. The infinitive precedes the *qatal* verb, emphasizing the action. Vg "I am full of bitterness" implies forms from *mārar* rather than *mārâ*. See the translation note on v. 18; also C. L. Seow, "A Textual Note on Lamentations 1:20," *CBQ* 47 (1985): 416–19.

d. The *k* indicates identity (GK 118x).

20 For the first time since v. 11, Zion addresses Yahweh, as she will through vv. 20–22. Again she pleads with Yahweh to *look* (cf. v. 9), with the implication of taking notice and taking action (see vv. 21–22, which bring out the implications of v. 9 itself). The poem has several times referred to the city's adversary/adversaries (*ṣar*); here it uses that same word as a verb to denote the *distressing* effect of the adversary's action. The word also recalls the "narrows" of v. 3 (*məṣārîm*). It suggests a sense of being trapped, of claustrophobia, of being hemmed in without escape.[154] The repetition and paronomasia are complemented in the parallel, second colon by a colorful new image: the feeling of distress is conveyed by means of a unique form of a rare word (*ḥāmar*) that suggests the frothing of water or wine.

The novelty of expression continues in the middle line in the declaration that *my heart turned over* (this expression otherwise comes only in Exod 14:5; Ps 105:25; Hos 11:8[9], where it suggests a change of mind). The language thus takes the physiological imagery further. Its second colon then provides an explanation for the distress, the churning, and the overturning. The explanation is conventionally expressed, in that it takes up the verb from v. 18 that justified Yahweh's action, though it doubles it; it is also a verb (*mārâ*) that both recalls the word for things being tough (v. 4) and resembles that word for churning. Ms. Zion thus "complains to YHWH about her anxiety that has come about as a result of her rebellion."[155] Only here does the First Testament link emotional pain and rebellion against God.[156]

The third line returns to describe in more outward terms the city's distressing experience, with some concrete indication of the reason for it. Al-

154. M. L. Mitchell, "Reading of the Imagery of Lamentations," 65, 66.

155. Thomas, "Poetry and Theology," 160 (in italics in the original).

156. Berges, *Klagelieder*, 90.

though the actual fall of Jerusalem seems not to have involved slaughter in the streets (though see Jer 52:27), reference to the sword is a standard element in threats about attack on the city. In such threats, "death" and "sword" can come together (Jer 15:2; 18:21) in contexts where "death" seems to suggest epidemic. The "Lamentation over the Destruction of Sumer and Ur" speaks of destruction both outside the city and inside it.[157] Here Lamentations points rather to bereavement by the sword out in the city and by epidemic in the home. "Death has crossed the final border and entered even the safe haven of the house."[158]

shin [21]*People listened*[a] *because I was crying out—*
there was no one comforting for me.
When all my enemies listened to my dire fate, they celebrated,[b]
because you yourself acted.
You brought[c] *the day you summoned,*
but may they become[d] *like me.*

a. LXX's imperative implies *šimʿû* for MT *šāməʿû*.

b. The word order (subject before verb) and the asyndeton within the colon suggest that the first clause is subordinate to the final verb.

c. Tg translates the *qatal* as future, while DG 60c takes it as precative, which makes the third line smoother.

d. LXX "they became" perhaps makes the third line smoother in an opposite way, though not the relationship with the first two lines, and it makes the meaning more difficult to discern.

21 The poem is working toward a climax and conclusion. The anonymous listeners in the first line might be no one in particular—maybe passersby. The point is that Zion had appealed for people to listen (v. 18), and it seems as if they have done so. They listened when Zion was *crying out*, which picks up from vv. 8 and 11. They listened when there was *no one comforting*, which picks up from vv. 2, 9, 16, 17. The first line suggests that Zion might be in a position to say something positive. But really the poem is playing with its audience.

The second line either establishes who the listeners were or adds some more listeners and makes clear that there was actually no positive listening; the comment fits with the earlier reference to seeing and laughing (v. 7). Yes, it was a *dire fate*: more literally, it was simply "a bad thing" (*rāʿâ*), a favorite expression in Jeremiah whose double meaning will be significant in v. 22. So

157. *ANET*, 618.

158. Linafelt, *Surviving Lamentations: Catastrophe, Lament and Protest*, 41.

Zion had appealed for people to listen, and they have done so, and by implication they have confirmed the direness of her fate. Has she therefore found a comforter? The answer brings the colon to a dramatic and shocking close[159] in that actually *they celebrated*. One can imagine that they would feel justified, and actually the poem has made clear that they were indeed justified. They celebrated the fact that Yahweh had *acted*.

Here the parallelism between the lines means v. 21c–d raises a question that v. 21e–f answers. In what way did Yahweh act? Once more the poem refers to Yahweh's summons (cf. v. 15) and to his *day* (cf. v. 12) before the verse itself comes to a dramatic and shocking close, on which the final verse will elaborate.

tav [22]*May all their dire fate come before you,*
and deal[a] *out to them,*
Just as you dealt out to me
because of all my rebellions.
Because my cries are many;
faint is my heart.[b]

a. For LXX "glean" (cf. 2:20; 3:51; though not 1:12), cf. BDB, 760.

b. The noun comes before the verb, reversing the order in the parallel colon, so that the poem ends with an a-b-b'-a' line.

22 In spelling out the shocking drama as it brings the poem to a close, v. 22 completes an approximate a-b-b'-a' arrangement in vv. 21–22. The first two lines spell out v. 21e–f with its appeal for poetic justice, though they begin with a recollection of v. 21c–d and the usefully ambiguous Hebrew expression for something dire or bad. The word shares the ambiguity of the English word "bad" in that it can denote something morally bad or something experientially bad and can therefore suggest a link between the two—something bad may happen to people who do something bad. Verse 21 used the word in the experiential sense; v. 22 may imply both senses.

Yes, something bad should happen to those enemies because they did something bad, even though they were executing Yahweh's will in connection with Zion's *rebellions* (cf. vv. 5, 14) without realizing it. Their dire behavior/fate coming before Yahweh means its gaining his attention as something upon which he should take action. Yahweh *dealt* out pain to Zion (v. 12); now he should deal it out to them.

159. R. A. Parry, "The Ethics of Lament: Lamentations 1 as a Case Study," in *Reading the Law: Studies in Honour of Gordon J. Wenham*, ed. J. G. McConville and K. Möller, LHBOTS 461 (London: T&T Clark, 2007), 140.

Insofar as the first colon refers to dire behavior, v. 22a–d also works as a chiasm, though the poem closes by returning "for one last time"[160] to the suffering that encourages this plea for Yahweh to take action against the people who caused it, the groans (vv. 8, 11, 21) and the faintness (v. 13). It thus closes not with sin or confession, nor with a promise that might wrongly take the edge off the need to grieve, but (like some psalms) by depositing Zion's plea before Yahweh. By its nature as a prayer, the poem incorporates no response from Yahweh. It ends with silence, the silence of Good Friday and Holy Saturday. The response will come in Isa 40, on Resurrection Day. Thus Lam 1 does not solve; it affects.[161] Within the poem, then, "God's only response is silence,"[162] though in this poem "the LORD comes with a gift. Grief. Because grief is indeed a gift."[163]

A READER'S RESPONSE

Imagine someone who has taken part in reading Lam 1 at a worship gathering in Mizpah or Bethel.

> We went through the fall of Jerusalem again. We cried, quietly, thinking about the city we loved, which had once been teeming with people and vibrant with life, the city that had sometimes seen the visit of envoys from places like Ammon and Moab that wanted us to ally with them. We cried, quietly, remembering our howls back then as Zedekiah's troops were breaking down a section of the wall in order to escape and we were facing the fact that it really was now all over, that the Egyptians were not going to come and rescue us and that the Ammonites and the Moabites were working with the Babylonians rather than against them. It was so easy for them, in the end. We cried, quietly, thinking about our family members and friends who had run for it during one of the breaks in the siege but who had been caught by the Babylonians anyway. We cried as we remembered having nothing to feed our children.
>
> We cried as we thought about our young men, the pride and the future of the city, slaughtered. We cried as we thought about the priests and members of the royal family who had been frog-marched off to Babylon after the city's fall. We cried as we thought about the roads

160. Koenen, *Klagelieder*, 91.
161. Koenen, *Klagelieder*, 92.
162. Berlin, *Lamentations*, 49.
163. A. Phipps, "Lamentations 1:1–6," *ExpT* 121 (2009–10): 611.

empty of pilgrims coming for Sukkot, of the priests who were still here but who could no longer make the morning and evening offerings, of the girls who could no longer sing in the festival processions. We cried as we thought about the careless pagan feet that had trampled the sanctuary and about the accoutrements that were destroyed or plundered. We cried as we imagined people laughing at us. We felt like someone who had been exposed, forced to march naked off to prison. It was like being the grapes in a wine press.

We cried, because we knew that it was Yahweh who had made it happen. And we cried because we knew we deserved it. Some of us had sometimes trusted in Yahweh, sometimes not. We knew that we had sometimes taken advantage of the people who lived around us in Judah, who produced the food that we ate but often didn't live as well as we did. We knew there were people who engaged in forms of worship that Yahweh loathed, but we tolerated it. We knew there were people in the city who had not just lost their livelihood in the course of these events but had lost their lives. And we knew we were ineradicably stained by these enormities.

We deserved it, but that fact doesn't excuse those invaders who just wanted to turn us into an outpost of their empire. We want to see the same thing happen to them. It's only fair.

LAMENTATIONS 2: "HE POURED OUT HIS WRATH LIKE FIRE"

> Such men surely do greatly overshoot themselves who think that there is no art, or skillful handling, in the proceedings of the holy scriptures. . . . For are there any passions, descriptions, comparisons, and such other like things taken or appertaining for or to any matter or purpose, whereby to move and stir up the hearts and minds of men, which are not to be found in these Lamentations? Namely in this second Chapter?[1]

Lamentations 2 is a further response to the affliction of Ms. Zion. Israel's splendor was thrown down from the heavens to the earth, the kingship and its officials were stuck to the earth, Zion's gateways sank into the earth, its elders were sitting down on the earth, its girls lowered their head to the earth. Of Lamentations' fifteen references to "Zion," with Zion usually treated as feminine ("Mount Zion" comes only once in the book), seven come in Lam 2.[2] One possible analysis sees it as comprising

- a description *of* Jerusalem (vv. 1–12);
- an address *to* Jerusalem (vv. 13–19); and
- a speech *by* Jerusalem herself (vv. 20–22).[3]

By way of more formal analysis, it comprises

- a third-party report of Yahweh's bringing disaster to Jerusalem in his anger (vv. 1–10);
- an expression of grief by the third party who did the reporting (vv. 11–17); and
- an exhortation to the city wall to cry out to Yahweh (vv. 18–22).[4]

Initially, then, vv. 1–10 describe how Yahweh brought catastrophe to Jerusalem: v. 1 covers the city and country in general and the temple in particular; vv. 2–5 expand on the former, while vv. 6–10 put sharper focus on the latter. The chapter tacitly invites people to recognize the implication that Yahweh was not wedded to the city of Jerusalem or its sanctuary. It describes the hor-

1. Toussaine, *Lamentations*, 55–56, spelling updated.

2. Maier, *Daughter Zion, Mother Zion*, 141.

3. B. B. Kaiser, "Poet as 'Female Impersonator': The Image of Daughter Zion as Speaker in Biblical Poems of Suffering," *JR* 67 (1987): 176.

4. Berges's analysis (*Klagelieder*, 130) is a cross between these two; his divisions are vv. 1–10, 11–19, 20–22.

rific nature of the calamity and expresses (for the poet himself or herself, as far as one can tell) the insight that it issued from Yahweh and from his anger. It reflects the poet's coming to terms with the reality of God's anger, and it seeks to help other people come to terms with that reality. Within the context of the Scriptures, its stress on God's anger compares with that in Romans and Revelation. It relates how God has been active in history, but it does so not in the manner of a hymn celebrating his acts of deliverance but more in the manner of an "anti-hymn" to his violent intervention.[5] One implication is that the fall of Jerusalem did not happen by chance, nor was it a mere human action, nor did it issue from another deity. It was a purposeful expression of Yahweh's power (see "Theology," pp. 25–27).

With the move from Lam 1 to Lam 2, the focus shifts from the victim of the disaster to its perpetrator.[6] Yahweh is the subject of a series of forceful verbs: "threw," "swallowed up," "tore down," "cut off," "burned," "killed," "devastated," "did violence," "destroyed" (vv. 1–6). He acted against "strongholds," "kingship," "officials," "horn," "citadels," "walls," "rampart," "gateways," "gate bars" (vv. 2–9). It is possible to speak of God only as enemy and powerful lord of a history that he makes work against Ms. Zion. Yet the poet has not lost faith in God but stands with Job in saying, "It is Yahweh who gave and it is Yahweh who has taken," though not in adding "Yahweh's name be blessed" (Job 1:21; one might rather compare Job's declaration in 16:9).[7] Theodicy is again not a focus of the poem, but neither is antitheodicy.[8] While some readers might infer that reference to Yahweh's anger implies the assumption that his action responds to his people's guilt,[9] the poem does not say so. It refers only to the way anger issued in the bringing of devastation; it does not raise questions about the reason for the anger.

There follows in vv. 11–17 a first-person expression of grief on the part of the third party who has been doing the reporting. This third party's heart is also poured onto the earth. The section expresses to Zion the speaker's grief about the terrible nature of the catastrophe. One implication is to offer its people permission and encouragement to grieve, notwithstanding their being the victims of Yahweh's wrath—or because of it. In the context of the Scriptures, it helps other people empathize with the suffering of Jerusalem and of other cities, and with the suffering of mothers and little children. As vv. 1–10 could compare with a protest psalm (but one with no praise, no statement of trust, no petition, and no looking forward to praise in the fu-

5. Koenen, *Klagelieder*, 105.
6. Berlin, *Lamentations*, 67; what follows also reflects Berlin's comments.
7. Koenen, *Klagelieder*, 184, 185.
8. Bier, *"Perhaps There Is Hope"*, 78.
9. J. Krašovek, "The Source of Hope in the Book of Lamentations," *VT* 42 (1992): 223.

ture), vv. 11–17 express the pain that can be a further element in such a psalm. As was the case in vv. 1–10, the expression of pain here has no indication that the speaker is expressing anger with Yahweh or thinks that Yahweh is motivated by unjustified rage.[10]

Third, vv. 18–22 is a second-person exhortation to the city wall to cry out to Yahweh. It thus urges Zion to express its own grief to Yahweh and to protest at what happened, and it gives it the words to do so. In the context of the Scriptures as a whole, it has the potential to help people pray for Jerusalem and for other devastated cities. Once again, then, the poem compares with a psalm. Only in the last three verses does it address Yahweh, as psalms address other people and the self as well as Yahweh. One implication is that the divine anger and the human grief can encourage prayer rather than inhibit it.

Lam 2 does not provide a comforting response to the plea at the end of Lam 1. It simply starts again.[11] It does form a pair with Lam 1, as is especially clear when the two are set over against the other three poems with their difference in form and in content. Lam 2 compares with Lam 1 in a number of ways:

- It begins with the same exclamation, and it comprises twenty-two verses, with a different letter of the alphabet beginning each verse.
- It focuses on a description of the events involved in the fall of Jerusalem, with Jerusalem being systematically personified as a woman, Ms. Zion or Ms. Jerusalem, but also with references to Ms. Judah. It also personifies parts of the city itself, such as its gateways, and in its speaking of the city as a person it invites readers not to confine themselves to an interest in the human beings who are affected by the disaster.[12]
- It mixes *qatal* and *yiqtol* verbs (and participles and noun clauses). I again follow LXX in mostly translating *qatal* verbs with English aorists, taking them to refer to the event of destruction rather than the ongoing situation.
- It combines the voice of a witness and the voice of the woman-city so that it again combines an intrinsically engaged first-person perspective and a more distant (though not detached) third-person report.
- It combines reference to God as Yahweh and as the Lord and em-

10. Conway, "Daughter Zion," 113.

11. Janzen, *Trauma and the Failure of History*, 100.

12. E. Boase, "Grounded in the Body: A Bakhtinian Reading of Lamentations 2 from Another Perspective," *BibInt* 22 (2014): 292–306.

phasizes his anger in the action he took, using a number of different words for anger.

- It sees the fall of Jerusalem as "the day" but also emphasizes the activity of the enemy/adversary and pictures adversaries and others mocking the devastated city. It speaks of fire.
- It mourns over the city's downfall, speaks much of crying, tears, and hunger, and emphasizes the unparalleled nature of the city's suffering. It is perhaps reproachful toward Yahweh but not exactly complaining that Yahweh's action was excessive or unreasonable. Its perspective and spirituality correspond to those of Jeremiah; the entirety could be something out of Jeremiah.
- It closes with a prayer urging Yahweh to look at the city's sufferings, but it eventually stops rather than ends.
- All but one of the verses comprise three bicola; the single exception comprises four bicola (2:19, like 1:7). The *athnah* comes after the first or second line except in vv. 2 and 18. The verses often have some unity of theme within themselves, and there is often parallelism between the lines.
- The lines average five stresses, with a tendency for the first colon to be longer than the second but with many lines where the two cola are of similar length, some lines where the second is longer (1:3ab, 7ab; 2:3ab, 4ef), and examples of single-stress cola (1:2d, 5f; 2:1b, 16b). Its prosody (e.g., word order, asyndeton, syntax) compares with that of Lam 1.
- It makes much use of repetition (e.g., "swallow up," "dandle," "spare"), picks up some rare words from Lam 1 ("churned," "things she valued"), uses the hyperbole of "all/every," and has other phrases in common with Lam 1 (e.g., "days of old"; "my girls and my young men"; "my insides"; "look, Yahweh, and take note, Ms. Judah").

In other respects, Lam 2 contrasts with Lam 1.

- There is little parallelism within the lines; typically, the second colon simply completes the first. Many verses lead into one another rather than being quite separate (e.g., vv. 6–7, 8–9, 11–12). The *pe* verse precedes the *ayin* verse (as happens in Lam 3 and 4) rather than following the usual alphabet order in which *ayin* precedes *pe*.
- Whereas Lam 1 more systematically maintains and develops the personification of the woman-city, Lam 2 does not directly portray Ms. Zion's suffering as a widow or as a victim of sexual assault. It makes less reference to comfort. Its focus lies more on the one who acted than on the victims of the action.

- It speaks more of battle and destruction, and it puts more emphasis on Yahweh's anger. It develops more systematically the motif of Yahweh's acting as warrior but makes less use of distinctive images such as "hunter" or "yoke" or "press." It refers less to captivity or exile.
- While Judah's enemies are still Yahweh's agents (as in 1:2, 5, 7, 10, 16), they are the subject of verbs only once (v. 16), and it is Yahweh who is like the enemy and adversary (vv. 4, 5). Is he even *the* enemy (see v. 22)?
- It makes more reference to the sanctuary and worship events and to people such as priests; it especially mentions prophets, and it refers several times to the temple as a "meeting" place. It thus puts more emphasis on the calamity's effect on worship and on different groups within the city.
- It talks more about the fate of little children, and it puts more emphasis on the witness's grief and tears—in other words, it does not separate out the roles of witness and city in the manner of Lam 1.
- It makes less reference to Judah's waywardness as lying behind her devastation, and it stresses the way she was misled by her guides. It makes no reference to her friends letting her down.
- It addresses Yahweh less, and it does not appeal to him to put down Zion's adversaries. The content of its prayer is different.
- On the whole, it manifests a greater rawness, which might mean it is closer to the events and older than Lam 1. If so, it is striking that the newer poem precedes it, as Matthew precedes Mark and Gen 1 precedes Gen 2. But the obvious inference from the order in the scroll is that Lam 2 came second, and within the scroll the order may suggest it is more feasible to face the anger of God when one has articulated one's pain. Either way, the two poems complement each other in these respects.
- Notwithstanding the rawness, the poem manifests its own literary skillfulness, making links between the stanzas that complement the separation effected by the alphabetic arrangement. Thus *Lord* recurs from v. 1 to v. 2, *Jacob* from v. 2 to v. 3, *fire* from v. 3 to v. 4, *enemy* from v. 4 to v. 5, and so on.[13]

The pairing of the two poems compares with pairings elsewhere in the Scriptures—such as the two (or more) accounts of creation, of God appearing to Moses, of Solomon's prayer at the temple dedication, of the fall of Jerusalem, of the birth of Jesus, and of Jesus's appearing to Paul. While some differences between such accounts reflect differences in context, they also

13. Bergant, *Lamentations*, 56.

reflect how a given event may benefit from being portrayed in more than one way and how a given event may be of such importance as to deserve retelling in order to bring home that importance. While there is a sense in which Lam 1 and 2 both incorporate dialogue, between a reporter and Ms. Zion herself, the dialogue does not suggest differences of conviction or insight. Within Lam 1, both voices make the same assumptions about what has happened; the difference is that one speaks as observer, the other as victim. Within Lam 2, there is a tension over recognizing Yahweh's anger and protesting against it, but it is a tension within the reporter (who encourages Ms. Zion to protest) rather than a tension over an understanding of what has happened.

In contrast, the juxtaposition of Lam 1 and 2 does generate an implicit dialogue. To a greater extent than Lam 1, "Lam 2 is shaped by hopelessness"; it "presents neither consolation nor hope." It offers no promise and expresses no prayer for a better future. There is no light at the end of the tunnel; indeed, it is not a tunnel but something that ends in darkness. It thinks the unthinkable and says the unsayable. It offers a knowledge of God as one who acts in a history of disaster rather than a history of blessing. It thus speaks with reality about what has actually happened. In this respect it compares with Ps 89, with which it has a number of phrases in common.[14]

Lam 2	**Ps 89**
He tore down . . . Ms. Judah's strongholds (v. 2)	you made its strongholds a ruin (v. 40[41])
she made the kingship ordinary (v. 2)	you made his crown ordinary (v. 39[40])
to the earth (vv. 2, 21)	to the earth (vv. 39[40], 44[45])
he rejected . . . disdained (v. 7)	you rejected . . . disdained (vv. 38–39[39–40])
all the people who passed your way (v. 15)	all the people who passed your way (v. 41[42])
he let the enemy rejoice (v. 17)	you let all his enemies rejoice (v. 42[43])
he let your adversaries' horn rise (v. 17)	you let his adversaries' right hand rise (v. 42[43])

aleph [1]*How*[a] *the Lord with his anger was beclouding*[b]
Ms. Zion![c]
He threw from the heavens to the earth

14. Koenen, *Klagelieder*, 116, 119–20, 183.

Israel's splendor.
He was not mindful of his footstool
on the day of his anger.

a. As in 1:1 (see the translation note), *'êkâ* is part of the first line, not an anacrusis.

b. Tg "loathed" perhaps suggests that it links the *hapax legomenon* verb *'ûb* with the verb *tā'ab*, while Aq "thickened" suggests a link with *'ābâ*. I follow LXX, Sym, Vg in taking it as a denominative from *'āb* and in assuming that the *yiqtol* has past imperfect reference; it is the background to the past verbs in the next two lines.

c. See the translation note and commentary on 1:6. The word order is "How he was beclouding with his anger the Lord Ms. Zion," which generates a harsh clash between the subject and the object.

1 Even more clearly than was the case in 1:1, *how* is not an expression of grief or desperation but an indication of astonishment. "Jerusalem, the city-woman, may have sunk into sobbing silence (1:22c), but the Poet has plenty of voice left."[15] Whereas Lam 1 followed the *how* with description of the city's suffering and mentioned Yahweh only in v. 5, Lam 2 begins from Yahweh's action. It opens by summarizing the nature and significance of that action; vv. 2–10 will fill out the picture. As in Lam 1, "there is no disagreement between the narrator and Zion as to the causes of suffering."[16] But whereas Lam 1 referred only once to Yahweh's anger, Lam 2 speaks of it twice in the first verse. Speaking of *the day of his anger* does come close to the earlier allusion to "the day of his angry blazing" (1:12), but the reference is doubled up in a way that almost makes these references the frame for the verse as a whole. And "the most stunning feature of Lamentations 2 is its *Leitmotif*: the wrath of Yhwh."[17] The report gives no explanation for the anger, and the repeated allusions to it in the context of the poem's understated reference to Judah's waywardness (v. 14) may suggest that it refers here and subsequently to Yahweh's anger more as an objective force than as a personal reaction to wrongdoing. Lam 2 points in that direction to a greater extent than Lam 1 does, but it does so in a manner comparable to Paul's way of speaking in Romans when he talks about wrath (see "Theology," pp. 25–27). Wrath suggests a terrible event that feels to the victim like an expression of someone's anger. So, the implication is that reference to *his anger* need not indicate that God has a feeling of anger; it denotes his doing the kind of thing that an angry person does. But it is *his anger*. And he is here *the Lord* as opposed to Yahweh. Each term comes seven times in Lam 2; *the Lord* is thus more frequent than

15. C. J. H. Wright, *Lamentations*, 77.

16. Provan, *Lamentations*, 57–58.

17. Rong, *Forgotten and Forsaken by God*, 76.

it was in Lam 1 (see the commentary on 1:14). The difference corresponds to the emphasis in this poem on the sovereign power of God, which relates to that emphasis on wrath and violent action.[18] "Let it be said as clearly as word and trope can convey: God has wrought this horror."[19] "Yahweh's day," which was supposed to be a day of blessing and celebration, had been turned by the Prophets into a day of darkness (Amos 5:18–20), and the day that arrived in Judah was that angry day. How, then, did this anger express itself? The first line provides a sort-of answer that raises more questions. The second line provides another sort-of answer that raises further questions. The third line provides something more like an actual answer. But neither this verse nor the rest of the poem gives much consideration to the question of why he is angry. Thus Lamentations takes up the motif of Yahweh's day in such a way as to rework or "subvert" it,[20] by emphasizing the way it brings affliction to Judah rather by seeing it as a response to Judah's waywardness, as well as by seeing it purely as a past event rather than a coming one.

First, then, the opening *yiqtol* verb refers to the ongoing reality that lay behind everything that follows. Yahweh's anger led to a cloud hanging over Jerusalem. "Of the relationship between the Lord and Zion/Israel there remains only the cloud of his anger."[21] While the noun for cloud (*ʿāb*), from which the unique verb *beclouding* comes, commonly denotes the kind of dark cloud that can be a welcome herald of rain, it can also suggest a symbolic dark cloud that both indicates and conceals Yahweh's active, dynamic, forceful presence. That presence, too, can be great news when it means Yahweh is going to act against his adversaries and against his people's adversaries (Ps 18:11–12[12–13]). But for the people who are the adversaries, it is therefore horrific news. So it was for Ms. Zion when Yahweh became her adversary and when the beclouding came *with his anger*. There is thus a strong tension between the first two cola (see the translation note).[22] Beclouding Zion is fine; anger toward Zion's adversaries may be welcome; but an angry beclouding of Zion . . .

What does the beclouding mean for Ms. Zion? In what way does it affect her? It expresses itself in the way Yahweh *threw from the heavens to the earth Israel's splendor.* Given that the Northern Kingdom ceased to exist more than a century before the fall of Jerusalem, Lam 2:1, 3, 5 can apply the name *Israel* to Judah. *From the heavens to the earth* suggests the maximum distance possible, from a position of highest significance to one of no significance at

18. Koenen, *Klagelieder*, 122.

19. Berrigan, *Lamentations*, 35.

20. Boase, *The Fulfilment of Doom?*, 138.

21. M. L. Mitchell, "Reading of the Imagery of Lamentations," 80.

22. House, *Lamentations*, 376.

all (cf. v. 2e–f);[23] so there is some correspondence between the beginning of Lam 2 and the beginning of Lam 1. Israel's *splendor* or "beauty" or "glory" (*tip'ārâ*) can refer to a number of things, such as the Davidic monarchy, the city of Jerusalem, the temple, and the nation itself. So the middle line continues to raise questions.

The third line clarifies them in turn. On his angry day, Yahweh *was not mindful of his footstool.* A king sits on his throne and has somewhere to put his feet up that reflects his status (cf. Ps 110:1). For Yahweh, who lives in the heavens, his *footstool* can mean the earth itself (Isa 66:1), but more concretely it means the sanctuary where he comes to meet with Israel (Tg; cf. Ps 132:7), perhaps more specifically the chest that symbolizes the relationship between Yahweh and Israel (1 Chron 28:2; the other reference to Yahweh's footstool in Ps 99:5 may also denote the earthly temple, but it is more likely a metaphor). Is there an allusion to the disappearance of the covenant chest that apparently happened sometime during the troubles that lie in the background of Lamentations?[24] There was a sense in which the temple belonged in the heavens. It linked the earth and the heavens. The earthly temple was a kind of portal. When people entered the temple, they entered Yahweh's heavenly dwelling. But Yahweh has thrown it down from the heavens to the earth. The Babylonians did not demolish it in the way they demolished the city walls, but they did devastate it in a way that reflected how Yahweh was overturning its significance. So the beclouding meant Yahweh acted in such a way as to indicate that he did not care what happened to the temple and did not bother to think about it. *He was not mindful* is a litotes: actually he cared very much, thought a lot, and was quite deliberate in his action.

The declaration that Yahweh's *day* has come, the day when Yahweh in his wrath brings great catastrophe, recalls the Prophets' prophecies about other nations (e.g., Jer 46:21; 50:31), and the opening part of the poem thus suggests this comparison rather than one with lament or mourning rites.[25] Those prophecies, too, focus more on the fact of bringing catastrophe than on the reasons for it. Those prophecies, too, conversely focus on affirming the sovereign power of Yahweh—Jerusalem has not been destroyed through the action of some other deity who is more powerful than Yahweh.[26] In contrast to those prophecies, however, the grim fact is that the object of Yahweh's action is Israel itself, as is the case when Jeremiah adapts that kind of prophecy (e.g., Jer 4:5–31; 6:1–26). And the action is not merely declared as something coming (maybe!) but as something that has happened, in ac-

23. Koenen, *Klagelieder*, 124.

24. Cf. Renkema, *Lamentations*, 221.

25. Thomas, "Poetry and Theology," 171.

26. Cf. Thomas's contrast with some of the city laments in "Poetry and Theology," 179–82.

cordance with Jeremiah's warnings. "The storm had passed over the poet's head," and around him he can see the desolation that resulted.[27]

After the Great Fire of London in 1666, a "Day of Humiliation and Fasting" was held, and Edward Stillingfleet preached at a service that day at St. Margaret's, Westminster. Lamentations 2:1 was the first passage of Scripture that he quoted.[28] His assumption was that God's action as interpreted in connection with a disaster within Scripture could provide a template for understanding other disasters.[29]

bet [2]*The Lord swallowed up,*[a] *and did not spare,*[b]
all[c] *Jacob's habitats.*[d]
He tore down in his fury
Ms. Judah's strongholds.
He stuck to the earth, made ordinary,
the kingship[e] *and its officials.*

a. The translation *swallowed up* recognizes the fact that the verb is *bālaʿ piel* (resultative), not simply *qal.*

b. The *ketiv* lacks the *waw*, which generates an asyndetic construction: "The Lord swallowed up—he did not spare" (cf. v. 21f).

c. Not only does the text include the object marker (unusually in poetry), but in addition MT keeps it as a separate word from *all Jacob's habitats*, with its own accent, which puts some independent stress on the entire phrase. This reading joins with the *qere*'s inclusion of a *waw* in the parallel colon (see note b) in having the effect of slowing down the entire line.

d. LXX, Vg, Tg "beautiful things" derives *nəʾôt* from *nāʾâ* rather than *nāwâ.*

e. LXX's "king" for *mamlākâ* may be a (not inappropriate) interpretive translation (Schäfer, "Lamentations," 120*), influenced by v. 9 (Kraus, *Klagelieder*, 37); LamR on the passage identifies this as referring to Zedekiah.

2 Given that v. 1 has covered city and country in general, and temple in particular, vv. 2–5 will expand on the former and vv. 6–10 will pay more attention to the latter. What immediately follows spells out further the way *beclouding* and *anger* found expression. The verse begins from a broad horizon: *Jacob* suggests the people as a whole, and *habitats* (*nāwâ*) strictly denotes the places where their sheep and thus their shepherds live. So the line as a whole begins from the devastation of Judah as a whole. *Swallowed up* (*bālaʿ piel*) is the poem's favorite verb (vv. 2, 5 [2×], 8, 16); nowhere else in the First Testament is there such a dense set of occurrences. This "drastic"

27. Ellison, "Lamentations," 711.

28. E. Stillingfleet, *A Sermon Preached before the Honourable House of Commons at St. Margarets Westminster* (London: Mortlock, 1666).

29. Cf. Joyce and Lipton, *Lamentations*, 71–73.

verb,[30] with its "aggressiveness,"[31] suggests an action that is eager, rapacious, avid, thorough, and overwhelming. It hardly needs the additional comment *and did not spare* (*ḥāmal*), though this verb is another that will recur (vv. 17, 21). While that second verb implies "did not pity or have mercy," its direct point is that Yahweh made no exceptions (cf. the literal usage in 1 Sam 15:3, 9, 15, in the only other chapter that uses the verb three times). The negative also repeats from the preceding line (*was not mindful*) and it will recur in the chapter: *did not turn back* (v. 8) and twice more in the reiterated *did not spare* (vv. 17, 21).

It would follow from the reference to *all Jacob's habitats* that *Ms. Judah's strongholds* are the fortified towns in the country as a whole. The metaphor of swallowing up meant for them more literally that Yahweh *tore* them *down* (*hāras*), the verb that goes back to Jeremiah's commission (Jer 1:10). The Lord's *anger* (v. 1) is here the Lord's *fury*, a more powerful expression.

The third line then speaks of what happened to the city's leadership. In this context, *kingship* (*mamlākâ*) denotes not "the kingdom" in the sense of the nation but what the crown stood for (Deut 17:18, 20; Ezek 17:14). The crown, the Davidic kingship, was something special and extraordinary, set in place by Yahweh. But Yahweh *stuck* it *to the earth*, along with *its officials*, who serve the king: the verb *stuck* (*nāgaʿ hiphil*) suggests making one thing touch or reach another. He thereby *made* it something *ordinary*. There is nothing wrong with being ordinary and everyday: the world is full of ordinary people, ordinary time, ordinary buildings, and ordinary food. But when Yahweh makes people, time, buildings, or food special and sacred, then things change. In 587 Yahweh turned the crown back into something ordinary. He profaned it. He brought this special thing into direct contact with the earthy and turned it into something everyday and disposable rather than out-of-the-ordinary and protected.

gimel [3]*He cut off in angry blazing*
Israel's every horn.
He turned his right hand backward
from before the enemy.
He burned against Jacob like a flaming fire
that consumed all around.

3 The poem refers again to Yahweh's *angry blazing* (cf. 1:12) and continues to speak of the nation as a whole rather than simply Jerusalem. The significance of the verb *cut off* emerges when the noun *horn* follows: the horn of an animal such as a bull is the secret of its aggressive strength, so it provides

30. Kraus, *Klagelieder*, 42.
31. Berges, *Klagelieder*, 136.

an image for the fighting strength of a nation. Yahweh's action involved more than merely sitting back and letting Judah be defeated, failing to defend her. He took positive action to ensure her downfall.

The second line makes the point in a different way. Syntactically, *his right hand* could be Israel's right hand, but allusion elsewhere to Yahweh's right hand suggests this reference here. Yahweh was supposed to have *his right hand* extended against Israel's enemies (Exod 15:6, 12). But he *turned* it *backward* so that instead of assailing Israel's enemy, it was assailing Israel itself.

To put it yet another, more metaphorical way, *he burned . . . like a flaming fire that consumed all around*, and acted that way *against Jacob* instead of against its attacker. Whereas Jer 6:29 speaks of fire as a means of refining, by removing what spoils, here it is simply a means of destruction.[32] Whereas Lam 1 spoke much of Yahweh acting by means of human enemies, Lam 2 speaks more about Yahweh's own direct action. His instrument is fire, and thus the literal objects of his fiery anger are mostly buildings (cf. 2 Kgs 25:9)[33]—but the metaphor of fire reaches much further.

dalet 4*He directed*[a] *his bow like an enemy,*
  taking his stand with[b] *his right hand*[c] *like an adversary.*
He killed everyone,
  the people the eye valued.[d]
In Ms. Zion's tent
  he poured out his wrath like fire.[e]

a. *Dārak* suggests treading on the bow to increase its tension and thus its reach, though J. A. Emerton argues rather for "stringing" ("Treading the Bow," *VT* 53 [2003]: 465–86).

b. LXX, Vg, Sym "he made firm," as if the verb were *hiphil.*

c. Tg specifies that it is Nebuchadnezzar's right hand, but the context suggests Yahweh's right hand, as in v. 3 (B. Blayney, *Jeremiah and Lamentations: A New Translation with Notes Critical, Philological, and Explanatory*, 2nd ed. [Edinburgh: Oliphant, 1810], 461).

d. In isolation one would take this line as a single colon, but the verse then ends up as five rather than six cola. Construing the line as a bicolon makes for a more plausible understanding of the verse as a whole even though this line's rhythm is an unusual 2-1. Removing the hyphen joining "the ones valued" and "the eye," in keeping with usage elsewhere, would make the line 2-2, but there are other single-stress cola in the poems (see "Poetic Form in the Poem," pp. 7–9), and the brevity of the line in MT draws attention to it in a fashion opposite to how MT punctuates v. 2a–b as 4-1 (see the translation note there). MT locates the *athnah* at the end of this line.

e. Whereas the first two lines began with the verb, the third line holds it back until the second colon and thus brings closure to the verse (cf. 1:1).

32. Boase ("Grounded in the Body") notes the implications of Lam 2 for the suffering of earth itself.

33. A. Labahn, "Fire from Above: Metaphors and Images of God's Actions in Lamentations 2.1–9," *JSOT* 31 (2006): 246.

4 To put it even more concretely, Yahweh acted as an expert and ruthless warrior. He was a skilled archer who knew how to aim his bow and how to stand and shoot it, and he took no prisoners. The problem is that he did so *like an enemy* and *like an adversary* in relation to Israel itself, not like Israel's own warrior-God who fights on Israel's behalf. The comparison with an enemy follows up the reference to the human enemy in v. 3. Does the poem mean that he fights *like* an enemy/adversary or *as* an enemy/adversary? Maybe it makes little difference; even if it is the former, it is still a frightening statement. Would it be a shocking and revolutionary one? Lamentations is not in the same position as Isaiah or Jeremiah, who lived among people who believed Yahweh was simply gracious and committed to Jerusalem and needed to convince them that he could act against it; events have shown that he could do so. On the other hand, the poem might need to convince some people that Yahweh could have been the one who acted as or like an enemy in causing the city to fall rather than letting them infer that some other god made it happen (see Jer 44:15–18).

So the *everyone* whom he *killed* were *the people the eye valued.* This is the expression that came earlier to denote things that Judah valued (1:7, 10, 11). While "Yahweh's tent" would denote the temple, *Ms. Zion's tent* denotes the city itself. The verse cannot close without another assertion that the havoc Yahweh thus wrought there was an expression of his *wrath.* The combination of arrows and fire suggests flaming arrows and again recalls 2 Kgs 25:9.[34]

he [5]*The Lord became like an enemy*[a]
that swallowed up Israel.
He swallowed up all her citadels,
devastated her strongholds.
He made great in Ms. Judah
mourning and moaning.[b]

a. Gordis understands *hāyâ kə'ôyēb* to mean "became an actual enemy" (cf. *Song of Songs and Lamentations*, 162; and see the translation note on v. 4). But for that meaning, the Hebrew would more likely be *hāyâ lə'ôyēb* (Salters, *Lamentations*, 127). LamR on the passage notes that the text has "became as" not "became."

b. The alliteration in the translation follows that in the Hebrew: *ta'ăniyyâ wa'ăniyyâ*, both from *'ānâ*.

5 The first two lines mostly resume expressions from vv. 2 and 4; *swallowed up* and *strongholds* in particular round off the exposition of Yahweh's action against the city that has occupied vv. 2–4. The third line brings the poem's

34. Salters, *Lamentations*, 126.

first mention of the affective aspect to the results of Yahweh's action. The words for *mourning and moaning* come only in this combination and only here and in Isa 29:2, where they refer to a threat Yahweh issues to Jerusalem. In that eighth-century context, deliverance for Zion came along at the last minute. In 587 it did not come.[35] Yahweh has now *made great* the grief of which he warned, thoroughly fulfilling his threat.

waw [6]*He did violence to his bivouac*[a] *like one in*[b] *an orchard,*[c]
devastated his appointed place.[d]
Yahweh caused to be forgotten[e] *in Zion*
appointed time and Sabbath.
In his angry condemnation he repudiated
king and priest.

a. *Śōk* comes only here; it looks like an alternative spelling for *sōk* (*śākak* and *sākak* seem to be alternative spellings of the same verb), and both are hard to distinguish from *sukkâ*.

b. For the pregnant use of *kə* meaning "like in," see BDB, 455; GK 118s–t; also v. 7f below.

c. For MT *gan*, LXX "vine" implies *gepen*; cf. I. W. Provan, "Feasts, Booths, and Gardens (Thr 2,6a)," *ZAW* 102 (1990): 254–55.

d. For *môʿădô*, LXX understands "his appointed time," as in the next line.

e. *Šākaḥ piel* comes only here; with LXX, I take it as causative rather than resultative.

6 If v. 5 provided a kind of breathing space and rounding off, this next verse resumes startling statements as it comes to focus on the temple. The first declaration is the most shocking. While the First Testament generally has no problem with speaking of Yahweh acting aggressively and ferociously, it reserves the noun *ḥāmās* for violence that involves wrongdoing. Yahweh is never engaged in *ḥāmās*. Only here is Yahweh the subject of the rarer verb *ḥāmas*, though Job 15:33 does apply the verb to aggressive treatment of a vine, which overlaps with the imagery in this verse. Farmers need bivouacs from time to time (Job 27:18; Isa 1:8), and they may, for instance, erect them as harvest time draws near and they want to protect their produce from animals or from the thieves in the next village. They may then also ruthlessly demolish them from time to time. The poem makes a link between the regular collocation of orchard, bivouac, and doing violence and the occasional description of the temple as a bivouac. To say that Yahweh *did violence to his bivouac like one in an orchard* does not quite accuse Yahweh of wrongful violence, but it is a strong statement. Strictly or etymologically, a bivouac is a shelter made of interwoven branches, so it is not an impressive term for the temple, and not a regular one, but it is a recurrent metaphor for a place

35. Cf. Renkema, *Lamentations*, 238.

where Yahweh protects his people (e.g., Ps 27:5). So the poem declares that Yahweh attacked the place of safety and security that he provided, as if it were just a flimsy temporary shelter. The parallelism describes the temple in a less metaphorical way but underlines the point: it is *his appointed place* (*môʿēd*), the place he designated for meetings between him and his people and for festivals. He *devastated* it!

The result was to make impossible *in Zion* the observance of any *appointed time* (*môʿēd* again), such as that of the morning and evening offerings. The addition of *Sabbath* is more surprising, since the destruction of the city and the devastation of the temple did not prevent observance of the Sabbath. But threats and warnings in Isa 1:13 and Hos 2:11(13) associate the Sabbath with other occasions that were marked by observances in the temple,[36] and Num 28 refers to special offerings on the Sabbath. Those connections suggest the same implication here.

The third line provides the reference to Yahweh's anger expressing itself in these events that we would half expect in light of the way these verses are unfolding, with their repeated allusions to that anger. *Condemnation* (*zaʿam*) relates to words for uttering a curse; it suggests denunciation that issues in acts of judgment.[37] It thus links well with *he repudiated* (*nāʾaṣ*). He determined to have nothing to do either with *priest*, which follows from the rest of the verse, or with *king*, which restates v. 2f; perhaps the line mentions the king here because of his important place in Judah's faith and worship. LamR on the passage identifies king and priest as Zedekiah and Seraiah.

zayin [7]*The Lord rejected his altar,*
disdained[a] *his sanctuary.*
He delivered into the hand of the enemy
the walls of her citadels—
They gave voice[b] *in Yahweh's house*
like an appointed time.[c]

a. *Nāʾar* comes only here and in Ps 89:39(40); the meaning is guessed from the context.

b. The asyndeton combined with the word order, in which the object precedes the verb, suggests that this clause is subordinate to the one that precedes.

c. Tg specifies Pesah.

7 The poem continues to focus on the temple. *The Lord rejected his altar* in the sense that he made a decision that led to its demolition. The sanctuary complex actually had two altars, but unqualified reference to "the altar"

36. Renkema, *Lamentations*, 243.

37. B. Wiklander, "זָעַם, *zāʿam*," *TDOT*, 4:106–11.

would denote the altar of sacrifice in the courtyard as opposed to the incense altar, so that Yahweh's action would mean that no sacrifices would be offered there. To put it another way, he *disdained his sanctuary*. The two nouns *altar* and *sanctuary* function as a merism for the temple and its various elements as a whole; as usual, there is no reference to a destruction of the temple, which was devastated but not demolished. While the language of rejection and disdain recalls the prophetic critique of Israel's worship in a passage such as Isa 1:11–15, the dissimilarity in the situation gives the language different significance. In the Prophets, Israel is offering worship in the temple, and the prophet is saying that Yahweh does not want it. In Lamentations, Israel is no longer able to offer worship in the temple, and the poet is saying that Yahweh brought this situation about.

The middle line broadens the focus with its reference to Yahweh's surrendering the walls of Zion's *citadels*. If the line simply read "its citadels," we might take the expression as a unique pointer to a destruction of the temple, but *her citadels* indicates the usual reference to the city's own impressive buildings.

The point in the context, however, is that letting *the enemy* get control of the city meant as a consequence that *they gave voice in Yahweh's house like an appointed time*. The point parallels the one in 1:10: when the enemy forces overwhelmed the city, they stormed into the temple itself with their shouts. The noise was as celebratory and loud as the shouting at *an appointed time*, a great festive occasion, but it was a quite different kind of shouting (contrast the "shout," *tərûʿâ*, of Jer 4:19 with that of Ps 89:15[16]).[38] Once again, *the enemy* has become the human enemy (compare and contrast vv. 3, 4, 5); Jerusalem's divine enemy and its human enemy work together.

khet [8]*Yahweh decided*[a] *to devastate*
Ms. Zion's wall.
He stretched out a line,
did not turn back his hand from swallowing up.
He made rampart and wall lament,[b]
as together they languished.[c]

a. For MT *ḥāšab*, LXX "returned" implies *hēšib*.

b. *ʾĀbal hiphil* comes only here and in Ezek 31:15, and LXX, Vg imply the more usual *qal*.

c. The word order with the verb second suggests that this clause is subordinate to the preceding clause, which makes sense, as languishing or growing weak precedes the actual collapse that led to lament. But the word order also means that the verbs *ʾābal* and *ʾāmal* enclose the line. LXX, Vg have a singular verb, suggesting that the rampart lamented as the wall languished.

38. Kraus, *Klagelieder*, 44.

8 The poem now focuses on the city itself, and tells a three-act story. First Yahweh made a decision; there is no suggestion in the poem that "Yahweh is out of control in a rage that lacks proportionality to anything she might have done."[39] He made an assessment and came to a determination.[40] The decision was a logical one for Yahweh and for the imperial power: the city wall is key to the city's defense and to its status, so it must go.

Second, he made plans, and he implemented them. Stretching out a line sounds like an action related to building rather than to demolition (Zech 1:16), but the expression is used in this other way elsewhere in a threat about Jerusalem (2 Kgs 21:13); this threat has been implemented. A king does need to do careful calculations about the resources needed to besiege and demolish a city, as he does in order to build one. So Yahweh made the calculations, and *did not turn back his hand from swallowing up*—another litotes.[41] He razed "the very architecture that served as the visible token of everything for which the Zion tradition stood and about which the psalmist implores his audience to 'walk' and 'go all around,' to 'count its towers,' 'consider well its ramparts,' and 'go through its citadels' (Ps 48:13–14)."[42]

Third, Yahweh thereby caused the kind of grief to which v. 5 referred. The *rampart* (*ḥēl*) may be a slope made of earth or rock that leads up to the *wall* built on it, from which the city's defenders can shoot at the attackers climbing up; or it may be an outer wall, a different form of second line of defense (so LXX, Vg) such as Jerusalem did have at some periods on some sides. Nebuchadnezzar's forces actually contented themselves with blockading the city until it had no more resources and had to give in, and then they demolished the defenses. Yahweh thus *made rampart and wall* themselves *lament*, as the city was crying and its approaches were mourning (1:2, 4). To say they *languished* or "grew weak" is another litotes.

tet [9]*Her gateways sank into the earth,*
he obliterated and broke up her gate bars.[a]
Her king and her officials were among the nations[b]*—*
there was no instruction.[c]
Her prophets, too—they did not find
a vision from Yahweh.

a. Seeing the line as a little long, R. B. Salters discusses ways of shortening it ("The Text of Lam. ii 9a," *VT* 54 [2004]: 273–76).

b. In the absence of a verb in this colon, LXX, Vg take *her king and her officials* as a further

39. K. M. O'Connor, "Lamentations," *NIB*, on 2:1–10.

40. Cf. Renkema, *Lamentations*, 210.

41. Koenen, *Klagelieder*, 142.

42. Dobbs-Allsopp, "*R(az/ais)ing Zion in Lamentations 2*," 45.

object of the verbs in the previous colon, which at least provides a logical link between the lines (see the commentary).

c. LXX, Vg have "there is no law"; I infer the past time reference of the noun clauses in both cola from the lines on either side. Tg infers logical links here: it was because there had been a failure in heeding the instruction in the Torah that king and officials were in exile, and this failure also lay behind the withholding of vision from the prophets to which v. 9e–f refers.

9 The first line continues the theme of v. 8 while the succeeding lines go in a different direction. Like the wall and the rampart, the *gateways* and the *bars* on the gates are crucial to the defense of a city. Whereas Ps 24:9 urges the gateways to lift their heads because Yahweh is coming in, here the gateways *sank into the earth.*[43] The result of the siege and its aftermath was that the gateways collapsed and the gate bars were broken. If the twofold demolition happened in the course of the siege, it might have taken place in the opposite order, but if it issued from the city's capture and the Babylonians' subsequent act of destruction, this order could be chronological. The doubling of the *piel* verbs to describe Yahweh's action against the gate bars and its consequences suggests the magnitude of the catastrophe and brings to an end the description of the physical devastation of the city's defenses.

Perhaps the second line, following from the first, implies that the breaking down of the city's gateways and gate bars meant the capture of *her king and her officials* and their being taken off to Babylon (see Jer 52), or perhaps this line moves from the elimination of the physical defenses to the elimination of the human resources. Likewise the city's capture meant that there were no priests to offer *instruction* (*tôrâ*): they had either been taken off in 597 (like Ezekiel's family), had taken refuge elsewhere, or had died in the course of the siege (1:19). Or perhaps they were dumbfounded by the events.

That reaction would link with the third line. It ignores Jeremiah in Judah and Ezekiel in Babylon, but they themselves talk about "the prophets" in a way that suggests people other than themselves (e.g., Jer 23:9–40; Ezek 13), and perhaps this line implies a snide judgment on the prophets in both locations who *did not find a vision from Yahweh* either because they shared messages that they said came from Yahweh but that actually came from inside them (cf. Jer 23:16; Ezek 13:16), or because they had nothing to say in light of the disconfirmation of their message by events. Tg paraphrases lines two and three:

> Her king and her rulers went into exile among the peoples because they did not keep the decrees of Torah, as if they had not received it on

43. Cf. LamR on the passage.

> Mount Sinai. Also her prophets had the sacred spirit of prophecy withheld from them and there was not said to them a word of prophecy from before YHWH.[44]

Tg thus plausibly assumes that the prophets are the ones who were functioning before 587, which would fit with what will follow in vv. 10 and 14. But maybe one should not seek too much precision in interpreting the poem. Here as elsewhere Lamentations does not name people such as king, priest, prophet, or enemy commander, as it doubtless could have done. While there is clarity and impact achieved by precision of reference and concrete naming, there can also be depth achieved and imagination encouraged by avoiding them.

yod [10]*They were sitting down on the earth,*
they were still,[a] *Ms. Zion's elders.*
They took up soil onto their head,
they wrapped on sack.
They lowered their head on the earth,
Jerusalem's girls.[b]

a. In light of the *qatals* on either side, I take the two *yiqtol* verbs as having past imperfect rather than present significance (LXX has aorist, Vg perfect); so also in v. 12a. With LXX, Syr, Vg, Tg, I take the second verb as the more common *dāmam* I ("be silent") as in v. 18, rather than *dāmam* II ("wail"; *HALOT*).

b. LXX renders "they lowered the leading girls in Jerusalem."

10 The allusion to *the elders,* the city's senior lay figures, complements the allusion to other leaders in v. 9. In 1:19 elders featured with priests, and just now v. 9 implicitly referred to priests. The elders were sitting in the city "dumbfounded,"[45] "traumatized,"[46] as v. 9 may have implied prophets and priests were.

They were garbed in the rough clothing that was fit only for manual work and that they certainly would not usually wear in public. When were they so sitting? Were they in a position to be doing so after the city's fall and the removal of people—especially its leadership? More likely the verse refers to the situation before the city fell. Jeremiah had urged people to put on sack and roll in ash at the prospect of the disaster that was coming (Jer 4:8; 6:26; cf. Est 4:1–3; Jonah 3). The poem then reports that the elders had done so,

44. A. Sperber, *The Hagiographa,* vol. 4a of *The Bible in Aramaic* (Leiden: Brill, 1968).

45. Renkema, *Lamentations,* 263.

46. Koenen, *Klagelieder,* 148.

though there is no indication that they had turned to Yahweh in the way that Jeremiah urged. The assumption that the poem refers back to the situation when the city's fall was imminent could link with the reference to the prophets in v. 9 (who had nothing true to say as the fall of the city drew near), and it will be confirmed by vv. 11–12.

The girls, too, bowed down *on the earth*; the reference to the most junior female figures of the city alongside the elders, its senior male figures, suggests the two extremes of the city's social spectrum so that it becomes a merism for the city's entire population.[47]

kaph [11]*My eyes failed with much crying,*[a]
my insides churned.
My guts[b] *poured onto the earth,*
on account of the breaking of my dear people,
As[c] *baby and suckling*[d] *fainted*[e]
in the town squares.

a. The (intensive) plural *dəmā'ôt* comes otherwise only at Ps 80:5[6].

b. Lit. "my liver." LXX, Syr "splendor" implies *kəbôdî* for *kəbēdî*, the opposite confusion between the two words to the one that seems to appear elsewhere (see M. Weinfeld, "כָּבוֹד, *kābôd*," *TDOT*, 7:23–24).

c. Perhaps like the English *as*, the preposition *bə* can hint at both the temporal and the causal.

d. While the formula "from baby to suckling" (1 Sam 15:3; 22:19) would imply that *baby and suckling* are not synonyms but rather denote a newborn and a child bit older, Lam 4:4 conflicts with that understanding and suggests that here, too, they are synonyms (Koenen, *Klagelieder*, 151).

e. Compounded with the preposition, *bē'āṭēp* is a compressed *niphal* infinitive (BDB); in v. 12, the infinitive is *hithpael*.

11 For almost half the chapter, the poem has used language like that of a prophet announcing in quite factual terms the threat that hangs over a nation, which the prophet portrays as if it has happened (e.g., Jer 4:5–31; 6:1–26). In this connection, the onlooker's voice has maintained quite an objective reporter's stance, with a form of expression something like a modern report of a war atrocity. Suddenly and dramatically, the reporter's tone now changes. Eyes are supposed to be keeping watch expectantly; it is troublesome if they have *failed* and stopped looking in that way. But much crying actually made it impossible to look for anything—maybe made it physiologically impossible, maybe made it psychologically impossible. In 1:20, the woman-city said *my insides churned*; now the reporter says it, recalling the awfulness of the siege

47. Salters, *Lamentations*, 145.

and the feelings it aroused. Possibly the poet is angry, but there is no indication of anger; what the poem rather expresses is grief.[48] The Jeremianic objectivity that appears in many of that prophet's messages gives way to the Jeremianic grief that he shows in others,[49] and this latter Jeremianic way of speaking runs through vv. 11–17. There is no doubt here that the poem identifies with the pain of Ms. Zion.[50]

My guts poured onto the earth is an even more vivid (not to say unpleasant) image. Like English expressions such as "it made me throw up," it might be metaphorical, but it gains its force from encouraging the reader to imagine something physical. *The breaking of my dear people* that was in progress had that effect on the reporter. *My dear people* are more literally "my daughter people" or "the daughter [who is] my people," my people who are (like) my daughter. Compared with "daughter Zion" (e.g., v. 10), the *my* makes the expression more explicitly a term of endearment; both kinds of expression recur especially in Jeremiah (e.g., 4:11, 31).

The particular aspect of that breaking that was so disturbing was the effect it had on little children.[51] There is no indication of the modern idea that they are "innocent children" or of their being the future of the nation. They are simply—children. Why was it that they *fainted*? The next verse will answer the question. This last line makes it particularly likely that the poem continues to recall the situation before the city's fall.

lamed [12]*To their mothers they*[a] *were saying,*
"Where is grain and wine?"
As they fainted away[b] *like someone run through*
in the city[c] *squares,*
As their life poured out
into the arms of their mothers.[d]

a. Tg makes "the young men of Israel" the subject of the verb, which makes the line as a whole more plausible.

b. The verb (*'āṭap*), *niphal* in v. 11, is here *hithpael*; the same applies to *šāpak* in v. 12e.

c. Whereas v. 11 used the rarer noun *qiryâ*, v. 12 has the more usual expression.

d. *Their mothers* begins and ends the verse and thus embraces it, as mothers do their babies.

48. It is at this point in the chapter that mourning becomes a key to understanding Lam 2, as Pham (*Mourning in the Ancient Near East*) argues for Lam 2 as a whole.

49. House, *Lamentations*, 385.

50. Linafelt, *Surviving Lamentations: Catastrophe, Lament and Protest*, 52.

51. On the pain associated with children in Lamentations, see T. Linafelt, "Surviving Lamentations," *HBT* 17 (1995): 45–61.

12 As the motif here in vv. 11–12, at the center of the poem, starvation might be seen as a central concern in the chapter.[52] The account of the babies' words is figurative—babies do not ask questions or eat grain, let alone drink wine. Perhaps the concrete expressions are a way of saying that the babies were appealing for sustenance; *grain and wine* could suggest the two staples that an adult would be longing for. But the combination would be puzzling even on the lips of an adult, because grain denotes the wherewithal to make bread rather than bread itself; one might expect bread and wine, or grain and new wine. Perhaps the question concerns whether there are any supplies left; or perhaps wine is what a person wants in distress (Prov 31:6–7);[53] or perhaps "wine is mentioned . . . because water would have been too polluted to drink";[54] or perhaps the sound sequence with its fourfold *ā* (*dāgān wāyāyin*) suggested the word sequence;[55] or perhaps the children are drawing attention to the fulfillment of the curse in Deut 28:51, which refers to grain, new wine, and oil.[56]

The move to *hithpael* verbs in the second and third lines adds to the intensity of the verse. The poem adds to this effect by means of the simile whereby it compares babies to men who have been *run through*, fatally stabbed. Such stabbing was a recurrent prophetic threat and no doubt a reality.

The implication of the third line might then be that the babies were almost like a wounded man dying in his mother's or wife's arms, but pouring out one's life (*nepeš*) can denote an experience of suffering that falls short of dying, and it links with the language of pouring out oneself in protest and crying (Job 30:16; Ps 42:4[5]),[57] which one can imagine the children doing.

mem [13]*With what can I bear you witness,*[a] *what can I compare to you,*
Ms.[b] *Jerusalem?*
What can I liken to you so I may comfort you,
young Ms. Zion?
Because your breaking was as big as the sea—
who could mend you?

a. Vg has "compare"; cf. *DCH*'s *'ûd* III. More likely the verb is a denominative from the noun *'ēd* (cf. LXX, Tg) with the suffixed *you* as its grammatical direct object (cf. Job 29:11). While one might then take the opening *mâ* as a second object, elsewhere the verb only has a

52. Renkema, *Lamentations*, 208.

53. Koenen, *Klagelieder*, 152.

54. P. M. Joyce, "Lamentations," in *The Oxford Bible Commentary*, ed. J. Barton and J. Muddiman (Oxford: Oxford University Press, 2001), 530.

55. Albrektson, *Studies in the Text and Theology of the Book of Lamentations*, 106.

56. Flanders, "Covenant Curses Transposed," 105.

57. Provan, *Lamentations*, 71–72.

personal object, and *mâ* can be used adverbially. LXX "what shall I witness for you" (cf. Tg) reverses the construction.

b. The article on *habbat* "ensures that we see [*bat*] as absolute and the relationship between the words as apposition" (Salters, *Lamentations*, 153).

13 In 1:12, the woman-city asked if there was any pain like hers; here the witness presupposes a negative answer to that question.[58] In both passages the question might be semi-rhetorical; in the cold light of day one might identify greater suffering. But the poems are expressing the absolutely horrifying nature of *this* city's pain in its objective nature and its subjective significance. It is not surprising that words fail the poet.[59] In the twentieth century, the rhetorical questions find an answer in the Holocaust.[60] "On a scale of one to ten, where would you place your pain?" "Eleven." The reporting voice acknowledges that reality. *Bear you witness* suggests the image of Ms. Jerusalem brought before the community elders or before the mountains and hills or before the heavenly court, as if under accusation for something. One would have to think of an accusation such as "she claimed she had suffered terribly, but it's not so." The witness imagines giving testimony for her: there is no suffering with which to compare hers.

The synonymy in the first two lines expresses emotion.[61] Paradoxically, although it is a strange comfort to have people acknowledge that one's suffering is uniquely horrendous, it can also be a comfort to find someone whose suffering is comparable; such a person is in a position to understand what one has gone through. "When adversity comes to a person, they say to him, 'It also happened to so-and-so.' These are comforts to him."[62]

But the third line reaffirms that there is no such person. The *breaking* or shattering of Ms. Zion has no parallel. She is a "bare life" figure.[63] The city's destruction is total. There is nothing left. The breaking was as big as the breakers in the Great Sea (Tg), the Mediterranean, the kind of breakers that can rise to an immense height at Jaffa. The verb for *mend* (*rāpā'*) means "heal," but it often applies to the mending of broken bones. In the verse's closing question, "the poetry backhandedly affirms YHWH as healer."[64] Is there the tiniest hint of hope in the "who"?[65]

58. Mintz, *Ḥurban*, 28–29.

59. Berges, *Klagelieder*, 151.

60. Joyce and Lipton, *Lamentations*, 82–84.

61. M. L. Mitchell, "Reading of the Imagery of Lamentations," 100.

62. Rashi, in MG.

63. A. Meverden, "Daughter Zion as *Homo Sacer*," in Kelle, Ames, and J. L. Wright, *Interpreting Exile*, 395–407.

64. Thomas, "Poetry and Theology," 187.

65. Salter, *Lamentations*, 154.

nun [14]*Your prophets, they beheld for you*
emptiness and besmearing.[a]
They didn't reveal your waywardness,
so as to bring about your restoration.[b]
They beheld for you
burdens of[c] *emptiness and provocations.*[d]

a. Tg "there is no substance to their prophecy" perhaps implies *tāpēl* I rather than *tāpēl* II ("plaster"); LXX, Vg "folly" looks like a guess (Alexander, *Targum of Lamentations*, 136).

b. For the *qere šəbûtēk*, the *ketiv* implies *šəbîtēk*, a common variant. LXX, Vg, Tg "your exile" links the noun with the verb *šābâ*, which fits most occurrences (the majority come in Jeremiah and Ezekiel), but not, e.g., Job 42:10. More likely the noun derives its meaning from its similarity to *šûb*: the compound phrase is "a sonorous expression of *šûb* with a cognate accusative" (J. R. Lundbom, *Jeremiah 21–36*, AB 21B [New York: Doubleday, 2004], 355). In Jeremiah and Ezekiel, it would include bringing people back from exile, but even there it implies more. Vg, Tg take it to denote a turning back to Yahweh, to repentance (cf. 5:21).

c. I follow MT in the accents and LXX in taking *maśśʾôt* as a construct, and I thus construe the line as 2-3 (cf. 3a–b, 8c–d, 10a–b, 14e–f).

d. The *hapax legomenon maddûḥîm* presumably derives from *nādaḥ*, which can denote being propelled away from Yahweh to go after other gods (Tg) or being driven into exile (LXX, Vg).

14 The poem jumps in a new direction. It mentioned *prophets* in v. 9, with the implication that they were the shalom-prophets (Jer 6:14; 8:11; 28:9; Ezek 13:10), the people LXX and Tg often call "false prophets" (e.g., Jer 2:8; 6:13; so Tg here). It now speaks more trenchantly, though the prophets are not here morally disqualified as in 4:13.[66] The witness's voice grants that they *beheld* something (*ḥāzâ*). While this verb can refer to ordinary seeing, it especially denotes a prophet's kind of seeing, the kind that goes beyond what the ordinary eye sees (e.g., Isa 1:1; 2:1). It is related to the word for a vision (*ḥāzôn*, v. 9). But these prophets' beholding was not the real thing. They beheld *emptiness* (*šāwʾ*), a favorite word in Ezekiel to describe their visions (13:6–9). The word is familiar in the context of the commandment not to take up Yahweh's name with regard to something empty (Exod 20:7; Deut 5:11), in the context of reference to empty witness (Exod 23:1; Deut 5:20[17]), and in connection with deities that have no substance (Jer 18:15). These prophets' visions of *šālôm* had no substance. The prophets were involved in *besmearing* (*tāpēl*) over the real situation in Jerusalem. The word comes otherwise only in Ezek 13; 22:28 to denote plaster applied to a wall in such a way as to conceal its cracks but not solve its real problems; it will not stop the wall collapsing in due course. A homonym suggests something that tastes nasty (cf. *tiplâ* in

66. Berges, *Klagelieder*, 153.

Jer 23:13, in connection with the shalom-prophets). The poem might make readers remember both meanings.

What follows suggests that Ezekiel's usage is in the forefront. The prophets declined to push people toward facing reality: *they didn't reveal your waywardness* but rather colluded with people in covering it up. The poem points to something close to a definition of prophecy here: prophecy means getting people to face their waywardness. Only here does the poem refer to the wrongdoing that issued in the catastrophe, and even here the allusion is indirect. "The emphasis on suffering over culpability" is even more pronounced in Lam 2 than in Lam 1, as "the vitriol unleashed at God" has hardly any parallel in the Scriptures.[67] Even here the critique relates to the prophets rather than the people. They didn't push people to face the danger they were in *so as to bring about your restoration*. The phrase recurs particularly in Jeremiah (e.g., 33:7, 11, 26) and in Ezekiel (e.g., 16:53), but there it especially denotes a restoration after the calamity. The grievous irony in the poem's taking up the expression is its implication that there could have been restoration without the community having to go through the catastrophe, if only the prophets had driven people to face facts.

Instead the poem repeats the charge that they *beheld for you . . . emptiness*, though it nuances it in one or two ways. First, it adds the word *burdens* (*maśśʾôt*), which is a regular enough word for a prophecy (e.g., Isa 13:1; 15:1), but also has a homonym denoting something burdensome. Jeremiah 23:33–40 works with the potential of these alternative meanings, and the poem may be inviting people to bear them in mind. Second, it adds the *hapax legomenon provocations*, which suggests messages that encourage people to turn away from Yahweh and serve other deities.

samek [15]*People slapped the palms of their hands at you,*
all the people who passed your way.
They whistled and shook their head
at Ms. Jerusalem:
"Is this the city of which they used to say:
Totality[a] *of beauty, joy to all the earth?"*

a. For *kālîl*, LXX has "crown"; see *DCH*, 4:425–26; *DTT*, 642.

15 The poem's focus changes again. While clapping is a positive gesture in Israel as in other cultures, the slapping (*sāpaq*) referred to here is negative (Num 24:10; Job 34:26), like whistling (e.g., Jer 19:8; 25:9, 18) and shaking

67. C. R. Mandolfo, "Lamentations," in *The New Interpreter's Bible One Volume Commentary*, ed. B. R. Gaventa and D. Petersen (Nashville: Abingdon, 2010), 453.

the head (Pss 22:7[8]; 109:25). As usual, the picture of people passing by and reacting in this way is a figure of speech (see the commentary on 1:12).

The last line twists the knife in the wound, and the length of the line lengthens the mocking.[68] The people who *used to say* these things about Jerusalem were the Judahites themselves (Tg). Much later, after Herod's glorification of the city, other people said it, but there was nothing outstandingly spectacular about the material Jerusalem in First Testament times. Even though the temple of Solomon was a marvelous building, the wonder of Jerusalem mostly lay in what it meant as the place where Yahweh dwelt. In this sense, Zion was indeed "the total embodiment of beauty" (Ps 50:2), "the greatest joy in all the earth" (Ps 48:2[3]). Both phrases are similar to the expressions in this verse. In their worship, Judahites indeed used to acclaim Zion in this way. As Ps 48 as a whole puts it:

> Yahweh is great and much praised
> in the city of our God.
> His holy mountain is the most beautiful height,
> the greatest joy in all the earth.
> Mount Zion is Zaphon's heights,
> the town of the great king.
> In its citadels God
> has made himself known as a haven.
> For now: when the kings assembled,
> people passed over altogether.
> As those saw, they were stunned,
> they were terrified, they panicked.
> Trembling seized them there,
> writhing like a woman birthing.
> With an east wind you break up
> Tarshish ships.
> As we have heard, so have we seen,
> in the city of Yahweh Armies,
> In the city of our God
> which God will establish forever. (Rise.)
> We think about your commitment, God,
> within your palace.
> Like your name, God, so your praise
> reaches to the ends of the earth.
> Your right hand is full of faithfulness;
> Mount Zion rejoices.

68. House, *Lamentations*, 389.

The cities of Judah are glad
for the sake of your decisions.
Go around Zion, go about it,
count its towers,
Give your mind to its rampart,
pass through its citadels,
So that you may recount to the next generation
that this is God.
Our God forever and ever—
he will drive us against death.

The affirmations that run through Ps 48 as a whole form the background to Judahite faith as it is also affirmed, for example, by Isaiah, but they could gain a kind of independent life as a "Zion theology" that emphasized God's commitment to Jerusalem independently of Jerusalem's commitment to God. It was the Judahite equivalent to the stress on faith rather than deeds that is attacked in James 2. The 587 catastrophe means that this kind of Zion theology "has proved itself false in its central assertions."[69] After 587 it was inconceivable. Instead of being a place that could mean joy for all the earth, Jerusalem is a place that brings horror to anyone who passes by. "With Jerusalem and its temple lying in ruins, the conceptual foundation of the Zion tradition, the visible token of Yahweh's beneficence and potency, was wrecked and with it the validity of the tradition's entire theological enterprise."[70] It is not terminated; Isa 40–66 reaffirms it. The Zion theology expressed in Ps 48 is thus affirmed both in the first part of the book of Isaiah and in the last part. But the fall of Jerusalem indicated that it could not be taken out of context or allowed to stand on its own, as Isaiah and the Psalms themselves made clear.

pe[a] 16*They opened their mouth wide at you,*
all your enemies.
They whistled and ground[b] *their teeth,*
they said, "We've swallowed her up.
Yes, this is the day that we waited for,
we've found it, we've seen it."

a. The *pe* and *ayin* verses come in the opposite order to the more familiar alphabetical one; Lam 3 and 4 also have this order.

b. The two verbs *šāraq* and *ḥāraq* make for alliteration; *ḥāraq* does not denote "gnashing" their teeth in the usual English sense (Renkema, *Lamentations,* 297).

69. Koenen, *Klagelieder,* 118–19.

70. Dobbs-Allsopp, "*R(az/ais)ing Zion in Lamentations 2,*" 27.

16 The poem makes the picture even tougher. It was not just that passersby were horrified at what had happened to Zion, which contrasted with the way they had (purportedly) looked at it. Its actual attackers were naturally enthusiastic about what had happened. As was the case with king and priest in v. 9, we can guess at the identity of the attackers (people such as Moab, Ammon, and Edom), but it is rhetorically significant that they are anonymous. While opening the mouth could be another expression for horror or for speaking (Job 35:16), more often it is preliminary to consuming (e.g., Deut 11:6); it is the kind of thing a lion does before attacking someone (Ps 22:13[14]).

The next line fits this understanding. The whistling and teeth-grinding would be anticipatory of enjoying the meal (teeth-grinding is hostile in Ps 37:12, like a dog's bearing and clacking of teeth).[71] *We've swallowed her up* is then the subsequent satisfied retrospective.

The enemies are thus pictured realizing their own longstanding hope for *this day*. But for the poet and the audience, reference to *this day* would carry distinct connotations. The poem is implying a link with the "day" of 1:12, 13, 21; 2:1. The enemies did not realize it was the day of Yahweh that they were looking forward to, but it was. *This is the day* is a very different proclamation from the one in Ps 118:24, and a kind of inversion of the "this is the day" of Judg 4:14. In another context, the line as a whole could describe Judah's anticipation of the day of Yahweh that would be a day of blessing and triumph over its adversaries, but in this context the line has a quite different significance.

ayin [17]*Yahweh did that which he schemed,*
he executed[a] *his word.*
That which he ordered from days of old—
he tore down and did not spare.
He let the enemy rejoice over you,
he let your adversaries' horn rise.

a. *Bāṣa'* usually means "cut off"; the use here is unique. It has been hypothesized that the word's background lies in weaving (*HALOT*; D. Kellermann, "בצע, *bṣ'*," *TDOT*, 2:205–8).

17 The poem continues to reflect on what happened in a chilling way. The enemies may have thought that the city's destruction was their achievement, but it was not.[72] In Hebrew as in English, scheming (*zāmam*) suggests a plan to do something questionable. Likewise in Hebrew as in English, *executed*

71. Salters, *Lamentations*, 162.

72. H. Lalleman-de Winkel, *Jeremiah, Lamentations: An Introduction and Commentary*, TOTC 21 (Downers Grove, IL: InterVarsity, 2013), 348.

(*bāṣa'*) has negative connotations when applied to implementing a scheme. Ordinary expressions for Yahweh's fulfilling his word need not have worrying implications. But Yahweh had said, "I have spoken—I have schemed, and I have not relented, I will not turn back from it" (Jer 4:18). Indeed, Yahweh's executing his word may not be good news.

The middle line rephrases the first. It would make sense if *that which he ordered from days of old* were the temple, which he *tore down*,[73] but there is no parallel for this language. More likely his orders were the threats built into Yahweh's relationship with Israel since Sinai and the Plains of Moab, as Tg assumes (Lev 26; Deut 28–30). Like the Prophets, the Torah made clear that such threats did not need to be fulfilled unless Israel fell into or continued in the waywardness to which v. 14 referred; but it also made clear that if it did so fall or continue, the threats definitely would find execution. *He tore down and did not spare* constituted his executing his word, though it is prophetic rather than Torah language (see v. 2 and the commentary on it).

The third line then puts in more down-to-earth language how Yahweh's unwitting agents were the means of fulfilling his word. Whereas Israelites could sometimes pray that Yahweh will not let their enemies rejoice about them and could give praise that he has not done so (Pss 30:1[2]; 35:19), on this occasion he has—yes, he has let them rejoice *over you*. "Even the smiles on the faces of Zion's enemies were put there by Yahweh."[74] Letting Judah's adversaries' horn rise is the obverse of cutting Judah's horn (v. 3).

tsade [18]*Their heart*[a] *cried out toward the Lord:*[b]
"Ms. Zion's wall!"[c]
Let your tears go down like a wadi,
day and night.
Don't give yourself respite,
the tear in your eye[d] *must not be still.*[e]

a. Grammatically, one would take the *adversaries* in v. 17 as the antecedent to *their* (Ibn Ezra, "Commentary B," in D. Anderson, "Medieval Jewish Exegesis," 188), which could suggest the neat idea that the adversaries are mockingly pointing out to the Lord what a fine job they have done (cf. 1:21). But the idea that *their heart* called out, and indeed that it *cried out* (a term for a cry of pain; e.g., Gen 4:10; Deut 26:7) makes that interpretation implausible. Rather, cf. Tg's making explicit that "the heart of Israel" cried out; "modern commentators make too much of the lack of antecedent for the pronom[inal] suffix" (Alexander, *Targum of Lamentations*, 139). For the many proposed emendations of v. 18a–b, see Salters, *Lamentations*, 167–70; but the ancient versions correspond to MT and "any emendation seems highly questionable" (Schäfer, "Lamentations," 123*).

73. Cf. Gordis, *Song of Songs and Lamentations*, 166.
74. Salters, *Lamentations*, 164.

b. MT places the *athnah* here, perhaps implying that the direct speech that follows occupies the whole of the rest of the verse.

c. Vg has "over Ms. Zion's wall."

d. Lit. "the daughter of your eye" or "your daughter eye"; cf. Blayney, *Jeremiah and Lamentations*, 464. LXX takes "daughter" as vocative.

e. The suffixes and the verbs in v. 18c–f and v. 19 are feminine singular.

18 So far, the poem has spoken much *about* the Lord, but no one has spoken *to* him. Now it begins a transition to someone doing so. In vv. 1–7 *the Lord* had four times been the subject of strong verbs that indicated his acting with the power suggested by that title. Now the poem returns to this designation in connection with recording an appeal to him. I take the first colon as anticipatorily summarizing the cry of vv. 19–22, which will record a cry of protest to the Lord that people uttered. It is the kind of cry that Israel uttered in Egypt, but also the kind that Jeremiah envisages coming from Judah in this present context (Exod 3:7, 9; Jer 22:20). It was the people's *heart* that cried out, the heart that turned over and was faint (1:20, 22): so the heart here suggests the turmoil and pain of the person (cf. v. 19). The transitions in what follows are elliptical, but I have inferred that *Ms. Zion's wall!* summarizes that heart cry. It was an exclamation to the Lord about the terrible fate of the city, symbolized by an exclamation about its wall.

In isolation, the middle line might be continuing the address to Ms. Zion's wall. Yahweh had *made rampart and wall lament* as they collapsed (v. 8), so there would be special point in appealing to the wall to cry, given that it had been destroyed.[75] It would thus become a wailing wall; and in the twentieth century, Gentiles came to refer to the surviving section of the Herodian Western Wall of the Temple Mount as the "Wailing Wall" because it was a place where Jews would pray in heartfelt fashion. But by the time we get to v. 19, it will be clear that the exhortation is addressing Ms. Zion herself (both wall and city are feminine). So the witnessing voice is continuing to speak, but it is now not continuing its report but issuing an exhortation. It is urging Ms. Zion to continue the crying toward the Lord of which the first line spoke, in a way that is especially calculated to move him. After a storm, a torrent goes down a wadi that is otherwise dry. This happening in nature becomes an image to reinforce the exhortation about crying, except that these tears (unlike a wadi's flow) are to stream continuously, *day and night*.

So the one crying is not to allow herself to stop; it is the appropriate reaction to the disaster she has seen. The poem advises her to "create a scene"

75. Calvin, *Jeremiah and Lamentations*, 5:444.

before the Lord.[76] "God has done it; cry to him!"[77] "Teares and prayers are the very true armour and weapons of the servants of God: yea, armour and weapons of great effect, and terrible to the wicked."[78]

qoph [19]*Get up, chant in the night,*
at the beginning of the watches.
Pour out your heart like water
in front of the Lord's face.
Lift up your open hands[a] *to him*
for the life of your babies,
Who were fainting with hunger
at the beginning of all the streets.[b]

a. Lit. "your palms."

b. Scholars who think the verse must originally have comprised three lines most often delete the last (e.g., Kraus, *Klagelieder*, 37). Its reference to *the beginning of all the streets* pairs with the reference to *the beginning of the watches* in the first line.

19 As an alternative image to that of crying day and night, Ms. Zion is to get up each night *at the beginning of the watches*, the periods into which the night was divided so that a lookout would have responsibility for just part of the night. Judges 7:19 speaks of the middle watch, so one might imagine three watches running approximately from six until ten, from ten until two, and from two until six. Ms. Zion is not only to pray before bed and on waking but to wake up at ten and at two to chant (*rānan*) a prayer—maybe the kind that appears in the Psalms.

But she is indeed to continue crying, to *pour out your heart like water*, which suggests an intensity of emotion attributed to the city. There may be no human beings left in the city to pray, but despite the destruction of Zion, Zion still exists.[79] The second colon of this line is also striking, with its assumption that the Lord is still there in the city, too—still present like a king before whom a suppliant can appear.

As well as tears and the expression of feelings, prayer implies the physical gesture of opening one's hands before God so that he can fill them. Prayer is not only a mental and verbal act but a bodily one.[80] Once again, a focus of concern is the city's babies. "The death of children leaves parents with a sorrow

76. K. M. O'Connor, "Lamentations," *NIB*, on v. 18.

77. C. J. H. Wright, *Lamentations*, 94.

78. Ambrose of Milan as quoted in Toussaine, *Lamentations*, 229.

79. Dobbs-Allsopp, "*R(az/ais)ing Zion in Lamentations 2*."

80. P. D. Miller, *They Cried to the Lord: The Form and Theology of Biblical Prayer* (Minneapolis: Fortress, 1994), 50–51.

that differs from other kinds of grief. . . . Those who have lost a child suffer more intense grief for a longer period of time than those who endure other losses. . . . The death of children occurs in biblical literature as an indication of extreme punishment or doom" (1 Sam 2:34; Ps. 137:9; Isa 47.8–9).[81]

The babies are there, notionally, *at the beginning of all the streets*—that is, where the streets branch off from a square.[82] In reality, it is presumably too late to do anything for them; yet there is something about drawing Yahweh's attention to them. "One in such pain should not be able to sleep through the night. Let God know the pain. Appeal to God for the sake of the children."[83] The second voice's bidding to Ms. Zion thus continues into this fourth line (cf. 1:7). It "breaks the pattern of three-line verses, but Zion's agony also breaks every pattern,"[84] and it brings the poem to a pause before Zion's actual address to Yahweh. The unexpected fourth line thus adds force to the urgent exhortation in vv. 18c–19g before we get the content of the plea in vv. 20–22. It brings to an end a sequence of verses (vv. 13–19) that "focuses on discourse: what cannot be said (v. 13), what should have been said (v. 14), what is expressed or said in mockery (vv. 15–16), what was said by YHWH to determine this destruction (v. 17), what should be said by the city as mother to beg the Lord to have mercy (vv. 18–19)."[85]

resh [20]*Look, Yahweh, and take note,*
to whom you dealt out in this way.
Do women eat their own fruit,
the babies[a] *they dandled?*[b]
Is someone killed in the Lord's sanctuary,
priest and prophet?[c]

a. "Dealt out" was *ʿôlēltā*, "babies" is *ʿōlălê*: the "horrific" paronomasia (Dobbs-Allsopp, *Lamentations*, 99) underlines the scandal expressed in the two lines.

b. Lit. "babies of dandlings." But *tippuḥîm* comes only here, and the verb *ṭāpaḥ* with some such meaning comes only in v. 22; the words refer to babies in some way, but the precise meaning is guesswork. We do know that *tappûḥîm* is a kind of fruit, traditionally assumed to be apples, so that the word makes for another acerbic paronomasia (cf. Dobbs-Allsopp, "R(az/ais)ing Zion in Lamentations 2," 58).

c. Tg makes this line the divine response to the previous question: the horrific events in v. 20a–d were caused by the horrific events in v. 20e–f; Tg refers specifically to the incident described in 2 Chron 24:20–22, though it describes Zechariah as son of Iddo (cf. Ezra 5:1).

81. Bosworth, "Daughter Zion and Weeping," 229.

82. Salters, *Lamentations*, 174.

83. Bailey, "Lamentations," 41.

84. E. Nowell, *Song of Songs, Ruth, Lamentations, Ecclesiastes, Esther*, New Collegeville Bible Commentary: Old Testament 24 (Collegeville, MN: Liturgical, 2013), 31.

85. M. L. Mitchell, "Reading of the Imagery of Lamentations," 109.

20 It is not immediately clear who is speaking, as it was not immediately clear who was addressed in v. 18c–f, and in isolation it could again be the witness. But in the next verse, it once more becomes clear that it is Ms. Zion. In a "bold and grand prosopopoeia,"[86] then, the poem now has Zion responding to the witness's bidding and appealing to Yahweh. The unannounced transition to direct address to Yahweh also compares and contrasts with that at 1:20. Once again the appeal begins *look, Yahweh* (the colon as a whole corresponds to 1:11e). The exhortation to consider how *you dealt* with the person who is pleading parallels 1:22, though here there is no appeal for action against the enemy. Is it significant that the witness gets Ms. Zion to voice the challenge to Yahweh so that the witness does not personally do it?[87] But the positive significance of Ms. Zion finding her voice is that "in 2:20–22 the poem comes full circle" as "razing turns into raising," and through Zion's speech "the poem constructs a memory of resistance and transcendence to counter the literal reality of destruction and suffering." Thus "personified Zion serves the temple-less community as an imaginative surrogate—a *place*holder, if you will—until such a time as a more material temple of mud and brick can be rebuilt; a Zion of the mind and text is substituted (quite literally before the eyes of the poem's readers) for the Zion of myth and cult that now lies in ruin."[88]

After the first line, what Ms. Zion does is perhaps not exactly what she was bidden to do. It is more confrontation than pleading.[89] She draws attention to two scandalous victims of Yahweh's action. First, the poem continues its distinctive focus on the fate of the city's little ones. The middle line makes its point with distinctive sharpness in the images in the two cola; children are the fruit of a woman's womb (Ps 127:3). The motif of eating children appears in other Middle Eastern texts;[90] it is hard to know if we are to take it literarily, but there is no doubt that the image is designed to be a horrifying expression of the terrible nature of events.[91] In this sense, the assumed answer to Ms. Zion's question is yes (cf. 4:10). It would be another aspect of Yahweh's executing his word (Lev 26:29; Deut 28:53, 55). Yet the rhetorical significance of the inquiry is now to raise a question about the propriety of this action.

86. *CTAT*, 889.

87. Cf. M. Boersma's discussion of Leviticus Rabbah in "Mourning for Vindication," *Conversations with the Biblical World* 34 (2014): 101–17.

88. Dobbs-Allsopp, "*R(az/ais)ing Zion in Lamentations 2*," 56, 61, 65.

89. Hens-Piazza, *Lamentations*, 34.

90. See the discussion in Koenen, *Klagelieder*, 175–79.

91. H. J. Bosman, "The Function of (Maternal) Cannibalism in the Book of Lamentations (2:20 & 4:10)," *Scriptura* 110 (2012): 152–65.

The same then applies to the third line. Even if the priest teaches people in a misguided way, and even if the prophet is a misguided promiser of shalom, should the Lord's sanctuary be defiled by the shedding of their blood?

shin [21]*They lay down onto the earth in the streets,*
youth and elder.
My girls and my young men,
they fell by the sword.[a]
You killed them on the day of your anger—
when you slaughtered, you did not spare.

a. The first two lines work a-b-b'-a'. LXX also has "by hunger," assimilating to frequent usage in Jeremiah.

21 Ms. Zion looks around the city more broadly, making statements rather than asking rhetorical questions, but still confronting. Both *youth and elder* were the victims, which might be a merism or might denote the youths as the key to the future and the elders as the key to insight. *Girls* and *young men* then cover everyone of that age group. But the three lines come to their climax with the confrontational third line and its four horrifying expressions. *You killed* or "slew" (the verb in the Decalogue!) *on the day of your anger,* returning to the stress on anger in vv. 1–6. And *you slaughtered* as if they were animals (heightening the verb in the parallelism); *you did not spare.*

tav [22]*You were summoning as on an appointed day*
terrors[a] *for me from all around.*[b]
On the day of Yahweh's anger there was not
survivor or escaper.
Those whom I dandled and raised,[c]
my enemy finished them off.

a. Tg derives from *ʾāgar* ("gather"), LXX from *gûr* ("dwell")—perhaps we are to think both of neighbors and of terrors (Gordis, *Song of Songs and Lamentations*, 169).

b. In this context, it is natural to take the preposition *min* to mean *from*, whereas in Jeremiah it means "on" (see BDB, 578b).

c. The simple *waw* rather than *waw*-consecutive suggests that the two verbs refer to the same action.

22 Once again Ms. Zion expresses what Yahweh did in an acerbic, biting way. Yahweh acted the way he did or the way a priest did when inviting people to come for a festival. It is a feast day, but it is a "gruesome perversion" of a feast day.[92] The invitees are *terrors for me from all around*, a variant on a phrase that recurs in Jeremiah in the singular and thus more abstractly (Jer 6:25; 20:3, 10; 46:5; 49:29).[93]

Once again there is a reference to the day and to Yahweh's anger; the chapter began with "the day of his anger," and it almost ends with *the day of Yahweh's anger.* Ms. Zion adds a concrete reaffirmation of how Yahweh did not spare: *there was not survivor or escaper*. (The poem speaks in hyperbole; there were quite a few, as Jeremiah promised.)

Again, the poem almost closes with another reference to the babies and with two ways of describing the mothers' nurturing them or bringing them up; but it actually closes with *my enemy finished them off.* It is quite an ending for the poem. The enemy must be the human adversary, but the resonances of Yahweh's being at least "like an enemy" (vv. 4–5) linger. And it is quite an ending for a prayer. There is no "why" as there is in many psalms, no acknowledgment of sin, no plea for forgiveness or for rescue, but rather counterattack[94] or reproach.[95] As was the case with Lam 1, in due course the poem will find its response from Yahweh in Isa 40–55, but its stopping where it does means that it does not "too soon transport contemporary biblical readers to a happy ending that shortcuts the work of grief and anger that comes to the surface in lament."[96]

A READER'S RESPONSE

Imagine someone who has taken part in reading Lam 2 at a worship gathering in Mizpah or Bethel.

> You know what it's like when your spouse or your parents lash out at you, and you know you did something wrong, but you never expected them to be as tough as they are being? That's how we felt. Yahweh put a dark cloud over us. He made us a disgrace. He didn't care what he did to our city, which was supposed to be his footstool. He didn't care what he did to the temple, which was supposed to be the place where he stayed among us. He didn't care what he did to the place where he had bidden us make our offerings. He swallowed us up. He treated our leaders as

92. Linafelt, *Surviving Lamentations: Catastrophe, Lament and Protest*, 58.

93. See A. H. W. Curtis, "'Terror on Every Side,'" in *The Book of Jeremiah and Its Reception*, ed. A. H. W. Curtis and T. Römer, BETL 128 (Leuven: Peeters, 1997), 111–18.

94. Koenen, *Klagelieder*, 184.

95. Provan, *Lamentations*, 58.

96. K. M. O'Connor, "Lamentations," *NIB*, in her "reflection" on Lam 2.

if they were nothing. He made our army incapable of defending itself. It was as if he was the great warrior and archer firing at us. He invited pagan feet to come and trample his house. He calculated how much by way of resources would be needed to demolish the city's walls and allocated the resources to get the job done. He made it impossible for priests or prophets to guide us. He made our children suffer. In fact, he did exactly as he had said he would. And so he made people cry out to him about the devastated city.

Then the poem reminded us of another voice. It was as if the city itself was crying out. After all, the city hadn't done anything wrong. So it cried out about the children and the priests and the prophets and the young people and the old people, the girls and the boys. Maybe his anger will be satisfied . . .

LAMENTATIONS 3: "PERHAPS THERE IS HOPE"

The poem in Lam 3 is another imaginary two-hander. It begins with the words of someone who articulates an experience of affliction and pain that has come about through Yahweh's action, the speaker this time being a man. Initially it thus recalls the form of an I-psalm in which someone speaks of an experience of attack and voices a plea for Yahweh to act on their behalf. Out of its context in Lamentations, the prayer might be such a psalm. But it then incorporates the words of someone who speaks from a third-party perspective and in relation to the one who is afficted, and it subsequently incorporates a further first-person plural self-exhortation to turn to Yahweh before eventually returning to an "I" prayer. It thus utilizes several traditional forms of speech to tell a complicated story.[1]

While one can therefore perceive behind the poem traditional forms of speech with a background in worship, it seems unwisely complicated to hypothesize that the alphabetical poem came about through the bringing together of already existent examples of such forms. It is also difficult to imagine how it could itself be used in worship except as a reading designed to help people reflect and pray. It could be taken as a report, reflection, confession, exhortation, and prayer by Jeremiah, and it likely encouraged the attribution of Lamentations to Jeremiah.[2] Traditional Jewish and Christian commentators in fact vary over whether they see the "I" as Jeremiah or as the Judahite people in the 580s. The poem was the entry point into a reading of Lamentations in light of Jesus's experience; the man who speaks is one who learned obedience through things suffered (Heb 5:8).[3] On the other hand, Christian commentators vary over whether or how they see Jesus here;[4] John of the Cross quotes the entirety of Lam 3:1–20 and also 3:28, 44 as illustrating the sufferings of "the dark night of the soul."[5]

1. M. J. Bier sees it as embodying a dialogue within the "man" ("'We Have Sinned and Rebelled; You Have Not Forgiven': The Dialogic Interaction between Authoritative and Internally Persuasive Discourse in Lamentations 3," *BIbInt* 22 [2014]: 146–67; *"Perhaps There Is Hope"*, 105–41).

2. On the development of an understanding of Jeremiah and Lamentations that follows from this, see J. Kugel, "'I Am the Man': The Afterlife of a Biblical Verse in Second Temple Times," in *Jeremiah's Scriptures: Production, Reception, Interaction, and Transformation*, ed. H. Najman and K. Schmid, Supplements to the Journal for the Study of Judaism 173 (Leiden: Brill, 2016), 470–96.

3. Dearman, *Jeremiah and Lamentations*, on the chapter.

4. See A. J. Rosenberg, *The Books of Lamentations, Ecclesiastes*, vol. 2 of *The Five Megilloth* (New York: Judaica, 1992), 25–48; D. O. Wenthe, ed., *Jeremiah, Lamentations*, ACCS (Downers Grove, IL: InterVarsity, 2009), 284–93; Tyler, *Jeremiah, Lamentations*, 477–94.

5. John of the Cross, *The Dark Night of the Soul* 2.7.2; 2.8.1.

3 "Perhaps There Is Hope"

In the context of the Lamentations scroll, Lam 3 reads as another report, reflection, confession, exhortation, and prayer relating to the invasion of Judah and the fall of Jerusalem. In the poem as a whole, the pronouns appear in a complicated sequence. An "I" speaks in vv. 1–24. In vv. 25–39 someone speaks about "he." In vv. 40–47 "we" speak. An "I" then speaks again in vv. 48–66. This movement makes for a comparison with the transitions in voices in Lam 1–2. Here there are once again a voice that speaks as an embodiment of affliction and a voice that comments on that affliction. Here there is also room for more than one understanding of the transitions between the voices, but I suggest that the "man" speaks in vv. 1–24 and 40–66 and that the second voice speaks in vv. 25–39:

vv. 1–18 A man's detailed first-person report of how "he" attacked "me" and how "I" consequently lost hope in "you." Behind the figure of the man one may see the experiences of several people (Jeremiah, Jehoiachin, Zedekiah), but the man himself is an imaginary figure, a construct born of the poet's imagination. Like the "I" in some psalms, he describes his experience by means of a series of images, some of which might be literal but all of which might be metaphors for attacks of one kind or another. None of them indicates a sense that he is under attack because of his wrongdoing. Initially and out of the context one might imagine that he is a figure who typifies the experience of other individuals, but the way the poem develops and the context of Lamentations as a whole suggest that he stands for the Judahite community, as the woman in Lam 1–2 stands for Jerusalem.[6]

vv. 19–24 The man urges Yahweh to be mindful of "me" and tells of how "I" nevertheless live in hope: Yahweh's commitment means that "we" still exist. The man thus makes a transition from statements about the past to statements about the present. He reports engaging in the kind of argument with himself that sometimes appears in the Psalms (notably, Pss 42–43; one might also compare the alternation in Ps 22). He reminds himself about Yahweh's commitment, compassion, and truthfulness—all are words that appear in the Psalms more than anywhere else. Given the tension between the facts in vv. 1–18 and the facts in vv. 19–24, the man determines to live with both sets of facts, in a way that parallels those psalms.

6. See further C. M. Maier's discussion in "The Afflicted Man in Lamentations 3," in Melton and H. A. Thomas, *Reading Lamentations Intertextually*.

vv. 25–39 A third party "breaks into the first singer's lament in midstream"[7] to speak about Yahweh's characteristic dealings with the kind of person the man has shown that "he" is.
The third party's generalizations are neater in form, which corresponds to their content. Each stanza manifests some formal unity, which contrasts with the jerkiness of the man's account of what the enemy has been doing with him. The generalizations correspond to promises in Prov 3:5–12 and to many passages in the Psalms that speak of the commitment, compassion, and truthfulness of Yahweh that the man affirmed.[8] Structurally this central section of the middle of the five chapters might be seen as the center of the scroll as a whole,[9] though the last two poems are shorter than the first three, so it is not the spatial or physical center. The section closes with an unexpected reference to a "man's" wrongdoing, which opens the way to a transition to a different point in what follows.

vv. 40–51 The man responds by recognizing that "we" must turn to Yahweh and acknowledge to Yahweh "our" rebellion, which Yahweh has not pardoned, and he reminds Yahweh about his attacks and about the enemies' attacks on "us." He is thus redescribing the experience he related in vv. 1–18. In vv. 48–51, he resumes speaking in the first-person singular, as he expresses his grief at his people's affliction.

vv. 52–66 In the manner of some protest psalms, in vv. 52–58 the man goes on to recall how he had previously experienced attack, how he had called on Yahweh, and how Yahweh had listened and acted for "me." In light of what Yahweh has now seen by way of the man's further experience of unjustified attack, in vv. 59–66 he pleads for Yahweh to do so again and to give his attackers their deserts.

As was the case with Lam 2 in relation to Lam 1, it is illuminating to compare and contrast Lam 3 with Lam 1 and 2.

- Once again, the poem comprises a set of grouped lines, or stanzas, whose initial words begin with different letters in an order that follows the alphabet.

7. Lee, *Singers of Lamentations*, 174; though I would not say this new singer is "admonishing" the first.

8. T. Sensing thus closes his possible sermon outline on a lament with v. 25 ("How Lonely Stands the Preacher," *Restoration Quarterly* 57 [2014]: 235–46).

9. See, e.g., B. Johnson, "Form and Message in Lamentations," *ZAW* 97 (1985): 58–73.

- The contents of a stanza commonly belong together, sometimes in carefully wrought ways (e.g., vv. 25–27, 28–30, 34–36), and changes of theme and ways of speaking coincide with breaks between stanzas (vv. 22–24 and 25–27; 37–39 and 40–42; 49–51 and 52–54). But sometimes a transition happens within a stanza (vv. 58–60) or motifs carry on from one stanza to the next (vv. 12–13, 48–49, 54–55, 60–61), thus holding the poem together over against the possibly fissiparous effect of the alphabetic structure. Some other apparent exceptions to the rule that the contents of stanzas belong together and transitions happen between stanzas also turn out to prove the rule and hold the poem together by compromising the breaks between stanzas (see vv. 19–21, 46–48, 52–54). "'Enjambment' of ideas and images across the alphabetical boundaries is a counterweight to the formal structuring of the acrostic. It keeps the poem moving forward and prevents the poem from breaking up into three-line sets."[10]
- The lines average five stresses, with a tendency for the first colon to be longer than the second but with many lines where the two cola are of similar length, some lines where the second is longer, and one example of a single-stress colon (v. 2). The poem's prosody (e.g., word order, asyndeton, syntax) compares with that of Lam 1 and 2. In some verses, the two cola in a line are parallel; in many others the second colon simply completes the line, and in those cases, there is often parallelism between lines (e.g., vv. 1–3).
- The people's experience and possible understandings and reactions are expressed by portraying the community as an individual.
- A second voice in addition to the main speaker expresses his or her grief at the experience of the main speaker, but the poem incorporates no announcements of the transitions between the two voices. The chapter works more like Jer 14 than Isa 49:13–21.[11] The audience has to work out when the transitions come.
- The chapter speaks concretely and forcefully about the experience of attack and about being the object of anger.[12]
- It works by presenting the audience with a disconcerting and bewildering sequence of images to convey what has happened to the individual.
- The two voices are not exactly in dialogue in that they do not ad-

10. Berlin, *Lamentations*, 85.

11. On the relationship between Lam 3 and Jer 14–15, see Boda, "The Priceless Gain of Penitence," 92–93.

12. See R. Brandscheidt, *Gotteszorn und Menschenleid: Die Gerichtsklage des leidenden Gerechten in Klgl 3*, TThSt (Trier: Paulinus, 1983).

dress one another, though they are in reaction to one another. If there are addressees for the words of the two voices, they are the poet who speaks to him or herself, the community to which the poet belongs and with which the poet worships, and finally and most explicitly Yahweh himself.

- The two voices are not in disagreement; they have the same understanding of the horrific nature of the man's affliction. The man declares his trust in vv. 21–24, and in vv. 25–39 the second voice takes up his point and builds on it. It does not rebuke him or correct him for his outspoken statements. The main difference between them lies in their representing someone who speaks from inside the experience of affliction and someone who can be more reflective about it.
- It incorporates some acknowledgment of wrongdoing, rebellion, and defiance—less than Lam 1, more than Lam 2. In Lam 2, though, only the second voice articulates this acknowledgment. Lam 3 thus shares with the earlier chapters the assumption about a link between wrongdoing and affliction. The assumption is often characterized as Deuteronomistic, though it might in this context rather be seen as corresponding to the assumptions of Proverbs.
- Its references to wrongdoing are notably unspecific compared with 2 Kings and the Prophets,[13] though not compared with the Psalms.[14]
- Like Lam 2, it thus urges the community to turn to Yahweh.
- It does not begin by addressing Yahweh, but it closes with a prayer, specifically a prayer for redress like Lam 1.
- It has a sequence of distinctive verbal links with Lam 1–2: "directed his arrow" (3:12; 2:4), "humbling" and "being put down" (3:19; 1:7), "sitting" and "being still" (3:28; 2:10), "be sorrowful" (3:32, 33; 1:4, 5, 12), "you [Yahweh] killed" (3:43; 2:21), "opened their mouth against" (3:46; 2:16), "on account of the breaking of my dear people" (3:48; 2:11), "my eye runs down with water" (3:48; 1:16), "respite" (3:49; 2:18), "eyes being still" (3:49; 2:18), "deal out to" (3:51; 1:12, 22b, 22c; 2:20).[15]

Lam 3 contrasts with Lam 1–2 in that:

13. See Boase, *The Fulfilment of Doom?*, 173.

14. K. L. Nguyen, "Mission Not Impossible," in Boda, Dempsey, and Flesher, *Daughter Zion*, 271–74.

15. See further Thomas, "Poetry and Theology," 248–50.

- It opens with *I* rather than *how*. Thus it begins with the words of the individual who embodies the people's experience and reports the reactions and words of a third party only later, rather than vice versa. It is an assertive introduction to an assertive poem.
- In the three-line stanzas, each of the three lines begins with that stanza's letter, whereas in Lam 1–2 only the first line begins with its letter. "I am unable, nor do I care, to impart any particular reason for this fact."[16] But the "intensification" of the alphabetic form[17] is a feature that makes Lam 3 "the acrostic of acrostics,"[18] along with Ps 119.[19] In keeping with this difference, the versification in modern Bibles gives each line a verse number instead of letting the verse number apply to the whole stanza, which can convey the misleading impression that Lam 3 is longer than Lam 1 or Lam 2.
- Changes in the subject of the poetry several times begin or hint at a change within the stanzas rather than between them.
- Nearly half the lines have the 3-2 rhythm; three-quarters have a two-beat second colon.
- The individual in this poem is a man rather than a woman, and a macho or warrior man rather than a princess, wife, mother, or girl.[20] Whereas Lam 1–2 thus portray the community's affliction in terms of what can happen in war to a woman, such as widowing, sexual exposure, sexual assault, and loss of children, Lam 3 portrays this affliction in terms of what can happen to a man in war, such as being injured, struck down, shot, pursued, captured, chained up, terrified, defeated, and taunted.[21] One might see the man as standing for Judah (which can elsewhere be referred to as "he") as the woman stands for Jerusalem.
- But that point is not explicit. Lam 3 incorporates even fewer concrete references to people and situations than Lam 1 and 2 do. It makes no concrete allusion to attacks on city or temple or country, nor to priests or kings. These differences would make it easier for

16. Vermigli, *Lamentations*, 107–8.

17. Joyce, "Lamentations," 531.

18. J. T. Dennison, "The Lament and the Lamenter," *Kerux* 12/3 (1997): 30.

19. See D. J. Reimer, "Reading Psalm 119 and Lamentations 3 Intertextually," in Melton and H. A. Thomas, *Reading Lamentations Intertextually*.

20. W. F. Lanahan ("Speaking Voice in the Book of Lamentations," 45) nicely calls him "a veteran," perhaps a veteran of the siege of Jerusalem.

21. Cf. Berlin, *Lamentations*, 84–85. A. Kalmanofsky compares and contrasts the mother/woman's prayer and the man/captured warrior's prayer ("'Their Heart Cried Out to God': Gender and Prayer in the Book of Lamentations," in *A Question of Sex?* ed. D. W. Rooke, HBM 14 [Sheffield: Sheffield Phoenix, 2007], 53–65).

later communities to relate to the poem. They also open up the possibility of dating the poem later than the sixth century.

- The man in the poem is realized as a person more than is the woman in Lam 1–2. He is more than a personification. He resembles Job. This difference would make it easier for individuals to relate to the poem.
- The man does not make Yahweh the subject of verbs describing the current attacks (the attacker is simply "he"), and he makes no reference to Yahweh's anger.
- Lam 3 incorporates more psalm-like expressions than Lam 1–2.
- The poem incorporates substantial avowals of hope and statements about Yahweh's commitment and compassion,[22] though these do not close the poem or provide it with closure, as it subsequently returns to anti-testimony.[23]

This last difference is the most prominent aspect of the way Lam 1, 2, and 3 imply a conversation between different angles on the affliction of which they speak. While it is a conversation within each chapter, it is more markedly a conversation between the chapters. It continues in Lam 4–5 so that the poems as a collection do not seek to bring it to closure. In this poem, the community's affliction has been horrific and appalling even if deserved; it is attributable to earthly adversaries but also to Yahweh; Yahweh is both the God of commitment and compassion and the God of anger; the community is dared to trust in Yahweh even while protesting against its affliction by him; it may both protest to Yahweh and submit itself to Yahweh.

This difference relates to and coheres with another: the poem is systematically ambiguous about the meaning of each section.

vv. 1–18 As well as not being specific about the man's identity, it is not specific about the identity of the man's attacker. It leaves the audience to work out whether "he" is Yahweh or an earthly adversary. Both are true, as the audience might realize by the end of the poem.

vv. 19–24 The man comes to affirm that he has a basis for hope despite the experience he has described in his anti-testimony, but the poem is allusive about the process whereby he comes to that

22. C. Frevel thus sees Lam 3 as seeking to move people beyond Lam 2 ("Zerstörung bewegt," in *Im Lesen Verstehen*, 233–54; further, "Gott in der Krise," in *Im Lesen Verstehen*, 155–76).

23. See F. Villanueva, *The "Uncertainty" of a Hearing: A Study of the Sudden Change of Mood in the Psalms of Lament*, VTSup 121 (Leiden: Brill, 2008), 213–47.

realization. That allusiveness may correspond to the gradual way he comes to the realization. Perhaps it corresponds to the allusive way the poet himself or herself came to such a realization, which is characteristically mysterious.

vv. 25–39 The second voice is ambiguous about the yoke that the man needs to bear and the wrongdoing it describes. Is the yoke the consequences of the man's waywardness, and does submission mean turning? Is the wrongdoing in vv. 34–36 done to the man or by him?

vv. 40–51 A different form of ambiguity features as the man goes on both to acknowledge the people's waywardness and nevertheless to comment on Yahweh's not pardoning "us" and on the toughness of the way Yahweh has treated "us."

vv. 52–66 Is the man now redescribing the affliction of vv. 1–18 and pleading with Yahweh to take action against his attackers, or is he recalling past affliction and rescue and pleading for Yahweh to take the same action again? There is an element of both in the section as a whole.

The effect of the poem's various ambiguities is to drive the audience (the poet's fellow theologians, the congregation with which the poet shares it, the poet him or herself) into a different kind of interaction with the poem, to engage with the questions its allusiveness raises, and thus to see how different ways of resolving the ambiguities illumine its own situation, attitudes, and relationship with Yahweh. Is Yahweh its attacker? What is the nature of the process whereby it is developing in its relationship with its affliction—and with Yahweh in light of its affliction? How does it see the wrong done to it and the wrong it has done? How does it see what Yahweh has done for it in the past and how it might pray in the present?

> Statements about divine love and mercy are not fully borne out in the imagery of the poem, which largely portrays divine violence. There is no resolution of this incongruity. It is unclear whether the poet is setting this conclusion as a challenge to readers . . . or whether he does not himself know how to resolve the questions which he raises.[24]

The audience could not answer the questions the poem raises because it could not quiz the poet—or if it could, we cannot. We can only see the incongruity as a challenge to our thinking and response.

24. M. L. Mitchell, "Reading of the Imagery of Lamentations," 168.

aleph [1]*I am the man who saw humbling*
by his furious club.
[2]*Me he drove and made go*
into darkness and not light.
[3]*Indeed*[a] *against me*
repeatedly[b] *he would turn*[c] *his hand, all the time.*

a. Vg renders *ʾak* "only," but this meaning seems irrelevant.

b. For the use of *šûb* followed asyndetically by another verb, see GK 120g.

c. In light of the *qatal* verbs on either side, I interpret the *yiqtols* in this line as past imperfect (cf. LXX).

1 *I am* is a remarkable beginning, hard to parallel in the First Testament, though strikingly comparable with the self-introduction of a quasi-king in Eccl 1:12. Like the previous poems, Lam 3 gives no further clue to the speaker's identity, though the lack may seem more of a problem in Lam 3 because this opening voice is speaking not about someone else (e.g., Ms. Zion) but about himself. By the time we get to the end of the poem, it will have become apparent that he stands for the community, for Judah as a people,[25] as the woman in Lam 1–2 stands for Jerusalem as a city; and if we are reading Lam 3 in light of Lam 1 and 2, we might immediately infer as much. But initially and in isolation from that context, we are listening to the deposition of an individual unnamed man.[26] It does parallel a protest prayer such as Ps 22, which begins "My God, my God, why have you abandoned me?" And the original audience for this poem would be familiar with such psalms in which an "I" speaks of being under attack and either seeks Yahweh's deliverance or testifies to that deliverance. These parallels also draw attention to the fact that such prayers address Yahweh, whereas this deposition does not do so; it addresses no one in particular. The poem's audience would also be familiar with the fact that the person who speaks in such a psalm may be a king or someone who stands for the people as a whole, and it could have this possibility in the back of its mind. Such a possibility would be encouraged by the speaker's describing himself as a *man* (*geber*). It is not a potentially gender-inclusive term like "person/individual" or "human being" (*ʾîš*, *ʾādām*) but a masculine and slightly macho word. "Belt up your thighs like a *geber*,"

25. Or for Zion; so U. Berges, "'Ich bin der Mann, der Elend sah' (Klgl 3,1): Zionstheologie als Weg aus der Krise," *BZ* 44 (2000): 10–12.

26. Thomas ("Poetry and Theology," 211) lists fourteen identifications that have been proposed for him; K. L. Nguyen (*Chorus in the Dark*, 125–53) gives a whole chapter to the question.

Yahweh says to Job in Job 38:3; 40:7.[27] "What *geber* is like Job," Elihu asks (Job 34:7); in Lam 3 the answer might implicitly be, "This one."[28]

So the speaker is an important and impressive strong man, not someone ordinary. His self-description might encourage the idea that he speaks as a warrior-like representative of the people. Whereas "few strong male figures have appeared to this point in Lamentations,"[29] here is one. Yet as soon as he has described himself in this way, his declaration about himself deconstructs his self-description. His collocation of *geber* and *saw humbling* makes for a strong and provocative beginning to his anti-testimony, in that humbling (*ʿŏnî*) denotes weakness and powerlessness. The word came in 1:3, 7, 9, which gives a concrete indication that this man is in just as much trouble and is having just as afflicted a time as the woman in Lam 1. If violence against women is one key motif in Lamentations, so is violence against men.[30] And he can say that he has *seen* humbling. He knows what he is talking about. Further, if he is a king or warrior, it is further striking that he is the victim of someone who is evidently a stronger king or warrior, one wielding *his . . . club* (*šēbeṭ*). Such a means of humbling suggests a formidable weapon held by someone in a position of authority, like a mace or scepter. Its *furious* force as usual more likely reflects the ferocity of the way it is exercised than a feeling of anger on the part of the one who wields it. The suffix *his* might then refer to someone like Nebuchadnezzar, the enemy with whom the previous chapter implicitly closed, or to the angry Yahweh to whom 2:22 also referred.[31] If the speaker belonged to certain kinds of Jews or pagans or Christians, he might wonder if he is under demonic attack. But he leaves open the question of his attacker's identity, in the same way as he does not reveal his own identity. As with that question, the chapter will in due course clarify the point: yes, his attacker is Yahweh. "Though the savage antagonist is nameless, his identity is no mystery."[32] Perhaps there is some reverence about not making Yahweh the explicit subject of the verbs the man uses—it is more feasible to use these verbs if one does not give them a subject.

2 As will be the case through Lam 3, these next two lines also begin with the stanza's signature letter. *He drove me* might suggest a shepherd and his sheep, which makes one reconsider the imagery of v. 1. The weapon in v. 1 is then a shepherd's club, which in Ps 23:4 is a sheep's protection, but the club is now turned on the sheep. "These verses are a reversal of the image

27. Cf. LamR on the passage.

28. See W. Kynes, "Debated Suffering: The Voices of Lamentations Personified in Job's Dialogue," in Melton and H. A. Thomas, *Reading Lamentations Intertextually*.

29. M. L. Mitchell, "Reading of the Imagery of Lamentations," 119.

30. Parry, *Lamentations*, 52.

31. Ibn Ezra assumes the first, Rashi the second, each in MG.

32. Mintz, *Ḥurban*, 34; cf. Mintz, "Rhetoric of Lamentations," 11.

of God as the caring, protective, and providing shepherd found in Ps 23."[33] Thus "being led, i.e. *walking with guidance*, is here a metaphor, not for divine protection, but for disastrous deception."[34] Instead of behaving protectively, the unnamed shepherd drove the sheep *into darkness and not light*: the double noun-expression is the one applied to Yahweh's day in Amos 5:18, 20. It could describe someone being put in prison.[35]

3 That he *would turn his hand* then means he would turn around (1 Kgs 22:34; 2 Kgs 9:23). After the reference to driving in v. 2, the poem may be referring to the hand that steers a chariot. But anyway, the familiarity of the idea of Yahweh's hand acting for his people (e.g., Exod 3:19–20; Ps 10:12, 14) implies that the attacker is someone who might have been expected to be on one's side but who acted in the opposite way. The effect of the imagery in the poem is already "claustrophobic."[36]

bet [4]*He wasted away my flesh and my skin,*
he broke up my bones.
[5]*He built around me and closed in*[a]
with poison[b] *and exhaustion.*[c]
[6]*In dark regions he made me sit,*
like the people dead for all time.[d]

a. *Around me* in the sense of "against me" (*ʿālay*) also applies to this second verb; taking the nouns that follow adverbially makes better sense than taking them as direct objects.

b. LXX, Tg understand this word as the more familiar *rōʾš*, meaning "head." Gordis (*Song of Songs and Lamentations*, 176) understands it as an alternative spelling for *rēʾš*, meaning "poverty."

c. For MT *ûtəlāʾâ*, LXX "and it [my head; see note b] was exhausted" implies a form of the verb *lāʾâ*.

d. Cf. Vg; LXX "long dead" seems to under-interpret *ʿôlām*.

4 The testimony continues to interweave expressions that could refer in a down-to-earth way to military attack and expressions that suggest rather the significance of the action. Thus the first line could describe one warrior doing terrible injury to another. But *flesh*, *skin*, and *bones* suggest the devastation

33. F. B. Huey, *Jeremiah, Lamentations: An Exegetical and Theological Exposition of Holy Scripture*, NAC (Nashville: Broadman, 1993), on the passage.

34. G. Eidenvall, "Spatial Metaphors in Lamentations 3, 1–9," in *Metaphor in the Hebrew Bible*, ed. P. van Hecke, BETL 187 (Louvain: Peeters, 2005), 134.

35. Brunet, *Lamentations*, 50.

36. K. M. O'Connor, *Lamentations and the Tears of the World*, 47.

of the whole person; and the recurrence of "breaking" on either side of this chapter (2:11, 13; 3:47, 48; 4:10) invites readers to see a reference to the devastating of country and community. This possibility links with the portrayal in Ezek 37 of the community as a collection of bones that need to be covered in flesh and skin and then given breath.

5 The middle line begins as if it were describing the action of an invader besieging a city (as Tg makes explicit) then in the second colon becomes more metaphorical. But the word *exhaustion* (*təlā'â*) is commonly used in connection with Israel's tribulations,[37] and it resonates with the verb describing a life that hangs suspended (*tālā'*) in Deut 28:66. That threat sits close to a reference to poison in the people's midst (Deut 29:18[17]). So an audience familiar with the threats in Deuteronomy might see a link with what happened to the community in 587.

6 The third line focuses on the metaphorical. The man describes himself not as dead but as deposited in a place of Sheol-like darkness, which takes us back to v. 2; darkness is a "unifying metaphor" through vv. 1–6.[38] "GOD oftentimes leadeth his holy ones into hell, and as it were, into a bottomlesse depth of temptation and griefes."[39] The line corresponds to Ps 143:3 except that the two words in the first colon are reversed (the *bə-* word needs to come first); there the adversary is human.

gimel [7]*He walled me about and I couldn't get out,*
he made me a heavy bronze chain.[a]
[8]*Even when I would cry out and call for help,*
he shut up my plea.[b]
[9]*He walled my paths with hewn stone*
as he diverted my tracks.[c]

a. Lit. "he made heavy my bronze."
b. An elliptical expression for "shut up [his ears to] my plea."
c. The word order with the object before the verb combined with the asyndeton suggests that this clause is subordinate to the previous one.

7 It becomes more evident that the man speaks metaphorically: the first and third lines describe his humbling in a series of images that could not all be literally true, as happens in the Psalms. The poem thus achieves its impact by the kaleidoscope of images, though here *paths* (v. 9) is the governing meta-

37. Albrektson, *Studies in the Text and Theology of the Book of Lamentations*, 130.
38. House, *Lamentations*, 409.
39. Toussaine, *Lamentations*, 109; cf. Tyler, *Jeremiah, Lamentations*, 478.

phor (cf. vv. 10–12).[40] The man had been *walled about* so he couldn't go anywhere. He was constrained by *a heavy chain* (like Zedekiah in Jer 39:7).[41]

8 The middle line more or less makes inevitable the implication that his attacker is Yahweh, because he is the one to whom one would *cry out* and *call for help*.

9 But the man had been walled about with blocks of cut stone that formed obstacles to his going as he wished and made him go by *tracks* he did not want. They are not just any old rocks; they are blocks of *hewn stone* that have been deliberately shaped so as to fit together securely, like the stones of the wall around the temple and its enclosure. Indeed, perhaps, they are (metaphorically) those very stones, horribly recycled.[42]

dalet [10]*He was a bear lying in wait, to me,*
a lion in hiding.
[11]*My paths he sidetracked*[a] *and he mangled me,*[b]
he made me desolate.
[12]*He directed his bow*[c] *and stood me up*
as the target for his arrow.

a. With Vg, Aq I take *sôrēr* as *polel* from *sûr* (BDB); Rashi (in MG) takes it as a denominative from *sîr* ("he made thorny").

b. For MT *wayəpaššəḥēnî* (a *hapax legomenon*), Aq "he made me lame" implies *wayəpaśśəḥēnî* (the *ś* would then be a variant for *s*, so that the hypothesized verb is *pāsaḥ* II), which follows well from Rashi's understanding of the previous verb (see note a; Salters, *Jeremiah*, 205–8).

c. See the translation note on 2:4.

10 Two familiar but frightening metaphors make the point in a different way; *bear* and *lion* come together elsewhere as dangerous animals that one has to be wary of (e.g., Hos 13:8; Amos 5:19). They also hint at another link

40. House, *Lamentations*, 410.

41. N. W. Porteous sees Jehoiachin behind the chapter ("Jerusalem—Zion: The Growth of a Symbol," in *Verbannung und Heimkehr: Beiträge zur Geschichte und Theologie Israels im 6. und 5. Jahrhundert v. Chr. Wilhelm Rudolph zum 70. Geburtstage dargebracht von Kollegen, Freunden und Schüllern*, ed. A. Kuschke [Tübingen: Mohr, 1961], 244–45); M. Saebø sees Zedekiah ("Who is 'The Man' in Lamentations 3?," in *Understanding Poets and Prophets: Essays in Honour of George Wishart Anderson*, ed. A. G. Auld, JSOTSup 152 [Sheffield: Sheffield Academic, 1993], 294–306). LamR on the passage identifies the chain as produce tax, state tax, and poll tax.

42. G. Baumann, "'Er hat mir den Weg mit quadersteinen vermauert' (Thr 3,9)," in van Hecke, *Metaphor in the Hebrew Bible*, 139–45.

with the shepherd image: they are the kind of animals from which Yahweh with his club is supposed to be his flock's protector, but instead . . .

11 The middle line then restates v. 9 and picks up the possible implications of v. 10. Its reference to being made *desolate* might seem an anticlimax, but it could suggest an allusion to the 587 calamity (cf. 1:4, 13, 16).

12 The last line moves to a different image, used in 2:4. It also takes up from there the verb for standing up but uses it in a different way (*hiphil* rather than *niphal*) and adds a grisly simile. It is one of the verbal links between the man's anti-testimony and Job's anti-testimony in Job 16:7–17.[43]

he [13]*He made come into my guts*
the children of his quiver.
[14]*I became an object of fun to all my people,*[a]
the subject of their song all the time.
[15]*He gave me my full of bitterness,*
soaked me with wormwood.

a. For *'ammî*, one would expect *'ammîm*, the word that appears (with other expressions for opprobrium) in Deut 28:37, and a sebir (a marginal note in MT) provides this reading (cf. Syr). But there is little other indication that *'ammî* is not the original text. Perhaps it reflects an individualizing reinterpretation of the poem (*CTAT* 2:895).

13 The opening metaphor is the first example of a recurrent feature in this poem: one stanza may link with another—here through the image of bow and arrow from v. 12. The story of bow and arrow thus continues, with a chilling metaphor within the metaphor in v. 13b. One of Horace's poems speaks of a quiver pregnant with arrows (*Odes* 1.22).[44]

14 The middle line is a recurrent motif in laments and protests (e.g., Job 12:4), and Jeremiah says of himself, "I became an object of fun all the time" (20:7). The reference to *my people* is odd. It is a concrete pointer toward the poem being the testimony of an individual, such as Jeremiah, or another leader. But it compares with the later references to *my dear people* and to *all the daughters in my city* (vv. 48, 51). Perhaps the poem is semi-quoting an expression like the one about Jeremiah being an object of fun: this aspect of the suffering of the people embodied in the figure of the man is like that feature in the suffering of an individual such as the prophet.

15 We might see the third line as a restatement of the first, as happened in vv. 7–9, but it is also a line infused with irony. Yahweh *gave me my fill* or "filled me up" (*śāba'*) and *soaked me* (*rāwâ*): the verbs usually refer to being

43. See Balentine, "Prose and Poetry of Exile," 353.
44. Trapp, *Commentary*, on the verse.

filled up in a satisfying way with food and having one's thirst quenched with drink. So the man has been abundantly provided with . . . things that tasted bitter, drink that was pungent. *Wormwood* is a plant with a strong smell, a bitter taste, and a reputation for toxicity. It is another Jeremiah word (Jer 9:15[14]; 23:15).

waw [16]*He ground my teeth on gravel,*
bent me down into[a] *ashes.*
[17]*You rejected*[b] *my spirit from things being well*[c]—
I put out of mind[d] *good things.*
[18]*I said, my future*[e] *has perished;*
my expectation: from Yahweh.

a. LXX, Vg "fed me on" for the *hapax legomenon kāpaš* (a byform of *kābaš*?) is likely a paraphrase in light of the parallelism or in light of Ps 102:9(10) (Schäfer, "Lamentations," 125*).

b. To understand *wattiznaḥ* as second person, addressed to Yahweh, fits other occurrences of the verb with Yahweh as subject (2:7; 3:31; cf. Ps 88:14[15]). Vg "my spirit was repulsed" takes the verb as third-person feminine and implies *niphal wattizānaḥ*.

c. The preposition *min* attached to *šālôm* comes only here; one might see it as an example of the "pregn[ant]" use of *min* (BDB, 578a). To put it another way, the construction implies an ellipsis: "You rejected my spirit [and turned me away] from things being well."

d. Like the more common *šākaḥ, nāšâ* can denote a deliberate, not an accidental, forgetting.

e. LXX "my victory," Tg "my strength" presuppose meanings of *neṣaḥ* in Aramaic and later Hebrew (*DTT*, 928).

16 The stanza again follows from the one that precedes as it suggests eating. The line implies the image of the attacker throwing his victim down to the ground, so that (metaphorically speaking) he eats gravel as he lies prostrate in the ashes.

17 The second-person address is a surprise, though it compares with 1:10. Here it is the beginning of a process of transition in the man's testimony.[45] He does not name Yahweh as addressee (again, as in 1:10) but he will name him in the third person in v. 18, and he will address him again in vv. 19 and 23. Further, the phrase *you rejected my spirit* corresponds to Ps 88:14(15), and most other occurrences of the verb reject (*zānaḥ*) in the *qal* come elsewhere in psalms addressed to Yahweh as a protest (see, e.g., Pss 43:2; 44:9[10], 23[24]). Maybe this phrase is another instance of the poet taking up a familiar expression that is slightly odd in the context, like "my people" in v. 14. As in the psalms just noted, the idea of rejection is that people approach Yahweh with their pleas and he refuses to take any notice, like a subject approaching

45. Berges, *Klagelieder*, 193.

a king and being turned away.[46] As in Ps 88:14(15), then, the man speaks of Yahweh's rejection of him as a person, rejecting his *spirit* (*nepeš*), rejecting the idea of things ever again *being well* (*šālôm*) for him. The parallelism then suggests that the logical consequence of that rejection was to make him in turn *put out of mind* the idea that there would ever be *good things* in his life and also put out of mind the good things of the past: so *put out of mind* corresponds to *you rejected my spirit* and *good things* re-expresses *things being well.* A psalm will sometimes work by recalling Yahweh's great acts in the past (again, see Ps 44, with its two references to Yahweh's rejection). But the man has made no reference to the great things Yahweh has done in his life or in Israel's history. "What 'he' has been doing to 'me' seems to have been going on forever and feels like it will never end."[47]

18 *I said, my future has perished* restates the previous colon. The parallel colon is then ambiguous in several directions, but it adds to the hints of a transition in the testimony. For the first time, the man names *Yahweh,* who would be the key to things being well and to experiencing good things. But is Yahweh set on not making such things possible? The man saying to himself, *My future has perished,* is reformulated in the comment about *my expectation,* but the addition of *from Yahweh* could make the point even more somber. Does he simply mean he no longer has any expectation of receiving anything from Yahweh (cf. Ps 62:5[6]), so that he is restating the point about Yahweh rejecting his plea? Or has his expectation perished through Yahweh (Ps 80:16[17])? Either way, this first mention of Yahweh carries no positive connotation, and "this is perhaps the lowest point of the whole poem."[48] On the other hand, might he mean "but my expectation is from Yahweh," as vv. 21–24 will declare?[49]

zayin [19]*Be mindful*[a] *of my humbling and my being put down,*[b]
the wormwood and poison.
[20]*Mindful, mindful*[c]
was my spirit,[d] *and it would bow down*[e] *within me.*[f]
[21]*This I will bring back to my mind,*
as a result I will have expectation.

a. I follow Vg, Aq, Tg in parsing *zəkor* as imperative rather than infinitive, as it often is in the Psalms (Albrektson, *Studies in the Text and Theology of the Book of Lamentations,* 139–40).

b. See the translation note on 1:7.

46. H. Ringgren, "זָנַח, *zānach,*" *TDOT,* 4:105–6.

47. Owens, "Personification and Suffering in Lamentations 3," 79.

48. Provan, *Lamentations,* 90.

49. Koenen, *Klagelieder,* 239–40.

c. The infinitive absolute precedes the finite verb, emphasizing the actuality of the action.

d. A "scribal correction" has "your spirit," which might mark it as an earlier reading, but its status is subject to question (Salters, *Lamentations*, 222–23).

e. I follow the *qere wətāšôaḥ* and take it as from *šaḥaḥ* ("bow down"). The verb form might come from *šûaḥ* ("sink down"—physically or emotionally); the *ketiv* has *hiphil wətāšîaḥ* from *šûaḥ*. But links with Pss 42–43 in the context suggest *šaḥaḥ* (see the commentary).

f. Lit. "upon me."

19 The first naming of Yahweh in v. 18b, with the ambiguity of its reference to expectation, leads into an appeal to Yahweh that dares him to belie any gloomy understanding of that preceding colon. Given the apparent impossibility of things being well, of good things, of a positive future that is worth expecting, the man urges Yahweh to be *mindful* of the realities of his present experience instead of ignoring them, to be mindful of the realities of which he has been speaking through vv. 1–18—of the man's *humbling* (v. 1) and *being put down* (1:7), which had the taste of *wormwood* (v. 15) and *poison* (v. 5); the last two come together in Deut 29:18[17]; Jer 9:15[14]; 23:15.

20 He himself can claim to have been *mindful*, as vv. 16–18 implied, but is the mindfulness to which he refers positive or negative? Was it accompanied by a positive bowing down or a negative sinking down? If the man's *spirit* would *bow down* within him or upon him, it suggests someone bent over in depression or in submission, either of which might be a response to Yahweh's rejecting his spirit as regards things ever being good again (v. 17). The verb could point either way, so that the line continues to manifest the ambiguity that began with v. 18. It also takes further the links with Pss 42–44 with their references to being mindful (42:4[5]) and to a spirit bowed down within or upon the self (Pss 42:5–6[6–7], 11[12]; 43:5).

21 Likewise *this* could refer backward or forward. The man might mean that continuing to bring to mind the bowing down issued in having *expectation*: again the verb is one that comes also in Pss 42:5[6], 11[12]; 43:5. But could things have worked that way in his spirit? Does *this* rather refer to what will follow? There is thus some further "transitory ambiguity" about vv. 21–22.[50] Either way, "the man's sudden change of mood from despair to hope is due to his change of mind."[51] And either way, the man has become engaged in an argument with himself, which again parallels Pss 42–43 and compares with the alternating perspectives in Ps 44, and also Ps 73:23.[52] In-

50. B. Weber, "Transitorische Ambiguität in Threni iii," *VT* 50 (2000): 111–20. He finds further instances at vv. 33–34 and 54–55.

51. Rong, *Forgotten and Forsaken by God*, 93.

52. Kraus, *Klagelieder*, 62.

deed, it turns out that practically every word in this stanza links either with earlier verses within the poem or with Pss 42–44.

khet [22]*Yahweh's acts of commitment—that we have not come to an end,*[a]
that his compassion has not become spent.
[23]*They are new each morning—*
your truthfulness is great.
[24]*Yahweh is my share, my spirit said,*
as a result I have expectation in him.[b]

a. With MT *tāmənû*, cf. Jer 44:18 (!); Num 17:13[28] (see Rashi, in MG). Syr, Tg imply *tāmmû* ("they have not come to an end"), which looks like a "facilitating slip" (*CTAT* 2:903), though J. Greer argues for it on the basis of the chiastic structure of v. 22 ("A Chiastic Key to a Text-Critical Crux in Lamentations 3.22," *The Bible Translator Technical Papers* 60 [2009]: 184–86). In his sermon on this verse on the anniversary of the Gunpowder Treason in 1612, Lancelot Andrewes is able to rejoice in MT's text: indeed, "we were not consumed," by God's mercy (*Ninety-Six Sermons*, 4 vols. [Oxford: Parker, 1841], 4:262).

b. The oldest LXX MSS lack vv. 22–24, perhaps by homoioteleuton.

22 If *this* in v. 21 looks forward, then it refers to what v. 22 says. *Commitment* (*ḥesed*) is a noun denoting the allegiance or self-giving that one person may show to another when there is no established basis for doing so, or the faithfulness or constancy that one person may show to another when the other person has forfeited any right to it because they have been unfaithful. The conventional English translations are "steadfast love" and "constant love." The noun comes hundreds of times in the singular, and it makes for yet another link with Pss 42:8[9]; 44:26[27], but it occurs less than a score of times in the plural to denote *acts of commitment* that give concrete expression to the quality (e.g., Pss 17:7; 25:6; 89:1[2]; 107:43). Here, in the parallelism, the man recalls Yahweh's *compassion* (*raḥămîm*), the infinite mercies of God that are a "cape of good hope."[53] This word is also plural, and one might understand it to imply acts of compassion, but it is regularly plural to denote the quality it refers to. It is related to the term for a woman's womb, so that it can suggest the feelings a mother has for her child or that a child has for the other children who came from the same womb. The man's declaration, the *this* that makes it possible to avoid giving in to final despair, is that actions that emerge from commitment have meant *we have not come to an end* and that compassion on Yahweh's part *has not become spent.* The logic of the comment is that the fact that we have not come to an end (which is obviously true, otherwise he and the people who read or listen to this poem would

53. Trapp, *Commentary*, on the verse.

not be reading or listening) is evidence that Yahweh has not abandoned his commitment, that his compassion has not become spent. The man is not just making a bold statement of faith; he is making a logical inference from some facts (Tg's rendering, "Yahweh's commitments have not come to an end," likely has the same implication). The statement, along with the facts on which it is based, mitigates the doctrine of retribution[54] and at the same time "agrees with one of the most extraordinary teachings in the OT,"[55] expressed in Exod 34:6–7 at a moment of horrifying waywardness, horrifying chastisement, but manifest mercy. The man is haunted by the memory of this Yahweh,[56] whose mercy here presupposed in Lamentations has paralleled that mercy.[57] It is perhaps possible to make such affirmations too early, when one has not owned the despair-threatening nature of one's situation or has not allowed someone else to own it. While Yahweh *might* have been the subject of the statements in vv. 1–18, it is explicit that he is the subject here.[58] Positive namings of Yahweh are now possible; the man is now okay about making Yahweh the subject of affirmative statements. He moves from concrete experiential images for pain to key theological concepts for comfort. Lamentations as a whole has certainly not rushed to make these affirmations of God's faithfulness; it has waited until chapter 3.[59] And the development within Lam 3 parallels that within Job, where Yahweh's appearing to Job pulls him to submission by a different dynamic. In Lam 3, Yahweh does not appear; its testimony suggests that the faithful, if they are wise, will "with the one eye looke upon their owne miseries and with the other, upon the mercies of the Lord,"[60] as Pss 42–43 model.

The way these lines have inspired hymns reflects the way Lamentations melds theology and spirituality. Among many examples is John Keble's:

> New every morning is the love
> Our wakening and uprising prove;
> Through sleep and darkness safely brought,
> Restored to life and power and thought.

54. V. F. Fernández, "Tiempo de llorar para seguir esperando: Lamentaciones 3 en su contexto," *Revista Teología* 45 (2008): 120.

55. House, *Lamentations*, 414.

56. See J. Gericke, "Spectres of Yhwh: Some Hauntological Remarks on Lamentations 3," *Scriptura* 110 (2012): 166–75.

57. But A. Lo emphasizes the much greater stress on wrath in Lamentations in "Exodus 32–34 and Lamentations: A Comparison of Sin Punishment, and Confession," in Melton and H. A. Thomas, *Reading Lamentations Intertextually*.

58. M. L. Mitchell, "Reading of the Imagery of Lamentations," 139.

59. R. R. Roberts, "Lamentations 3," *Int* 6 (2013): 198.

60. Toussaine, *Lamentations*, 115; cf. Tyler, *Jeremiah, Lamentations*, 486.

New mercies, each returning day,
Hover around us while we pray;
New perils past, new sins forgiven,
New thoughts of God, new hopes of heaven.

Lamentations is not just theory, and it is not concerned with theodicy—certainly not as a theoretical exercise—but neither is it just piety. As the poem melds theology and spirituality, it makes key theological statements about God. But part of its point in doing so is to lean on Yahweh to be himself.[61]

23 The man restates the point by declaring that Yahweh's *truthfulness* (*'ĕmûnâ*) *is great*; truthfulness implies reliability and steadfastness. Yahweh's threats through Jeremiah had been that darkness would fall and it would be the end; creation would be undone (Jer 4:23–28; 13:15–17; see also, classically, Amos 5:18–20). But actually, the sun still rises each day. Yahweh's commitment and compassion are *new each morning*. Each new day is like a new day of creation, manifesting Yahweh's faithfulness.[62] Each morning there is a burst of new light.[63] The affirmation makes for a nice contrast with the reference to darkness in v. 2.[64] Perhaps more is implied by the word *new*. To put it in a superficially contradictory way, "God's new activity distinguishes itself radically from his old," like the new heavens, the new covenant, and the new mind (Isa 65:17; Jer 31:31; Ezek 18:31).[65] *New* (*ḥādāš*) thus implies "something unique and special . . . a new and hitherto unheard of deed of Yhwh, for example, which gives rise to a new song . . . something unexpected and unanticipated."[66] "His assured faithfulnesse, and constant veritie" are "the verie efficient cause of the renewing of the Church, and of the graces of the Lord."[67]

24 Whence come the man's convictions? Two considerations come together. One is that fact that the end did not come, that Yahweh's bite was not as bad as his bark. The other is that alongside this fact and against his "internally persuasive experience of pain" the man sets "the authoritative discourse of religious tradition . . . to assert Yhwh's ongoing fidelity and integrity, seeking an antidote to his extreme experience to the contrary."[68] It is, indeed, the

61. W. C. Bouzard, "Boxed by the Orthodox: The Function of Lamentations 3:22–39 in the Message of the Book," in *Why? . . . How Long? Studies on Voice(s) of Lamentation Rooted in Biblical Hebrew Poetry*, ed. L. S. Flesher, C. J. Dempsey, and M. J. Boda, LHBOTS 552 (London: T&T Clark, 2014), 68–82.

62. Cf. Alexander, *Targum of Lamentations*, 150.

63. Koenen, *Klagelieder*, 246.

64. Theodoret, *Thrēnoi*, PG 81:796.

65. Koenen, *Klagelieder*, 246.

66. Renkema, *Lamentations*, 388.

67. Toussaine, *Lamentations*, 119 (cf. Tyler, *Jeremiah, Lamentations*, 488).

68. Bier, "'We Have Sinned'," 161; cf. Bier, *"Perhaps There Is Hope"*, 125.

dynamic in Yahweh's speeches in Job. The man has reminded himself that commitment, compassion, and truthfulness are just part of Yahweh's being Yahweh and part of the fact that Yahweh is his *share* (*ḥēleq*). In a down-to-earth sense, a share is one of the expressions for the tract of land allocated to a clan (e.g., Josh 18:5–10), but Israel is also referred to as Yahweh's "share" (Deut 32:9) and Yahweh as Israel's (Pss 16:5; 73:26; 119:57). The man's point is that Yahweh belongs to him as surely as his family's tract of land belongs to his family. That fact underlies Yahweh's not having given up on his commitment, compassion, and truthfulness and is the basis for knowing that Yahweh will not do so. The man has reminded himself of these facts—or as he puts it, his self (his *nepeš*) has so reminded him. The picture of him and his spirit in conversation again recalls Pss 42:5[6], 11[12]; 43:5. There he is talking to his spirit (here alone does someone's spirit "say" something to them), but in both contexts, the expressions presuppose the odd but familiar idea of our arguing with ourselves. Here, the comment is a neat, gutsy, assertive footnote to his words in v. 17 about Yahweh rejecting his spirit and a gutsy follow-up to his ambiguous comment about his spirit being mindful and bowed down in v. 20. His spirit's assertiveness issues in his now having the expectation that had perished in v. 18, and the declaration *as a result I have expectation* forms a frame around vv. 21–24.

tet [25]*Yahweh is good to the person who has hopes of him,*[a]
to the individual who inquires of him,[b]
[26]*Good, yes, to the one expectant*[c] *and in stillness*[d]
regarding Yahweh's deliverance,
[27]*Good to a man*
when he takes up the yoke in his youth.

a. I follow the *ketiv*'s *lqww*; the *qere* has *ləqōwāyw*, "the people who have hopes of him."

b. Or is it "to the woman who inquires of him," since the verb is feminine? See M. I. Gruber and S. Yona, "A Male Speaker's Obsession with the Feminine: The Strange Case of Lamentations 3," in Embry, *Megilloth Studies*, 74–75. One would then render the preceding colon "good to the man who"; masculine and feminine would complement each other.

c. *Ṭôb wəyāḥîl* (lit. "good and expectant"). As the *ṭ*-word, *good* has to come first, which generates an odd word order; one could see the colon as involving a quasi-extraposition. LXX, Vg, Tg imply "it is good that one should be expectant."

d. *Dûmām* is apparently a noun used adverbially; BDB and *HALOT* give two different explanations. The relationship between *dûm*, *dāmâ*, and *dāmam* is also "controversial" (*HALOT*, 216), but the meaning of each would overlap in practice. The colon as a whole is elliptically expressed, but no single emendation commends itself (see Koenen, *Klagelieder*, 194–95; GK 107q).

25 The "I" now disappears until v. 49. While the poet might have the man speaking through vv. 25–39, the transition to speaking in the third person about *the person who has hopes of him* is pointed after the threefold *I/my* in v. 24, and the precedent of preceding poems suggests that the poet now has a different speaker uttering some generalizations on the basis of what the man has confessed. The transition parallels (in reverse) the move within Lam 1 between the more distanced reporting voice and the involved Ms. Zion voice. It is clearer than it was in v. 24 that we are hearing "the voice of tradition" here,[69] that the voice of wisdom speaks.[70] The poem turns from the narrative of a unique experience to an affirmation of teaching expressing generalizations that fit the narrative and make links with the man's recent experience. A further difference supporting the impression that we have a different speaker from vv. 1–24 is the way each of the following stanzas shows some consistency in the working of each of the three lines in a stanza. The form of expression as well as the content thus recalls Proverbs. First, each of the *tet* lines begins with *ṭôb*, the word *good* that the man put out of mind in v. 17. Far from allowing it to be put out of mind, the poem now says good, good, good. The statements thus also conflict with much of the rest of Lamentations.[71] This is not to say that they are an illegitimate distortion of the real message of Lamentations, as if the very word "tradition" implied something illegitimate. The polyphonic nature of the scroll means it embraces the truths expressed in these verses without allowing them to silence its characteristic laments and protests—as the last part of this poem will indicate. Here, the stress on Yahweh's goodness following on the reference to his commitment suggests another resonance with Ps 23,[72] of a more positive kind than the one evoked by vv. 1–3. The declarations about Yahweh's goodness also compare and contrast with the ones in the *tet* stanza of Ps 119, though there the stress lies on the link between goodness and Torah, whereas here the stress lies on Yahweh's goodness to the man who suffers but turns to him.[73]

First, Yahweh is indeed *good to the person who has hopes of him* (*qāwâ*); indirectly, the commentator refers to the man who has been giving his testimony, confirming his comment and turning it into a generalization for the benefit of people listening to the poem. The generalization sums up something of key importance that Israel knows about Yahweh, which the man's words have now reconfirmed despite the experience with Yahweh that he has been going through. To speak of having hopes (*qāwâ*; cf. v. 29) is another way to describe having expectations (*yāḥal*, vv. 21, 24; cf. vv. 18, 26) and looking to Yahweh. Yet another way of describing such a person is as one *who inquires*

69. B. Savarikannu, "A Polyphonic Reading of Lamentations 3," *Journal of Asian Evangelical Theology* 20 (2016): 31.

70. Kraus, *Klagelieder*, 55–56.

71. Cf. Bier, *"Perhaps There Is Hope"*, 124.

72. P. van Hecke, "Lamentations 3,1–6: An Anti-Psalm 23," *SJOT* 16 (2002): 274–75.

73. Berges, *Klagelieder*, 201.

of him. In the background here is perhaps the recognition that one of the failures that led to the catastrophe was that people made inquiry in other directions (e.g., Jer 10:21).

26 To put it that other way, Yahweh is good to the person who has this expectancy, which has become a key motif. In the circumstances, it had been hard for the man to be *expectant* for anything, let alone for Yahweh's deliverance, yet now he is being so expectant; again the commentator makes him an example. That expectancy goes along with stillness—a more positive stillness than the one to which 2:10 referred (see also 2:18), a positive quietism that issues from trust (though admittedly, "if the man had followed this advice, there would be no poem"[74]). The silent waiting gains its dynamic through the clear focus on Yahweh's help.[75]

27 The third *good* makes yet another different point. The word continues to apply to Yahweh, not to the man (see the translation note).[76] Wearing a *yoke* need not be a burden; it can be a means of discipline and training (see the commentary on 1:14). The Torah is a yoke in that sense (cf. Tg; and Matt 11:30). The statement might thus be ironic—it would have been good if the man (again he is a *geber*—indeed, "the *geber*"), who stands for the community, had worn the yoke instead of declining to do so. But the First Testament's references to yokes are usually negative (cf. 1:14), and what follows here has some negative implications. The *yoke* is the burden of trouble that the man has borne. Yet even this yoke can be a means of instruction and discipline. The man now has a new way of looking at his trouble. And Yahweh will be good to him as he accepts it. The reference to youth is still a little odd; perhaps the line is an aphorism. Both in form and content it represents the kind of thinking and speaking that appears in Proverbs: a son is not to discard his father's correction; a father reproves the son he favors (Prov 3:11–12).

yod [28]*He will sit alone and be still,*[a]
because he lifted it onto him.[b]
[29]*He will put his mouth in the dirt—*
perhaps there is hope.[c]
[30]*He will give his jaw to the one who struck down—*
he will have his full of reviling.

a. I follow LXX and Vg in taking the verbs in vv. 28–30 as *yiqtol* rather than jussive.

b. "It" has to be understood. For *ʿālayw*, Old Latin "a yoke" implies *ʿōl*; Syr implies the addition of *ʿôlô* (Koenen, *Klagelieder*, 195).

c. LXX lacks v. 29 by homoioarkton: *he will put* is the same as *he will give* (*yittēn*).

74. M. L. Mitchell, "Reading of the Imagery of Lamentations," 142.

75. Berges, *Klagelieder*, 202.

76. Renkema, *Lamentations*, 396.

28 The *yiqtol* clauses continue to spell out the submission to which Yahweh responds with his goodness. Whereas Lam 1 began with Ms. Zion sitting down alone at the time of the city's fall, in Lam 3 the man who submits to Yahweh's yoke will *sit alone* on an ongoing basis. On that ongoing basis he continues to be *still* (cf. v. 26; and compare and contrast 2:10). The second colon confirms that he accepts the trouble that has come to him. One would not be able to tell from v. 28 in isolation what kind of acceptance it was. Is it a bitter acceptance of the inescapable? The context on either side suggests rather a willing, positively submissive acquiescence. He has *lifted* the yoke onto himself. Or has Yahweh lifted it onto him? The form of expression could be read either way. And is the commentator speaking about the man of vv. 1–24 or about anyone who follows his example? The answer is surely both.

29 To *put his mouth in the dirt* sounds similar to grinding one's teeth on gravel and being bent down into ashes (v. 16), but here the words again suggest a willing submission. Putting one's mouth in the dirt is a figure for bowing low before someone whose status one thereby acknowledges (cf. Ps 72:8–11). That submission links with the possibility that there might be *hope* (cf. v. 25). The formulation indicates that hope is here not an attitude internal to the person but an objective possibility of something good that a person can therefore look forward to—it suggests things being good (cf. v. 17). Of course, "'perhaps there is hope' . . . is not exactly a solid avowal of confidence."[77] Quite properly, the man's expectation is like those of Moses, Amos, and Zephaniah (Exod 32:30; Amos 5:15; Zeph 2:3). There is a certain sense in which one can take Yahweh for granted but another sense in which one does not do so. There is a "contingent" aspect to Yahweh's relationship with his people.[78] Real relationships are that way.

30 *He will give* is the same verb as *he will put* in v. 29, and it is again followed by a part of the body. In other contexts the man might be giving *his jaw* or his cheek to *the one who struck down* as if to invite him to do it again if he wishes, but here the idea is rather that the jaw is the location for a yoke (Hos 11:4). The man is now willingly yielding submission to the one who knocked him down when he resisted him. As the first colon parallels v. 29a in the sequence of lines, the second colon parallels v. 29b. *Reviling* will have followed from the treatment he has received that has been described through vv. 1–18.[79] The promise of the colon is that bearing this yoke will not go on forever; a time will come when the man *will have his full* of it, will have had all that he needs to have.

77. Bier, "'We Have Sinned'," 160; cf. Bier, *"Perhaps There Is Hope"*, 124.

78. D. J. Reimer, "An Overlooked Term in Old Testament Theology—Perhaps," in *Covenant as Context: Essays in Honour of E. W. Nicholson*, ed. A. D. H. Mayes and R. B. Salters (Oxford: Oxford University Press, 2003), 326.

79. Cf. Koenen, *Klagelieder*, 254.

kaph [31]*Because the Lord*
does not reject for all time.[a]
[32]*Because even if*[b] *he makes sorrowful, he has compassion,*
in accordance with the vastness of his acts of commitment.[c]
[33]*Because he did not humble*[d] *from his heart*
and make human beings sorrowful.

a. The division of the cola in the 3-2 line ("because he does not reject/ for all time the Lord") is a striking example of the way the poems' "propensity for enjambment" between cola "effects a distinct feeling of forward movement as the syntax of the sentence carries over" from one colon to the next (Dobbs-Allsopp, *On Biblical Poetry*, 204; see "The Relationship between the Cola," pp. 9–10).

b. For the use of *kî 'im*, cf. *TTH* 143; GK 163c. In effect, I doubly translate the *kî* to reflect how this word begins each line.

c. For the *qere*'s plural *ḥăsādāyw* (cf. Vg), the *ketiv* has singular *ḥasdô* (cf. LXX).

d. LXX takes this verb as *'ānâ* I ("answer") rather than BDB's *'ānâ* III; Tg assumes *'ānâ* III but makes a human being the subject. One might take the *qatal* verb as "gnomic," as indicating something that is always true: "He does not humble." But in the context, the line likely refers to the humbling of vv. 1 and 19.

31 Once more the three lines in the stanza work in a similar way: these three all begin with *kî*. The basis for the hope expressed in vv. 28–30 lies in this stanza.[80] Further key theological affirmations feature here at the center of the chapter, which is, furthermore, the central chapter in Lamentations (though this is not the central verse in Lamentations as a whole, because the last two chapters are shorter than the first two). In v. 17, the man noted that Yahweh had rejected him in the sense of turning away his pleas and thus pushing him aside, and the commentator does not query that assessment. The question raised by other protests about rejection is whether such rejection is going to continue forever (Pss 44:23[24]; 74:1; 77:7[8]), and here the commentator affirms that the pushing aside need not last *for all time*. God is here *the Lord*, whereas so far in Lam 3 he has been Yahweh. *The Lord* will be less surprising in vv. 36–37; following on vv. 27–30, it reaffirms that he is the God to whom one submits.

32 Admittedly, then, waywardness may mean that Yahweh *makes sorrowful* (cf. 1:4, 5, 12). Most of this verb's occurrences come in Lamentations; it no doubt implies making people experience something physically painful, but it specifically refers to the inner suffering associated with such an experience. So how does one know that one's suffering and the rejection of one's appeals will not last for all time? It is because of who the Lord is. Acting in grace is, in Martin Luther's words, his *opus proprium*, the natural activity that

80. Salters, *Lamentations*, 236.

emanates from his being.[81] He cannot just leave people with their suffering. He also necessarily *has compassion* and necessarily acts *in accordance with the vastness of his acts of commitment* (see the commentary on v. 22). In his anti-testimony, the man gave a long list of things that did not count as acts of commitment, but the Lord's characteristic deeds are the acts of commitment that Israel's faith celebrated (cf. Pss 25:6; 89:1[2]), and they provide the model for imagining what he will do.

33 The poem restates the principle again. In 587, Yahweh did *humble* (vv. 1, 19), he did *make human beings sorrowful* (cf. v. 32), but the action did not come *from his heart.* When he acts that way, "'his heart' is not in it."[82] While the heart can denote the mind (v. 21) or the emotions (1:22), it can also denote the center of something, as in English, and that connotation makes sense here. There are things we do that come from who we really are and things we do because a situation requires us to act in a certain way, and so it is with God. The center of Yahweh is compassion and commitment. But he has the capacity to act in a way that humbles people and makes them sorrowful, and he can call on those capacities when necessary. They are just as innate in him, but they are not as central to his character. Lamentations is making the same assumptions about God as Isa 28:21 when it describes it as strange for Yahweh to act in judgment and wrath. In a sense they are alien to him, yet they are his actions. To put it Martin Luther's way again, acting in wrath is his alien activity, his *opus alienum,* rather than the activity that is most instinctive to him.[83] These assumptions also appear in Exod 34:6–7, when Yahweh describes himself as compassionate, gracious, long-tempered, committed, truthful, and forgiving (many of these are words that have come here in Lam 3) but also as taking action against waywardness. It is not the case that the love that issues in forgiveness and the justice that issues in judgment are equally matched in God, but neither is Yahweh simply love and forgiveness. The justice that issues in judgment is just as much part of God, but it is not as central to him.

lamed [34]*Crushing under his feet*
all earth's prisoners,
[35]*Turning away the exercise of authority for a man*
before the face of the One On High,
[36]*Cheating someone in his case*
while the Lord did not see . . . [a]

81. The phrase issued from Luther's Heidelberg Disputation in 1518 (Koenen, *Klagelieder,* 255).

82. Gottwald, *Studies in the Book of Lamentations,* 98.

83. See, e.g., V.-M. Kärkkäinen, *The Doctrine of God* (Grand Rapids: Baker, 2017), 102–3.

a. LXX, Vg take this colon as the main clause, but the asyndeton combined with the word order in which the subject precedes the verb suggests that it is subordinate to the clause that precedes. Tg takes it as an unmarked question, but "no syntactical marker suggests that it should be read in such a manner" (H. A. Thomas, "Poetry and Theology," 231—though he goes on to understand it thus), nor does the context require it.

34 The next three lines form a sequence of infinitival (gerund) phrases, covering similar ground in three different formulations, without syntactical connection to the verses on either side. They form a chilling follow-up to vv. 31–33 and also lead into what follows. They are critical observations about the way powerful people operate in the world—the kind of thing that other people say about such goings on (cf. 1:9, 11, 20; Isa 58:3),[84] the kind of thing the victims themselves might say.[85] The ambiguity about them concerns whose wrongdoing they are depicting and the related question of how they link with the stanzas on either side. In isolation, one might take this opening verse to refer to an invader such as Nebuchadnezzar and see it as redescribing in more literal terms the humbling and making sorrowful of v. 33 and the "man's" affliction from vv. 1–18. But if we take the following two verses literally, they look more like an indictment of the practices in Judah that led to the 587 catastrophe. So the audience can decide whether to see the verses as a further description of their humbling or as an indictment regarding what led to their humbling.

In Israel and elsewhere in the Middle East and in other traditional societies, incarceration is not a default punishment for criminal wrongdoing in the way it is in Western societies (theft, for instance, requires making recompense rather than imprisonment). Imprisonment is more often a political act, as Jeremiah's story shows (e.g., Jer 32–33). And no doubt Jeremiah was not the only victim of such incarceration in the centuries and decades that led up to 587. Such imprisonment would indeed be a *crushing* experience (cf. Jer 38)—both in the earth and in the land (*'ereṣ*), as one might with equal plausibility understand the reference. But crushing under foot is also the action of an army (Pss 18:38[39]; 47:3[4]; 44:19[20]), the action of a leader such as Nebuchadnezzar. So the verse might indeed also be a more literal description of the treatment the man has described in vv. 1–18.

35 Jeremiah's story again shows that it is quite likely that a person may end up in prison wrongfully. The administration's job is to see that *the exercise of authority* (*mišpāṭ*) happens in a proper way, but the administration may be involved in *turning away* that exercise. Judgment may not be justice. But this turning away happens *before the face of the One On High*, even though the

84. Koenen, *Klagelieder*, 261.

85. Renkema, *Lamentations*, 418.

administration may not realize it. The administration is therefore taking a big risk (cf. v. 38). Once again, the wrongdoing described here could thus also be part of a popular or prophetic critique of life in Judah before 587, or it could alternatively constitute another description of an invading army's action, another description of what happened to the *man* (vv. 1, 27). Its talk in terms of ignoring the proper exercise of authority on behalf of this "man" fits with the assumption that Yahweh should take redress on Judah's attackers and other national powers (e.g., Jer 46:10; 50:15, 28; 51:6, 36), redress being an idea from the realm of law. Yahweh is not just Judah's local deity; he is in a position of power and authority as the One On High, and he is therefore a threat to any power that thinks it can do as it likes in international relations and ignore what Western thinking might call international law and human rights.

36 So imagine someone bringing a case before the authorities—for instance, claiming that a neighbor (or the king himself) has appropriated part of his land. The two cola parallel the two cola in v. 35. The authorities may collude with the neighbor, dismiss the plaintiff instead of recognizing his case, and cheat him of his land. The second colon then articulates the assumption they will implicitly make: that it happened *while the Lord did not see*. They were of course wrong. "Is it possible that this is not revealed before the Lord?" (Tg). But one could also once again view the line as describing the way imperial forces treated Judah, expressed in the man's anti-testimony. An invading imperial army is engaged in a large-scale version of illicit land appropriation, again on the assumption that it can do as it likes because it takes no account of the sovereign Yahweh.

mem [37]*Who is it who said and it happened,*
when the Lord did not order it?[a]
[38]*From the mouth of the One On High there does not go out*
dire things and a good thing?[b]
[39]*Of what should a living person complain,*[c]
a man on account of his wrongdoings?[d]

a. The asyndeton and the word order with the subject preceding the verb together suggest that this clause is subordinate to the one that precedes.

b. In the context of vv. 37–39, this line is an unmarked question (GK 150a); contrast the translation note on v. 36, and see the commentary.

c. The verb *ʾānan* comes only here and in Num 11:1; Sir 10:25; its meaning is a matter of guesswork.

d. For the *qere*'s plural *ḥăṭāʾāyw* (cf. Vg), the *ketiv* has singular *ḥeṭʾô* (cf. LXX).

37 This time the three lines have in common that they are all questions. The logical link from what precedes is elliptical, like the syntax, but the lines thus again open up different ways for the audience to see their implications. Back at the Beginning, God "said" and "it happened"—numerous times (Gen 1:3, 9, 11, 14–15, 24, 29–30). For anyone who knew Gen 1, the answer to the question *Who is it who said and it happened, when the Lord did not order it?* (that last verb comes in this connection in Ps 33:9) would be obvious. Admittedly, Lam 3 quite likely antedates Gen 1, and it may also antedate Ps 33, so for an audience that did not know these two passages, the answer to the question might require more thought, and this wondering would lead neatly into the next line.

38 Creation issued in what is *good*, but surely not in what is *dire*, whereas history manifests both, but the pattern of God speaking/ordering and then things happening applies to history as well as to creation.[86] It would again be in keeping with Jeremiah's message to affirm that Yahweh, *the One On High*, by his command commissions both *dire things and a good thing*. While the statement recalls Isa 45:7, that prophecy must be taking up this statement rather than vice versa, and Jeremiah also loves the word *dire* (*ra*ʿ, traditionally "bad") and likes to set it over against the word *good* (*ṭôb*; e.g., Jer 32:42; also 21:10; 24:1–10; 39:16; 44:27). The poem does not think in terms of God merely permitting things in the context of history but in terms of ordering them, as he did at creation. Further, the implied declaration here in Lamentations thus also parallels the one in Amos 3:6: "Does something dire happen in a town when Yahweh has not done it?"[87] Admittedly, the parallels raise the question how universal such statements are. Amos 3:7 follows up that declaration with the further affirmation that Yahweh does nothing without revealing his purpose to his servants the prophets. Amos hardly invites readers to take this affirmation as the invariable truth that it might at first seem to affirm; he surely recognizes that Yahweh does many things without announcing them through a prophet. Amos's declaration relates to Ephraim in his context in the eighth century, though it might imply a broader truth about the general way in which Yahweh's revealing his purpose through the prophets gives people principles on whose basis to understand what he does. Here, too, Lamentations' apparently universal statement concerns what Yahweh was doing in the 580s, though it applies more broadly. If the community was complaining in vv. 34–36 about the way it has been treated, the poem implies that it needs to think again about the matter. Yahweh knows what has happened to Judah. He has not just seen it. He accepts, indeed claims, responsibility for it. As far as the invading army was concerned, it thought it made its own decision—in this case, to take action against Judah. But without realizing, it was implementing Yahweh's orders, even though it was acting

86. Koenen, *Klagelieder*, 262.
87. Joyce, "Lamentations," 531.

against international law. Lamentations shares the First Testament's characteristic stress on Yahweh's sovereignty without worrying too much about the rights and wrongs of his action. "For the ancients, events occur by divine causation."[88] And not just for the ancients: modern Western people make the same assumption and thus complain at God when tragedies happen to them. If the idea of divine causation feels uncomfortable, one might understand the line as a statement: the dire things did not come from Yahweh's mouth (because Judah brought them on themselves, as a consequence of the choice they made in light of the alternatives set before them in a passage such as Deut 30:15).[89] But this line is by no means the only one where Lamentations, like the prophets, attributes dire actions to Yahweh (in a moment, see vv. 43–45). More likely, the way Lamentations rescues Yahweh from any charge of being himself dire appeared in vv. 31–33, while the implicit exoneration recurs here in the declaration of the good news that, as well as claiming responsibility for the plural dire things of vv. 1–18, Yahweh also affirms that a good thing will be coming.[90]

39 The poem has a further response to any complaints about the idea that dire things issue from Yahweh's orders. This response presupposes the other way of understanding vv. 34–36. Okay, the invaders were involved in *wrongdoings*, but the ambiguity in vv. 34–36 opens up the possibility of Judahites facing the fact that they were engaged in wrongdoings too. So a Judahite can hardly *complain* at a series of events like those that came to a head in 587, especially as a person who is lucky enough still to be alive, *a living person* who was not swallowed up by those events. This reference to wrongdoings is the first indication in the chapter that the affliction of which it has spoken might be caused by the Judahites' waywardness, so that Lam 3 as a whole is hardly "rooted thematically in the idea of retributive justice."[91] The chapter rather compares with the other poems: they all make the assumption that Judah and Jerusalem deserve what happened, but they all focus on a freedom nevertheless to cry out in pain because of what has happened, and they thus parallel prayers such as Pss 38 and 39 (see the commentary on 1:9). In the parallelism in this verse, with its reference to wrongdoings, the living person becomes *a man*, the term used in vv. 1 and 27 and 35. The line thus makes a dig at the "man" who stands for Judah and who spoke through vv. 1–24, and it prepares the way for a further transition in who speaks.

88. K. M. O'Connor, "Lamentations," *NIB*, commenting on vv. 25–36.

89. Rashi, in MG; cf. M. P. Stone, "Vindicating Yahweh," *JSOT* 43 (2018): 101.

90. Koenen, *Klagelieder*, 264.

91. See Balentine, "Prose and Poetry of Exile," 353.

nun [40]*Let's search our paths and examine them,*[a]
and turn right back to[b] *Yahweh.*
[41]*Let's lift up our heart in addition to*[c] *our open hands*[d]
to God in the heavens.
[42]*We—we rebelled and defied;*
you—you did not pardon.

a. LXX takes the two verbs as *niphal.*
b. *Šûb ʿad.*
c. For this meaning of *lə*, see BDB, 40a; cf. Vg, Sym.
d. Lit. "our palms" (cf. 2:19).

40 It is not immediately clear whose voice now speaks as "we." In vv. 40–41 one might understand this self-exhortation as coming from the voice that has been speaking through vv. 25–39, but v. 42 will suggest that the reference to the "man's" wrongdoing has provoked him into making a response. So these are his words, though in uttering them he makes a move from first-person singular to first-person plural speech. He thus casts aside the veil whereby he presented himself as an individual and speaks overtly on behalf of the community. First-person plural speech thus appears in Lamentations for the first time (except 2:16, which tests and proves the rule) but it will have a place in Lam 4 and 5. It may be encouraged by the fact that first-person plural verbs begin with *nun,* the letter needed for this stanza. The stanza holds together by means of lines that all begin with a reference to "us": two first-person plural cohortatives and then the rare shortened form of the word for "we" (*naḥnû* for *ʾănaḥnû,* so as to begin with the right letter). From vv. 37–39 it follows that as a community "we" would be wise to *search our paths and examine them.* One can see why if we set Lam 3 against the background of events in the 580s and make a link with the possibility that vv. 34–36 refer to issues in Judah in the time that led up to 587. So "we" would be wise then to turn back to Yahweh. Turning was Jeremiah's exhortation; the formulation here, *turn right back* (see the translation note), indicates that it needs to be a proper turning, a turning right round.

41 Slightly surprisingly, the emphasis in indicating the nature of a proper turning lies not on the kind of change of community life that vv. 34–36 pointed to but on personal attitudes to Yahweh (though Tg thinks of hands that are now clean of theft and robbery). That proper turning will involve the inner person and the outer person, because both are essential aspects of a human being. The *heart* without the *hands* would be odd and might be an attempt to be secretive or might suggest a refusal to associate one's turning with other people; "prayers, when they are earnest, move the hands."[92] But

92. Calvin, *Jeremiah and Lamentations,* 5:516.

the hands without the heart would also be problematic; it would imply a turning that was exclusively external and symbolic. The worshiper "gives his heart as a gift in his hands."[93] The one on whom people are to bestow this gift is *God in the heavens*. That title incorporating the word *ʾēl* for God comes only here in the First Testament, but the title makes for a link with the description of Yahweh as One On High (vv. 35, 38); elsewhere Yahweh is God On High (*ʾēl ʿelyôn*; e.g., Ps 78:35). In the context of the mid-sixth century, people would know that God was not in the temple, which he abandoned in 587. Maybe this fact encourages a focus on his being the God of the entire cosmos.

42 The confession that the man articulates on the people's behalf fits with that focus on a change of attitude to God as opposed to a change in community life. The nature of confession in the Scriptures is to be narrative. Confession is not (for instance) a statement about how sorry we are but a statement about the fact that *we rebelled and defied*, two more Jeremianic words (e.g., Jer 2:8, 29; 3:13; 4:17; 5:23). And it is an acknowledgment that *you did not pardon* (Jer 5:7). How could the King have pardoned rebels who had not turned from their rebellion? The point and the contrast are underlined by the inclusion of the unnecessary explicit pronouns *we* and *you*. "In the same way that they confess that they have sinned, so they attribute justice to God, who punished them in this way."[94] The poem thus need not imply a protest or claim that Yahweh is unjust or imply the idea that repentance need not issue in pardon.[95] The poem agrees with Jer 18:5–12: if people do now repent and speak in this way to God, it will open up the possibility of pardon.

samek [43]*You covered us*[a] *in anger and pursued us—*
when you killed, you did not spare.
[44]*You covered over yourself with a cloud*
so that a plea would not pass through.
[45]*Offscouring and discarding you would make us*
among the peoples.

a. BDB takes the meaning to be "wrapped yourself," but the verb is usually transitive; I follow Tg in assuming that the object suffix on the following verb applies also to this one.

43 At the end of the three lines with first-person plural subjects (*let's search, let's lift up, we rebelled*), the second-person verb (*you did not pardon*) prepared the way for three lines addressed to Yahweh. They spell out the implications of his not pardoning and do so in quite confrontational statements about what Yahweh has done. The statements might indicate that the comment

93. Ibn Ezra, "Commentary B," 192.
94. Vermigli, *Lamentations*, 139.
95. So Berlin, *Lamentations*, 96.

about not pardoning was more confrontational than it seemed when following up the acknowledgment of rebellious defiance. In a chilling metaphor, Yahweh *covered us,* wrapped us, smothered us, *in anger* instead of the protective covering elsewhere noted by the verb (*sākak*; Ps 140:7[8]; the *hiphil* in Pss 5:11[12]; 91:4). It is the first reference to anger in Lam 3, after the six in Lam 2. Yahweh *pursued* the Judahites, like Zion's human pursuers (1:3, 6) and *killed* people (2:4, 20, 21) without sparing (2:2, 17, 21). So he did in 587. The man is now making Yahweh the explicit subject of these aggressive verbs, as he did not in vv. 1–18, while also continuing to formulate words that address Yahweh, as he also did not in vv. 1–18. Perhaps it is possible now that he has made the affirmations in vv. 22–24 and the second voice has generalized them in vv. 25–39. The poem thus continues to be at ease both with speaking of the community's waywardness and Yahweh's consequent chastisement and with articulating the harshness of what Yahweh did. Whereas one might have thought that the much-loved phrases at the center of Lam 3 would constitute the resolution of the chapter and the Lamentations scroll, they do not.[96] They are only the center of the middle chapter, which now reverts to the more characteristic tone that will run through the rest of the poems. In its structure, Lamentations parallels the Jeremiah scroll, where chapters 31–34 form a high point of hope but not the end or resolution of the scroll. "Lamentations is a poem of defeat."[97] Here, as elsewhere, it "refuses denial, practices truth-telling, and reverses amnesia."[98]

44 But it is Yahweh's essential nature to be committed and compassionate. Therefore, if Yahweh was not to pardon but to cover his people in anger and pursue, to kill and not spare, and to persist in rejecting appeals for clemency, then he had to put a veil over that essential nature, as much for his own sake as for anyone else's. He needed something to stop pleas getting to him, a cloud that discouraged people from taking the risk of approaching his fiery, electrifying presence, and that they would find impenetrable if they did bring their plea near. As Yahweh said a number of times in Jeremiah, he had no intention of listening to their prayers or to Jeremiah's. "The connection between Jerusalem and God is out of order."[99] As the hidden God, "deus absconditus, God stands over against his people."[100] It is another comment that fits with the man's not speaking to Yahweh in vv. 1–18. His omission hints at a recognition that his plea would not have got through that cloud. Yet the comment here has paradoxical

96. Roberts, "Lamentations 3," 198.
97. Owens, "Personification and Suffering in Lamentations 3," 83.
98. K. M. O'Connor, *Lamentations and the Tears of the World*, 94.
99. Koenen, *Klagelieder*, 272.
100. Kraus, *Klagelieder*, 66.

or hopeful implications: if Yahweh had made it impossible for prayer to get through, what does the man think is going on now when he prays?[101]

45 Yahweh's anger found expression in surrendering Judah to the peoples that attacked it. The man might have in mind neighbors such as the Moabites, Ammonites, and Edomites, or he might have in mind these same peoples and others as the ones among whom Judahites had come to take refuge, or he might have in mind the Babylonians among whom some Judahites had gone into exile.[102] Yahweh's inspiring Judah's attackers meant that at their hands he turned Judah into *offscouring* (the junk stuck to the side of the pan that one scrapes off to throw out) and *discarding* (which ironically anticipates the use of the related verb in 5:22). In 1 Cor 4:13 Paul describes himself in language that recalls these words;[103] the language would resonate for him and for Jewish believers at Corinth who were familiar with Lamentations.

pe [46]*Against us all our enemies*
opened their mouth.
[47]*Panic and pit*[a]*—it became ours,*
the wrecking and the breaking.[b]
[48]*With streams of water my eye runs down*
on account of the breaking of my dear people.

a. *Paḥad* and *paḥat*.

b. *Haššēʾt* and *haššāber*. The articles help the alliteration, make for variation between the cola, and contribute to the closing off of vv. 46–47 before the transition in v. 48 (cf. Salters, *Lamentations*, 256). The first noun is a *hapax legomenon*, but it recalls words such as *šāʾâ* ("crash in ruins") and *šōʾâ* ("devastation").

46 The man gives up the challenging tone in order to go on to a different way of describing what had happened to the people—not as something Yahweh did (though that will still be presupposed) but as something they experienced. In other contexts, to say *against us all our enemies opened their mouth* could be another way to describe becoming like offscouring, becoming like something that had been discarded: that is, their enemies opened their mouth to be insulting, or earlier they had opened their mouth to say things by way of threat that they then implemented. But more often, opening the mouth is preparatory to devouring, and so it was in 2:16.

101. Cf. L. Beach, "A Spirituality of Exile: Responding to God's Absence," *Journal of Spiritual Formation and Soul Care* 10 (2017): 48.

102. Salters, *Lamentations*, 255.

103. Broughton, *Lamentations*, on the verse.

47 A pithy, artful, disturbing pair of phrases characterized by alliteration and assonance sum up the community's consequent experience of disaster (see the translation notes). The assonance and alliteration may suggest an aphorism.[104] The first pair of words combine abstract and concrete, but they are metaphorical.[105] The second pair suggest something more literal and equally frightening in its way. So the whole line sums up the horror of the consequences of Yahweh's abandonment.

48 The man continues to speak in vv. 48–51. In the last line of this stanza, he first takes up the reference to *breaking* in v. 47 but then makes another transition to speaking once more as "I" in order to articulate another sort of comment about *my dear people*. He thus refers to some of the "we," but now speaks of them in the third person. He is explicitly addressing no one in particular, but we might think that he implicitly hopes that both Yahweh and the people are listening. *My eye was running down with water*, Ms. Zion had said (1:16); *with streams of water my eye runs down*, the man now says. It was *on account of the breaking of my dear people*, the earlier witness said (2:11); the man repeats these words. Like that earlier witness, the man is strangely able both to identify with and to distance himself from the people: he grieves for himself and he grieves for them.

ayin [49]*My eye—it poured and it will not be still,*
without respite,[a]
[50]*Until Yahweh looks out*
and sees[b] *from the heavens.*
[51]*My eye—it dealt out to my spirit*
more than[c] *all the daughters in my city.*

a. *Hăpugôt* is a "very strange" form (BDB) apparently from *pûg*, and related to the (also strange) *pûgat* in 2:18—both are *hapax legomenona*.

b. The verb is jussive, which can be used to suggest purpose (*TTH* 172).

c. Tg, Vg understand *min* to mean "on account of" (cf. *'al* in v. 48), and LXX's *para* might have this meaning. But *min* also allows "more than," which gives good sense here (so Ibn Ezra, "Commentary B," 192–93).

49 The man's reference to *my eye* and the substance of the line make for continuity with the preceding stanza. This motif, along with the reference in v. 50 to Yahweh looking out and the recurrence of *my eye* in v. 51 (*'ayin* conveniently begins with the letter *ayin*), runs through this stanza. The idea of my eye streaming down so that *it will not be still* takes up from the witness's words in 2:18 (the usage in 3:26, 28 was rather different); the talk of tears

104. Cf. Hillers, *Lamentations*, 132.

105. Koenen, *Klagelieder*, 274.

without *respite* also picks up from 2:18. There the witness urged Zion's wall to cry without respite; here the man cannot stop himself doing so because of the breaking of the people of which he is part but to whom he wants to minister.

50 In theory, no doubt, when *Yahweh looks out . . . from the heavens*, he does not do so because he needs to in order to see. The expression has two implications. He is like the king looking out from his palace; the verb (*šāqap*) commonly denotes looking out of a window. So Yahweh looks out from his palace in the heavens. The other implication is the connection between seeing and acting, which parallels the connection between hearing and acting. That link has already been implicit in 1:9, 11. The man looks forward to Yahweh seeing because it will imply his taking action on the basis of what he sees. "With God's seeing, the long history of his saving intervention begins."[106]

51 The stanza closes with another reference to *my eye*. Saying that my eye *dealt out to* someone is another expression taken up from earlier (1:12, 22; 2:20). Those earlier occurrences would suggest that crying *dealt out* things that were hard and painful *to my spirit*, and this idea follows well from the preceding references to crying. But the immediately preceding allusion to looking and seeing may also suggest the eye as the organ of sight. It is what the man's eye has seen that has brought such distress; by implication, the line expresses a wish that what his eye has seen may have the same effect on Yahweh (cf. v. 50). Only here does Lamentations refer to the city's *daughters*, whom Tg takes to be its daughter villages (e.g., Jer 49:2). But in other contexts, "Israel's daughters" are women engaged in leading mourning (e.g., 2 Sam 1:24), and that connotation makes sense here.[107] What the speaker himself sees is having more effect on him than the plaints of the mourners would have, or is having more effect on him than it would on a group of mourners.

tsade [52]*My enemies hunted, hunted*[a] *me like a bird,*
without reason.
[53]*They put an end to my life in a pit*
and threw rock at me.[b]
[54]*Water flowed over my head—*
I said, "I'm cut off."

a. The infinitive absolute precedes the finite verb, emphasizing the reality of what happened.

b. LXX, Vg "put a rock on me" fits the singular "rock" and generates a plausible picture (cf. Dan 6:17[18]), but "put" is too mild a translation of *yādâ* and "on" does not fit the preposition *bə*. It is easier to take the singular noun as collective.

106. Berges, *Klagelieder*, 218.

107. Ibn Ezra, "Commentary B," 192–93.

52 The man continues to speak but to speak as an embodiment or representative of the people. Out of the present context, vv. 52–54 and the lines that follow could seem to be describing once more his recent and present experience—the experience he described in vv. 1–18, the situation he needs Yahweh to rescue him from. But generally, Lamentations does not speak of Judah as currently under attack; its references to attack relate to the events that led up to 587. And *without reason* would be a bit rich in that connection. The continuation of his words in vv. 55–57 looks more like a recollection of a past act of deliverance than a description relating to the present.[108] It refers to the typical past occasion when Judah experienced attack and knew Yahweh's deliverance. Here the man more systematically evokes the language of the Psalms. He takes up the language of protest psalms and testimony psalms to recall the way Yahweh acted on a previous occasion, which is the pattern the Psalms themselves want to see repeated (e.g., Pss 9–10). A testimony psalm thus witnesses to the way Yahweh rescued Israel from its enemies so that people escaped "like a bird from the fowler's trap" (Ps 124:7). The *bird* (*ṣippôr*) is a vulnerable little creature (KJV sometimes translates "sparrow"), not an eagle or a hawk. The stanza's first image thus fits the Psalms in general terms, though this verb for hunting (*ṣûd*) does not come there; strikingly and ironically, it does come in Jer 16:16 to describe the threatened fate of Judah. The complaint that one was attacked *without reason* fits against that background in the Psalms (Pss 35:7, 19; 69:4[5]; 109:3; 119:161).

53 A second image sees threatening peril as like being thrown into a pit (see Ps 30:3[4], where the parallelism with a reference to Sheol suggests *the* Pit). The enemies thought they had *put an end to* the man's *life* by throwing him there. Again, the terminology recalls Jeremiah (37:16; 38:6–13). But here, metaphorically speaking, the enemies also *threw rock at me* there.

54 If the pit is actually a cistern, as Jeremiah's pit was, then this third image links with the second, though it is also of broader significance (see Pss 18:16[17]; 69:1–2[2–3], 14–15[15–16]; 124:4–5). Being *cut off* is a pregnant expression: Cut off from Yahweh's action (Ps 88:5[6])? Cut off from the land of the living (Isa 53:8)?

qoph [55]*I called*[a] *on your name, Yahweh,*
from the deepest pit.
[56]*As you listened*[b] *to my voice*[c]*:*
"Do not hide your ear regarding my relief (regarding my cry for help),"[d]
[57]*You came near on the day I would call you—*
you said, "Don't be afraid."

108. Cf. Koenen, *Klagelieder*, 278–780.

a. Whereas DG 60c sees this *qatal* as performative, following on the *qatal* in v. 54 it more likely has past reference. But taking the alternative view on the question covered by the next note would make a difference to this assessment.

b. This *qatal* verb is the first in a sequence in vv. 56–61 that I. W. Provan argues to be precative—that is, they are prayers in *qatal* form ("Past, Present and Future in Lamentations iii 52–66," *VT* 41 [1991]: 164–75). This possibility links with the way *qatal* verbs can refer to an event that is so real and actual that it can be referred to in the *qatal* even if it is actually future. But psalms can incorporate recollections of Yahweh's past answers to prayer, and it works well to take the *qatal* verbs in this way. And the audience would be so familiar with *qatal* referring to the actual past that it would surely understand the verbs this way, given that there is no difficulty about doing so (see, e.g., Parry, *Lamentations*, 120–24).

c. The word order in this colon (object before verb) combined with the asyndeton suggests that this clause is subordinate to the one that follows. The main clause might then be the parallel colon in v. 56b, which will be the plea the man is uttering now. But v. 56b then anticipates the plea that will come later. Rather, I take the second colon as spelling out what *my voice* said in the past (see the commentary); v. 56 as a whole is then subordinate to the main clauses in v. 57.

d. *Regarding my cry for help* may be an addition to explain *regarding my relief* (*rəwāḥâ* comes only here and in Exod 8:15[11]); without it, the line is a more plausible 2-3 instead of 2-4. With it, one could rework the MT division of the line by taking *do not hide your ear* with the first colon so that the line becomes 4-2.

55 In a testimony psalm, recollection may move from recalling one's predicament to recalling one's prayer (Ps 30:6–10[7–11]). So it does here. Lamentations is working with two levels of metaphor, as the pit is a metaphor in the man's testimony and the man himself is a metaphor. To put it another way, the pit is a metaphor for the man's enemies, but the enemies are only too real for the referent of the man-as-metaphor. In the past, Israel has known itself to be in a metaphorical pit, and it is now in one again; this stanza takes up the motif from the previous one. But in that pit it had prayed before. Indeed it was in *the deepest pit*. But it had *called on your name*. Shouting someone's name should get their attention. "Abrupt cries are fitly suited to occasions of great extremity. . . . And, for the most part, when 'his blessed Spirit makes intercession in us' with more than ordinary power, it is not by diversified and rhetorical language, but 'by groans which cannot be uttered.'"[109]

56 It did get Yahweh's attention (Pss 6:8–9[9–10]; 18:6[7]; 22:24[25]; 28:6). This account of Yahweh's answering prayer becomes part of the background for the renewed prayer in vv. 59 and 64–66, but at this point we are nowhere near the end of the recollection; v. 56b specifies what the *voice* was saying in that earlier prayer. *Do not hide your ear* is an engaging mixed metaphor suggesting the image of someone physically putting their hand over their ears so that

109. C. Simeon, "Lamentations," in *The Entire Works*, by C. Simeon, vol. 9 (London: Bohn, 1844), 338.

the ears are not even visible. The quote from the prayer in the second colon will be paralleled by the quote from the answer in the parallel second colon in the next line. Words related to the rare noun for *relief* suggest having space (see, e.g., Jer 22:14), and space makes for a nice contrast with confinement in a pit. That is the content of the *cry for help* that the man had uttered.

57 *You came near,* and did something, which contrasts with staying away and doing nothing. The man testifies to Yahweh's having regularly acted in that way. It meant that Yahweh could also give the man the familiar First Testament reassurance, *Don't be afraid.* Maybe logically the reassurance should appear in the first colon, but alphabetical considerations encourage *you came near* (*qārabtî*) to come there. The second colon tests the rule that God does not speak in Lamentations[110] as the poem recalls the "performative" words Yahweh has uttered before—words that "have the capacity to remove the fear and anxiety that are at the center of the trouble and distress of those who cry out to God."[111]

resh [58]*You argued my causes, Lord—*
you restored my life.
[59]*You have seen*[a] *the cheating done to me, Yahweh—*
exercise authority[b] *for me.*
[60]*You have seen all their redress,*
all their plans for me.

a. LXX has aorist verbs through vv. 59–61, implying that the recollection of past deliverance continues (see note b). But in MT, the imperative in the next colon indicates a move from past deliverance to the need for deliverance now, and I take the verse's first colon as the beginning of this move so that the verse as a whole set the agenda for vv. 60–66 (see the commentary).

b. For MT *šopṭâ*, LXX "you exercised authority" implies *šāpaṭtā*, which makes for a smoother *qatal* sequence through vv. 59–62.

58 The testimony ends with yet another metaphor, or one taken up from vv. 34–36. Yahweh is now like someone who acted as witness or advocate on behalf of a defender in a case that came before the gathering of the village elders, and thereby *restored* him. The plural *causes* compares with the *yiqtol* verb in v. 57: on Judah's behalf, the man can look back on a number of such occasions.[112] The verb (*gāʾal*) suggests he acted like the near relative who can make life possible again for someone within the family, as Boaz did for Ruth

110. J. A. Gladson, "Postmodernism and the *Deus absconditus* in Lamentations 3," *Bib* 92 (2010): 329–30.

111. P. D. Miller, *They Cried to the Lord*, 144.

112. Salters, *Lamentations*, 271.

and Naomi. The fact that there were cases that needed arguing suggests that the man was in danger of losing his land to someone who was claiming it, perhaps because of debt, or perhaps through fraud. But Yahweh protected him from the loss.

59 Once more the movement within the chapter ignores the alphabetical transitions, incorporating a transition within the stanza. As happens in a psalm, the man moves from recalling what Yahweh did in the past to appealing for the same kind of action in the present. Initially, he stays with the metaphor of community dispute resolution. He is like someone who has been cheated, defrauded of his land (cf. v. 36). He needs Yahweh to *exercise authority* for him in the way the elders would, or were supposed to. The first colon will be expanded in vv. 60–63; the second colon will be expanded in vv. 64–66.

60 Talk of *redress* again recalls the language of the Psalms (44:16[17]) but also the way Ezek 25:14–15 speaks of Israel's adversaries. The parallel colon and the lines that follow could suggest that the man is talking about some adversaries' current intentions to take redress rather than something that has yet happened, as can be the case in some psalms. But in this context, the man is speaking about plans they had that were implemented in the 580s.

shin [61]*You have listened to their reviling, Yahweh,*
all their plans against me.
[62]*The lips of my assailants and their murmuring*
have been against me all the time.[a]
[63]*At their sitting and their rising,*[b] *take note,*
I have been the subject of their song.

a. LXX, Vg, Tg see the noun expressions in v. 62 as further objects of *you have listened to*, but such enjambment is rare in Lam 3. Rather, v. 62 as a whole is an independent noun clause referring to the past; v. 63b will be another.

b. LXX, Vg take *their sitting and their rising* as the object of *take note*; but see rather Hillers, *Lamentations*, 119.

61 Through this penultimate stanza, the man continues to remind Yahweh of the affliction he has received, speaking in metaphor of the suffering of Judah in the 580s. The new stanza picks up the closing theme of the previous one. The first colon has the same shape as v. 60a: *listened* is equivalent to *seen*, and *reviling* is equivalent to *redress*. He has had his full of this *reviling* (v. 30), and he knows that Yahweh has heard it. But has Yahweh listened? He longs for Yahweh to take action against his attackers in light of the *plans* they made and executed. The second colon then corresponds to v. 60b, with the verb once more applying to both cola, except that the understated *plans for me* becomes the sharper *plans against me* (*lə* gives way to ʿ*al*).

62 The *murmuring* might further refer to the plans that the adversaries implemented, or it might alternatively denote the reviling that followed the military victory.

63 The same alternative will apply to their singing about the man and his people (cf. v. 14): it might be their dismissive and confident military chanting before their attacks, partly designed to embolden the attackers and demoralize the defenders, or it might again refer to the mocking that followed. *Their sitting and their rising* is a merism: it covers their entire life, their relaxation and their activity, "everything they do."[113] Given that the man has known in the past what it was like to have Yahweh pay attention to his cry (vv. 55–57), Yahweh's doing so in the past is the basis for his appeal for Yahweh to *take note* and therefore take action in relation to what he has *listened to* again. His recollection of Yahweh's past response is both an encouragement to the man himself and a reminder to Yahweh that looks to him to be consistent with his past action.

tav [64]*May you give them back their remuneration, Yahweh,*
in accordance with the deed of their hands.
[65]*May you give them a wrapping*[a] *over their mind,*
may your oath[b] *be for them.*
[66]*May you pursue them in anger and destroy them*
from under Yahweh's heavens.

a. BDB derives the *hapax legomenon meginnâ* from *gānan*; LXX, Vg "shield" implies a link with *māgēn,* also from *gānan.* Tg has a word for grief, but that translation looks like guesswork deriving from the puzzling nature of the expression and related to Tg's understanding of the next colon (see note b).

b. LXX, Vg, Tg "toil/weariness" suggests *təlā'ātəkā* for *ta'ălātəkā.*

64 The poem closes (as a protest psalm often does) with a move from an appeal for Yahweh to pay attention (vv. 60–63) to an appeal for action against the adversaries. The recollection of Yahweh's past action (v. 58) as well as his past listening and drawing near (vv. 56–57) thus becomes a further part of the background to a renewed prayer and an appeal to him to act again, as happens in psalms (Pss 10:17; 40:1[2]). The prayer takes the form of an appeal for redress that parallels the prayer in 1:22. The man's adversaries deserve their *remuneration,* as Paul sees someone who did wrong to him deserving their remuneration from God (2 Tim 4:14).[114]

65 A *wrapping over their mind* might sound like something rather mild, but it is something horrifying if it is the opposite to a circumcising of their

113. Hillers, *Lamentations,* 119.

114. Broughton, *Lamentations,* on the verse.

mind (see Jer 4:4; 6:10; 9:25–26). It would make it impossible for them to see the truth or change. If Yahweh took an *oath* along those lines, it would indeed be a frightful curse.

66 The man's closing wish asks that Yahweh may treat his attackers as Yahweh has treated him (v. 43); the verse is combined with Ps 79:6–7 in some versions of the Pesah liturgy. The phrase *Yahweh's heavens* comes only here, and the third-person reference to Yahweh in a prayer addressed to him is unexpected. But there are many parallels, in speaking to God and to human beings (e.g., 1 Kgs 22:15), including the final verse of Lam 2.[115] The poet is ending with a flourish[116] and indicating that the man who walks in darkness and has no light trusts in Yahweh's name and relies on his God (Isa 50:10).[117] The man stands "not triumphant, but alive."[118]

A READER'S RESPONSE

Imagine someone who has taken part in reading Lam 3 at a worship gathering in Mizpah or Bethel.

> My main reaction is a kind of sense of relief, as if a weight has been lifted from my spirit. It was all very well to be drawn into going through the terrible events of the first fall of Jerusalem and the siege, and some of my neighbors deciding to go off to Ammon and Moab, and then hearing that things hadn't worked out very well there, and then the shortages and the sickness and the final siege and the surrender and the king fleeing and being caught and the humiliation and the shame . . . I was thinking, "Enough already!" Then this poem began by taking us through the whole story again in a different way. And it was all very well to picture it as the suffering of a man instead of the suffering of a woman and being reminded that it was the kind of thing that men had often gone through, as it was the kind of thing that women had gone through over the ages. But it made me think again, "Enough already!"
>
> Yet then the poem pictured the man going through the kind of struggle I went through: to imagine that there might be any kind of hope for the future and to face the possibility that Yahweh had turned his back on us forever. I knew we couldn't complain if Yahweh had. But I also knew that, actually, we are still alive. Jeremiah had kept saying

115. Koenen, *Klagelieder*, 199.
116. Salters, *Lamentations*, 281.
117. Koenen, *Klagelieder*, 200.
118. Dobbs-Allsopp, *Lamentations*, 128.

that we would all be dead, and actually we weren't. It was as if Yahweh couldn't bear to do what he had said he would do. Our life continued, new every morning.

And in the poem, there was this other voice affirming that our experience of Yahweh's continuing to show compassion to us and continuing to be committed to us, and our becoming aware that we needed to submit to him, wasn't so odd. It fitted with what we often sang in the Psalms. They reminded us that the tough way Yahweh had acted toward us wasn't a reflection of his essential nature any more than when a father or mother disciplines their child. Really, his heart wasn't in it. You can sometimes picture one of your parents as the tough one and the other as the soft one, and maybe they are like that, but with God, there is only one of him. We knew it to be so even though our neighbors didn't. So Yahweh has to be the one who does the tough things as well as the compassionate things. And we couldn't complain about him doing some tough things, given that we were the people that we were.

So it seemed that the man listened to that voice affirming what he had said about himself and about Yahweh and about us, and then he came back to talking about us and inviting us to identify with what he said about us. It was not just about the extraordinary fact that we were still alive. It was about the paradoxical fact that therefore we have to come to Yahweh with our confession and repentance as well as with our laments and protests. It wasn't one or the other, it was both.

And he reminded us about something else in the Psalms and in our experience. When we looked back over our story as a people, we couldn't see anything as terrible as what had happened to us. But we could see occasions that the people at the time probably thought were just as bad. They sounded just like the things the man described. But then the Psalms describe how Yahweh rescued them from the people who attacked them, and they go on to press Yahweh to do it again. That's how the man talked. It was as if he was identifying with them, and he was remembering how they prayed when they were under attack, and how Yahweh listened and put down those attackers. And then he moved seamlessly to us being the people who were in that position, and us being able to pray that way . . .

LAMENTATIONS 4: "HE LIT A FIRE IN ZION"

"It would be satisfying if we could stop the book here, at the end of chapter three, and cling to faith and hope even in the midst of the great suffering attributed to God. But the grieving of Lamentations continues, pressing beyond this moment of hope, almost appearing to forget it has even been spoken."[1] Lam 4 thus makes a key contribution to the structure and balance of the Lamentations scroll.

We may gain some appreciation of the fourth lamentation by again comparing and contrasting it with the ones that came before:

- Like them, it comprises twenty-two stanzas structured by the letters of the alphabet, though its stanzas comprise two rather than three lines, so that it is one-third shorter than them.
- Like them, it has "attempted to restore a necessary balance between stability and adaptability" for people "by describing the chaos they experienced in a structured manner. The effect in this instance is an experience of catharsis and a regaining of control, restoring stability and adaptability to a proper balance."[2]
- Like them, it moves between speaking about "them" (the Jerusalemites and their attackers), speaking about "him" (Yahweh), speaking to "you" (Edom and Judah, but not Yahweh), and speaking as "I" and as "we." Like them, it might be read as a two-hander: a first-person singular voice speaks about Zion in vv. 1–16, 21–22; a first-person plural voice speaks about "us" in vv. 17–20.
- Like them, it both grieves or protests at the city's suffering and recognizes its waywardness without implying that the suffering is necessarily proportionate to the waywardness.
- Like them, it attributes the city's suffering to Yahweh's angry blazing and his wrath.
- Like them, it sometimes describes Zion's trouble as brought by Yahweh, but it does not do so as systematically as Lam 2 and 3.
- Like them, it utilizes hyperbole, both in the portrayal of how great things were before the siege and in the portrayal of the reversal that followed.
- Like Lam 1–2, it begins only the first line in each stanza with that stanza's letter; like Lam 1–2, one of its stanzas has a supernumerary

1. J. Peters McCurry, "Grieving Together with Lamentations," *Lutheran Forum* (Summer 2017): 14.

2. I. G. P. Gous, "Mind over Matter: Lamentations 4 in the Light of the Cognitive Sciences," *SJOT* 10 (1996): 70–71.

line (v. 15; cf. 1:7; 2:19); and like Lam 1–2, it begins with *how*, which it repeats in v. 2.

- Like Lam 1–2, it puzzles and protests over Yahweh's acting in ways that clashed with his own revelation to them: his prohibition on unbelieving foreigners coming into the sanctuary, his establishing his altar and sanctuary, and now his anointing of the Davidic king.
- Like Lam 2–3, it has the stanzas in the unusual alphabetical order that puts *pe* before *ayin*.
- Like Lam 3, it has expressions in common with Lam 1–2, but mostly the latter: e.g., *at the beginning of all the streets* (4:1; 2:19), *the breaking of my dear people* (4:10; 2:11), *priests* and *elders* (4:16; 1:19), mothers eating their children (4:10; 2:20), *Ms. Zion* (4:22; 1:6; 2:1, 4, 8, 10, 13, 18), *reveal* in relation to the community's offenses (4:22; 2:14).
- Like Lam 3, it eventually offers the community some encouragement, in the last two stanzas and on a smaller scale.
- Like Lam 3, it begins with a puzzling figure, an allusive metaphor that has an "unrealistic" tone[3] (whereas Lam 1 and 2 begin in a way whose meaning is clear).

It is distinctive in that:

- Its opening metaphor does introduce its running motif of reversal, of things being turned upside down, of the impossible becoming actual: gold tarnished, hewn stone tumbling, parents not feeding children, well-to-do people feeding on trash, flourishing bodies emaciated, a secure city being overwhelmed, prophets and priests engaged in murder, Yahweh's anointed captured. "Blessings of the covenant become human carnage."[4]
- After that opening stanza, it moves briskly into being more down-to-earth and concrete in its description of the situation of Jerusalem before and after its fall. Thus, whereas Lam 1–2 personalize the city as a woman and Lam 3 makes a man a figure for the country's affliction, Lam 4 talks directly about the experience of ordinary people, especially during the city's siege and fall. It is more interested in what is going on in the streets and the squares (vv. 1, 5, 8, 14, 18).[5]
- Thus "the narrator acts like a traumatized guide to the devastated

3. Brunet, *Lamentations*, 66.

4. Hens-Piazza, *Lamentations*, 60.

5. Koenen, *Klagelieder*, 308.

city."[6] The concrete nature of its portrayal might indicate that it comes from soon after the event or might reflect the memory and imagination of a poet working a decade or two later.

- Whereas Lam 3 focused on an individual, Lam 4 broadens things by focusing on various segments of the population and finally breaking into the "we" that will also characterize Lam 5.[7]
- It thus talks about the fate of the people as a whole, of the ordinary people, of the well-to-do people, of the children, of the women, of the men, of laypeople, and of priests and prophets.
- It is distant and objective in its portrayal, though that characteristic does not mean being remote. It conveys an impression of the horrific nature of what is going on like a television news report. "The unimaginable is played out before our eyes."[8]
- It puts a focus on the responsibility of priests and prophets for the disaster and on their fate, with a distinctive stress on the priests and on uncleanness and its implications.[9]
- It conveys a sense of the tragedy of the lives of individuals: compassionate women who cook their children, prophets and priests who cannot see.
- Whereas a protest psalm may comprise address to Yahweh, complaint, statement of trust, petition, words of assurance, and vow of praise, Lam 4 virtually comprises only complaint,[10] addressed to no one in particular.
- Thus, whereas the rhetorical "you" in Lam 1 and 3 is Yahweh and in Lam 2 is Zion (but words to Yahweh are put on Zion's lips), in Lam 4 the first rhetorical "you" is Edom and the second is Zion. Yahweh overhears what is said about him and about Zion's affliction.
- Its moving between "I" and "we" does compare with some protest psalms, and one might see it as having in its background the forms of individual protest (vv. 1–16), communal protest (vv. 17–20), and prophetic response (vv. 21–22).[11]

Within the lengthy section that compares with an individual protest in vv. 1–16, the train of thought, the different perspectives, and some verbal markers suggest subdivisions, so that the poem as a whole works as follows:

6. K. M. O'Connor, "Lamentations," *NIB*, in her introduction to Lam 4.

7. Dobbs-Allsopp, *Lamentations*, 129.

8. Berlin, *Lamentations*, 103, 104.

9. See S. E. Balentine, "'Away! Unclean! Do not Touch!': Defiled and Defiling Priests in Lamentations," in Melton and H. A. Thomas, *Reading Lamentations Intertextually*.

10. Bailey, "Lamentations," 55.

11. Kraus, *Klagelieder*, 73.

vv. 1–6 The perspective is the period before the actual fall of Jerusalem, a time especially marked by starvation. The speaker uses the first-person singular. The lament focuses on the fate of children. The section closes with a kind of moral comment on what happened.

vv. 7–11 The speaker continues in the first-person singular, describing more generally the reversal of experience that came on people in the city—well-to-do people, ordinary people, mothers, and children again. The section closes with a theological comment on what happened.

vv. 12–16 The section starts from an implicit question, which it implicitly answers by recalling the wrongdoing of prophets and priests; it suggests a recollection of the period between 597 and 587, when many or most prophets and priests had already gone into exile. Once again, the section closes with a theological comment on what it has related.[12]

vv. 17–20 Here the speaker uses the first-person plural in recalling how things were for "us" on the eve and in the aftermath of the fall of the city, as "we" looked in vain for help and then were subject to pursuit. It again closes with an implicit theological comment as it notes the disappointment of hopes in Yahweh's anointed.

vv. 21–22 Again the theme changes: the poem closes with declarations to Edom and to Zion of what Yahweh intends to do with them that compare with messages to other nations in the Prophets. The voice is perhaps again that of the original "I." The perspective may be not the immediate aftermath of the city's fall but circumstances a little later.

aleph [1]*How the gold was being made dim,*[a]
the fine gold was changing.
The sacred stones[b] *were pouring out*
at the beginning of all the streets.

a. *Yûʿam* is apparently *hophal* from *ʿāmam* II. I translate the three *yiqtol* verbs as past imperfect in light of the past reference of the event they refer to (see v. 2).

b. With LXX I take the construct phrase as adjectival; Vg has "the stones of the sanctuary."

1 While it would be natural enough for a Jerusalemite to lament the destruction of the temple with its gold and its well-hewn stone, it might seem an odd starting point for the lament. But in due course, the second stanza with

12. Kraus (*Klagelieder*, 75–80) also subdivides vv. 1–16 in this way.

its further allusion to gold and its use of pots as a metaphor will suggest that gold and stones are a metaphor here. *Gold* is supposed to shine brightly, and so were the people of Jerusalem, but the gold has lost its sheen or has been covered in smoke.[13] In the parallelism, an alternative, rarer term for *gold* is also enhanced by the addition of the word *fine* (the word literally means "good"), while the new verb *was changing* makes an understatement. Gold does not actually go dim or change, so the poem begins with a telling impossibility. "The power of the metaphor derives precisely from the fact that gold, unusually impervious to tarnishing, here loses its luster."[14] The impossibility anticipates the hyperbole that runs through the poem. "Something which is known to be against nature is taking place."[15]

The main body of the temple is made of the impressive *stones* to which the second line refers, which are *sacred* by virtue of being structurally part of Yahweh's sacred palace. They once fit together tightly, but just now they *were pouring out*, tumbling from their place in the structure. They were doing so *at the beginning of all the streets*, the center of the city from which the streets branch off, and thus throughout the city (see 2:19). It makes for a frightening image, bringing to mind the effects of an earthquake, but the hyperbole also prepares the way for the coming interpretation of the figure in terms of people. It will turn out to suggest human beings collapsing all over the city. But the audience does not know it yet. To rediscover what the gold and the stones stand for, the audience must listen on.[16] The relationship between the stanzas in the first section of the poem (vv. 1–6) parallels the relationship that sometimes obtains within a line, when the first colon raises a question that the second colon answers.

bet 2*Zion's children, valuable,*
weighed out in refined gold—
How they came to be reckoned as like clay vessels,
the work of a potter's hands.

13. Rashi (in MG) finds a reference to Josiah here, though R. B. Salters notes that Rashi does not think in terms of Josiah in the main body of his comments on the chapter ("Using Rashi, Ibn Ezra and Joseph Kara on Lamentations," *JNSL* 25 [1999]: 205–7), except in connection with v. 20.

14. Gordis, *Song of Songs and Lamentations*, 188.

15. M. L. Mitchell, "Reading of the Imagery of Lamentations," 171; cf. M. L. Mitchell, "Reflecting on Catastrophe," in *The Function of Ancient Historiography in Biblical and Cognate Studies*, ed. P. G. Kirkpatrick and T. Goltz, LHBOTS 489 (London: T&T Clark, 2008), 79, 82.

16. If it knew the poem in Song of Songs about gold (Song 5:10–16), the question might be all the more puzzling; see M. F. Strollo, "The Value of the Relationship: An Intertextual reading of Song of Songs and Lamentations," *RevExp* 114 (2017): 190–212.

2 The stones, then, represent people (cf. 1 Peter 2:5),[17] *ʾabnê* for *bənê*. They stand for *Zion's children*. That expression comes otherwise only in Ps 149:2 and Joel 2:23, where it denotes the people of Jerusalem in general. Zion's earlier reference to *my children* (1:16; cf. Jer 10:20; also Baruch 4:12, 19, 21, 25, 27) would encourage that understanding. Yet what will follow will again cause a reconsideration of the assumption, because actual little children will be the focus of the subsequent verses and of much of the chapter as a whole.[18] It "is most graphic and blistering in its account of their suffering."[19] The stones themselves were *valuable*; *stones* can denote precious stones,[20] but the context in v. 1 with its reference to stones pouring down the streets suggests valuable building stone (cf. 1 Kgs 5:17[31]). Whereas gold and stone would have suggested two separate things in v. 1 (the stone of which the temple was built and the gold with which parts of it were enhanced), here the children for whom the stones stood, the stones themselves, and the gold have become conflated, as gold becomes the measure of the children's value. At least, it was the way they were supposed to be valued, by Yahweh (Pss 72:14; 116:15; Isa 43:4). To underline the point further, Lamentations adds yet another word for gold, a term that perhaps especially denotes *refined gold*.

The heightening of the point about value prepares the way for the contrast: the people, and specifically the children of Jerusalem, have been treated like disposable clay containers—not even fired but quickly shaped by a potter and easily thrown onto the trash heap without a second thought. They aren't even broken pots![21] The *yiqtol* verbs of v. 1 give way to *qatal* verbs, and what follows is more overtly a recollection of the situation in Jerusalem in the months leading up to the city's fall.

How was the devaluing expressed? The audience must again listen on.

gimel 3*Even jackals*[a]*—they pull out the breast,*
they nurse their babies.[b]
My dear people[c] *turned cruel,*[d]
like ostriches[e] *in the wilderness.*

a. The *qere*'s *tannîm* is the usual word for jackals; the *ketiv* implies *tannîn*, which is usually the singular word for a sea monster (cf. LXX, Vg. Tg). The verbs are plural, and while the *qere*'s text may not be original, its implied interpretation is surely right.

b. The two *qatal* verbs are "gnomic": a single instance exemplifies something recurrent (*IBHS* 30.4b).

17. Cf. Re'emi, "Lamentations," 120.

18. Renkema, *Lamentations*, 489.

19. K. M. O'Connor, "Lamentations," *NIB*, on the verse.

20. Cf. J. A. Emerton, "The Meaning of *ʾabnê-qōdeš* in Lamentations 4 1," *ZAW* 79 (1967): 233–36.

21. Cf. Renkema, *Lamentations*, 497.

c. LXX "daughters of my people" implies *bənôt-ʿammî* for MT *bat-ʿammî*, assimilating to the context.

d. Lit. "the daughter my people into cruel."

e. It is difficult to make sense of the *ketiv*'s division of the word into two: *ky ʿnym*.

3 *Jackals* are an unhappy comparison in the First Testament (see, e.g., Job 30:29; Jer 9:11[10]; Mic 1:8), so it is forceful to set them forward as a model for mothering. *Ostriches* appear elsewhere in the company of jackals (e.g., Job 30:29; Mic 1:8). Etymologically, the word (*yāʿēn*) may suggest they were thought to be greedy creatures,[22] and Job 39:13–18 (using another term for "ostrich") gives them an unfavorable profile. What had made the people of Jerusalem, *my dear people* (cf. 2:11; 3:48), seem to have turned from gold to clay was that they had come to behave more cruelly than jackals and as cruelly as ostriches.[23] "Something against the natural order is happening."[24]

How had they done so? The audience must again listen on.

dalet [4]*A baby's tongue stuck,*
to its palate, with thirst.
When infants asked for bread,[a]
there was no one breaking it[b] *for them.*

a. The asyndeton combined with the placing of the subject before the verb suggests that this clause is subordinate to the following one.

b. The verb is *pāraś* ("spread"), but Vg, LXX imply it is a variant spelling for *pāras* (cf. Mic 3:3); the tense of the verb in the first colon suggests the time reference of this participle.

4 The image of jackal mothers had a more precise significance than we might have realized. Whereas jackals fed their babies, *a baby's tongue stuck to its palate with thirst* in Jerusalem. It was not (one may assume) because its mother was deliberately cruel but because she could not produce any milk and had to behave as if cruel. Her baby is then either so dry from thirst that its tongue sticks to the roof of its mouth or it is so weak from starvation that it no longer cries.[25]

Neither could anyone give the slightly older children something to eat. The idea of ostriches being cruel is probably a myth; the Jerusalem mothers, too, were likely grieved rather than happy at not being able to provide for their children.

22. See BDB.

23. On these animal comparisons, see A. Labahn, "Wild Animals and Chasing Shadows," in van Hecke, *Metaphor in the Hebrew Bible*, 77–82.

24. M. L. Mitchell, "Reading of the Imagery of Lamentations," 175.

25. Berlin, *Lamentations*, 106.

he [5]*People who ate gourmet food—*
they became desolate in the streets.
People who were raised in purple—
they clung to trash heaps.

5 The transformation from refined gold to disposable pottery extended beyond ordinary children. In the months of the city's siege, well-to-do families were also affected. For them, the deprivation made for a bigger contrast over against their usual experience. The context and the reference to how the subjects were *raised* suggest that the poem continues to speak of the children in particular. These children were used to eating really well and were *raised in purple* (the word literally suggests scarlet). In describing them, the two lines work a-b-b'-a'. Instead of eating *gourmet food,* they were foraging on *trash heaps,* as really poor people often have to. *Desolate* (*šāmēm,* here *niphal*) is one of the default descriptions of Jerusalem's material state and of its people's consequent emotional state after the city's fall (the *qal* comes in 1:4, 13, 16; 3:11; 5:18). The children's desolation contrasts with their upbringing in their finery.

Why was it so? The audience must again listen on.

waw [6]*So*[a] *the waywardness of my dear people was greater*
than the wrongdoing of Sodom,
Which was overturned as in a moment
when no hands whirled[b] *against it.*

a. If v. 6 provides an answer to the question why things had been turned upside down, one might expect it to begin "because," but the alphabetic sequence suggests a *waw*.

b. LXX "labor" suggests *ḥālâ,* and Sym "wounded" suggests *ḥālal,* but more likely the verb is *ḥûl.*

6 The meaning of the words for *waywardness* and *wrongdoing* (*ʿāwōn* and *ḥaṭṭaʾt*) can glide into denoting punishment for the relevant offenses, and both aspects of the words' meaning would be appropriate here. The deprivation just described establishes how grim Judah's offensiveness was and illustrates how grim the consequences were. *Sodom* is a regular and appalling image for both waywardness and catastrophe (e.g., Gen 18–19; Deut 29:23; Isa 1:9–10; 3:9; 13:19; Jer 23:14; 49:18; 50:40). So it could be a standard for measuring a city such as Babylon and describing its fate. Lamentations follows Deuteronomy and some Prophets in referring to it in connection with Israel. Indeed, the poem says that Judah's offensiveness and overturning (the word in Gen 19:25) were actually greater than Sodom's. A further difference between Jerusalem and Sodom was that Yahweh acted directly against Sodom, whereas it was the *hands* of earthly adversaries that *whirled* against Jerusalem. Along with the opening *waw*-consecutive, the move to providing a theological/moral comment and the picking up of the phrase *my dear people* advertise that this line is bringing a section of the poem to a close. "With this appraisal the poet puts on the mantle of a prophet."[26]

zayin [7]*Its special people*[a] *were purer than snow,*
they were brighter than milk.
They were ruddier in body than coral,
their hair[b] *was sapphire.*

a. While *nəzîrîm* are usually people dedicated to Yahweh in a distinctive way ("Nazirites"), that meaning does not fit here. But *nēzer* can mean a crown, which suggests a meaning such as princes here.

b. Etymologically, *gizrâ* should have something to do with cutting, but the meaning in this context is a matter of guesswork.

7 In this second section, the poem moves from the fate of the children, and specifically the well-to-do ones, to that of their parents; it will come back to the children. The *special people* may be the members of the royal family or whoever might count as nobility. The word for *were purer* (*zākak*, with related words) commonly denotes moral or religious cleanness, but it can also denote physical purity; the context and the parallelism with the word for *were brighter* suggest that idea here. In climates other than those in much of Europe and the United States, having fair skin can be a sign of status. It means you do not spend your day working in the fields (cf. Song 1:5–6). The line is referring to people who looked good and were in good health.

There might thus seem to be some tension with the next line, which could suggest being tanned, but coral is often pink in color, so perhaps the idea is that their skin is pink rather than brown. *Sapphire* or lapis lazuli implies blue; while the princes may not have had literally blue hair, hair or eyebrows (for instance) could be portrayed as blue to signify their splendor (cf. Song 5:14).[27]

What is the point of this comment on their impressiveness? It is necessary to read on.

khet [8]*Their appearance became darker than black,*[a]
they were not recognized in the streets.
Their skin shriveled on their body
as it became dry as wood.[b]

26. Berges, *Klagelieder*, 246.

27. Koenen, *Klagelieder*, 333–34.

a. LXX, Vg make the comparison more concrete by translating the *hapax legomenon* *šəḥôr* "soot" or "coal."

b. The word order with the adjective preceding the verb combined with the asyndeton suggests that this clause is subordinate to the preceding one.

8 Whatever the uncertainties of v. 7, the contrast is clear. *Darker than black* contrasts with *brighter than milk*. It is a hyperbole; more literally, they looked gray. Being members of the well-to-do or the royal family changes to *they were not recognized in the streets* because they no longer looked royal and impressive. Their healthy bodies became emaciated, and their skin hung off their bones.

Again, why was it so? It will be a while before the poem says.

tet [9]*Better were the people run through by the sword*
than the ones run through by hunger;
Better were those people who would flow, wounded,
than the ones without the produce of the countryside.[a]

a. The second line simply reads "those people who would flow, wounded, without the produce of the countryside"; the parallelism with the first line presupposes an ellipsis of the phrases at the beginning of each colon (cf. Gordis, *Song of Songs and Lamentations*, 190–91).

9 Jeremiah commonly refers to the two threats of enemy attack as "sword and hunger" (e.g., 5:12; 14:15–16). They feature here with an extra nuance in speaking of who is "better off." Whereas *run through* literally signifies death *by the sword*, here it also metaphorically signifies death *by hunger* or starvation.

The second line expands on the point more concretely so that the verse as a whole works a-b-a'-b'. It pictures people who *would flow*; more literally, their blood would flow. It thus adapts a term for fluid flowing from a man or woman's body, including discharges of blood (Lev 15:25), and adds *wounded* because it is referring to this different reason for blood flowing. The other familiar use of the verb refers to the country of Canaan flowing with milk and sweetness (e.g., Jer 11:5), which facilitates another contrast between dying in battle and dying because *the produce of the countryside*, food in general, is not flowing.

yod [10]*The hands of compassionate women—*
they have cooked their children.
They became something to devour[a] *for them*
through the breaking of my dear people.

a. BDB takes *bārôt* as *piel* infinitive, which suggests "eating up" or "devouring," though Schäfer ("Lamentations," 132*) takes it as a composite of the noun *bārût* and the *qal* infinitive construct *bərôt* .

10 There is a coup de grâce to the description of the grim transformation with which the poem began, as it affects children and mothers.[28] These are *compassionate* women, women with a womb and with the feelings for the offspring of that womb that go with it (see the commentary on 3:22). Not calling them mothers here perhaps suggests that it is too horrific any longer to see them that way. Describing them as *compassionate* is then either sarcastic or tragic,[29] in that they have *cooked their children* to eat them (see the commentary on 2:20). In case the audience has failed to get the point, the poem adds that thus the children *became something to devour for them*. The line involves a contradiction like the contradiction in v. 1: it is impossible for gold to tarnish, and it is impossible for mothers to cook their children.[30]

> Throughout Lamentations, conflicting images—the merciful YHWH, the angry YHWH; the protesting sufferer, the penitent sufferer—alternate. Here in Lam 4, incompatible images—precious children, abandoned as worthless in the streets; compassionate women, consuming the fruit of their womb—are given in the very same breath, increasing the intensity of disorientation. Rather than an indictment of the women then, the imagery graphically portrays the desperation of the situation: even a mother's compassion for her child is a sheer impossibility.[31]

Such is one mark of *the breaking of my dear people* (cf. 2:11, 13; 3:47, 48). Perhaps the verse is another hyperbole; but compare 1 Kgs 3:16–28; 2 Kgs 6:26–30.[32] If it is, the poem nevertheless invites its audience to imagine the literal reality in order to appreciate the grimness of that transformation. Here the "rhetoric of hunger" that appeared in Lam 1–2 reaches its most intense. Starvation itself is a regular policy implemented by besieging armies; it appears in the city laments. It issues in people's "psychosocial dehumanization." In light of v. 9, perhaps cooking their children actually was an expression of compassion—providing them with a quicker death and providing the survivors with one more bitter meal—rather than an action that contrasted with compassion.[33]

kaph [11]*Yahweh expended his wrath,*
poured out his angry blazing.

28. Berges, *Klagelieder*, 249.

29. Koenen, *Klagelieder*, 338.

30. M. L. Mitchell, "Reading of the Imagery of Lamentations," 182.

31. Bier, *"Perhaps There Is Hope"*, 151.

32. M. L. Mitchell, "Reading of the Imagery of Lamentations," 181–82.

33. L. L. Wilkins, "War, Famine and Baby Stew: A Recipe for Disaster in the Book of Lamentations," in *By Bread Alone: The Bible through the Eyes of the Hungry*, ed. S. E. McGinn, L. L. E. Ngan, and A. C. Pilarski (Minneapolis: Fortress, 2014), 71, 79, 81.

Thus he lit a fire in Zion
and it consumed its foundations.

11 The poem's second section, like the first, comes to a close with some theological interpretation of what we have been reading. The horror of the image in v. 10 fits with and finds interpretation in the horror of what here follows. "What has happened is too much, unprecedented and beyond expression."[34] Those actions of compassionate women were an expression or result of the fact that Yahweh *expended his wrath,* held none of it back, as that horror suggests. He gave total expression to it, and thus *poured out his angry blazing* (cf. 2:4, 11). The pouring out of the stones (v. 1) is an articulation of the pouring out of this wrath, and his expending his wrath thus stands in tension with his not having expended all his compassion (3:22). Whether it makes it worse or better, once more "by Yahweh's wrath is meant not a spontaneous emotion of God, but a calculated reaction to human guilt."[35] Given that redress and recompense thus belong to Yahweh, "falling into the hands of the living God is frightening" (Heb 10:31, quoting Deut 32:35).[36]

The final catastrophe involved a literal burning down of the city by Nebuchadnezzar and his agents (Jer 52:13), but the poem is not here interested in the Babylonians' burning but in the fact that Yahweh *lit a fire in Zion* so that it *consumed its foundations.* A city fire would commonly consume roofs and walls; to say that the fire consumed a city's foundations is to say how radical its effect was. There would surely be no hope for the rebuilding of that city.[37] Yahweh's expending all his wrath meant he destroyed the city down to the ground and below it. And he did it to *Zion.* With this pronouncement we come to the halfway point in the poem, to the end of the first half, in which it has described the realities of life during the siege and then summed things up in this verse.

lamed [12]*The kings of the earth did not believe,*
any[a] *people living in the world,*
That adversary or enemy would come
through Jerusalem's gateways.[b]

a. For the *qere*'s *kōl,* the *ketiv* has *wkl* ("or any"), an easier reading.

b. The word order would permit "that adversary would come/ or enemy through Jerusalem's gateways," against MT accents, which would make for parallelism (Koenen, *Klagelieder,* 305), but the poems' lines sometimes work so that the second colon simply completes what is begun in the first (e.g., v. 4a); see the translation note on 3:31.

34. M. L. Mitchell, "Reading of the Imagery of Lamentations," 185.

35. Koenen, *Klagelieder,* 340.

36. Kraus, *Klagelieder,* 84.

37. Calvin, *Jeremiah and Lamentations,* 5:565.

12 Whereas the stanzas in the first half of the poem were often interlinked, v. 12 makes a new start; there is no specific connection with what preceded. One could say that it recalls v. 1, where there were gold and intact stone in Jerusalem, or v. 7, where the special people were in good shape. Once again the poem speaks in hyperbole. One doubts whether many kings or peoples in the ancient Near East thought about the question this verse raises,[38] though they may have recognized that Jerusalem was a tricky town to take (Sennacherib and Nebuchadnezzar left Jerusalem until last when seeking to conquer Judah). But the point about the poet's statement is to signify that "Jerusalem's destruction is simply unthinkable,"[39] like other things the poem has said. Yahweh had given Judah reason to hold the conviction expressed here. People knew that he had chosen Jerusalem as a permanent place to settle down (Ps 132:14). They knew that he loved Zion's gateways (Ps 87:2; see Ps 48 and the commentary on 2:15). Although *adversary* and *enemy* got close to the *gateways* of Jerusalem in Isaiah's day, they had not come through them (see Isa 29:1–8; 31:1–9; 36:1–37:38; it is Jerusalem, not Zion, that the poem names here).

mem [13]*Because of its prophets' wrongdoings,*
its priests' wayward acts,
People who had poured out within it
the blood of the faithful.

13 So why were the expectations of v. 12 not fulfilled? For that matter, why did Yahweh's fury have to pour out? Why did the stones pour out? Why had things gone so wrong in Judah? Verses 13–16 have a distinctive explanation. The verse begins in an abrupt way, and its two lines do not comprise a complete sentence. We might need to understand "it happened because . . ." or assume that the lines follow from the sentence in v. 11 or that they lead into v. 14.[40] However the syntactical question should be resolved, the verse implies the problem that people could easily forget the "if" attached to Yahweh's commitments to David and Zion (e.g., Ps 132:12). In this connection, Lamentations here places the entire blame for the catastrophe on *prophets* and *priests*, which largely agrees with Jeremiah's account. "Prophets and priests were two eyes as it were in the Church"; and "the very prophets and priests were the cause of ruin."[41] The poem picks up the words *wrongdoing* and *waywardness* from v. 6 but associates them in particular with the city's religious leaders. And it turns them into the plural so that they suggest concrete acts.

38. Cf. Clines, "Lamentations," 621.
39. K. M. O'Connor, "Lamentations," *NIB*, on the verse.
40. Hillers, *Lamentations*, 141.
41. Calvin, *Jeremiah and Lamentations*, 5:568.

What are these acts? The second line answers the question raised by the first. It is a partly different answer to the one we might have expected in that it says nothing about uttering false prophecies or serving other deities (which Tg mentions). The unexpected nature of the logic is thus the converse of that in 3:40–42. Prophets and priests were people *who had poured out within it the blood of the faithful*: here is that verb *pour out* yet again. The pouring out of vv. 1 and 11 finds its explanation; the prophets and priests make us think of the "murderous clerics" of church history.[42] How had they poured out blood? Jeremiah might have had several sorts of answer. One is that they were engaged in or had colluded with the offering of human sacrifice, though there is no pointer in that direction here. Another is that they were engaged with or had colluded with people swindling others of their land and thereby their livelihood and thus in due course robbing them of their lives; the reference to *the faithful* suggests people who were in the right, which fits with this possibility. *The blood of the faithful* is what Jeremiah calls "the blood of the innocent" (e.g., Jer 7:6; 19:4; 22:3, 17). Their killing is what makes Jerusalem a bloody city (Ezek 24:9).[43] Yet a further Jeremianic context in which there is reference to priests and prophets potentially shedding the blood of an innocent man is Jer 26:15, where they are wondering about shedding a prophet's blood, and such shedding follows in 26:20–23. This motif also appears in Matt 23:35—one of the links between Matthew and Lamentations that points to Lamentations being a significant "Matthean intertext."[44]

nun [14]*They*[a] *roamed blind through the streets,*
they had defiled themselves with blood.
People that they should not,[b]
they would touch[c] *their clothes.*

a. Grammatically, "they" might be the faithful, but v. 13 implied that the faithful had been killed, and anyway they were hardly people who "had defiled themselves." "They" might be people in general; but who, then, are the people in v. 14b? "Blind people" might be the verb's subject; but who are these people? It makes sense for it to be the priests and prophets of v. 13 who are roaming, which leads well into what follows.

b. For MT *bəlōʾ*, 5QLam has *bal*, an easier reading (Schäfer, "Lamentations," 132*).

c. Sym "so that they could not touch their clothing" takes the second verb as asyndetically dependent on the first (cf. GK 120g), but there are no parallels for this usage with *yākōl*, and the division between the cola is hard.

42. C. J. H. Wright, *Lamentations*, 140.

43. See further A. Kalmanofsky, "The Sound and the Fury: Women and Suffering in Ezekiel and Lamentations," in Melton and H. A. Thomas, *Reading Lamentations Intertextually*.

44. D. M. Moffitt, "Righteous Bloodshed, Matthew's Passion Narrative, and the Temple's Destruction: Lamentations as a Matthean Intertext," *JBL* 125 (2006): 299–320; see more broadly R. A. Parry, "Jesus and Jerusalem: Christological Interpretations of Lamentations in the Church," in Melton and H. A. Thomas, *Reading Lamentations Intertextually*.

14 Throughout the section comprising vv. 12–16, the links are elliptical and the audience has to connect some dots. Whether or not v. 13 leads grammatically into v. 14, I take it that *they* are the prophets and priests of v. 13 and that the stanza's point is that the actions of priests and prophets had led into what v. 14 describes. Those actions described in v. 13 meant that priests and prophets *had defiled themselves with blood*, and as a result (through Yahweh's action?) they became people who *roamed blind*. They were bewildered, and they did not know where they were going (cf. Zeph 1:17; also Isa 56:10; 59:10). As priests and prophets, they were supposed to be able to open people's eyes to the right way to walk, but they are themselves unable to see.

In the second line, the poem continues to imagine the fate that befell them, but here it is trickier to identify who is who, though the logic of the line is clear enough. While "the background to the sentiments expressed here (and in v. 15) is to be found in strict ancient taboos among primitive peoples,"[45] the taboos are not just ancient ones and they are not just found among primitive peoples. In Shakespeare's play *Macbeth*, Lady Macbeth knew that she had blood on her hands through her involvement in the plot to murder King Duncan (even though she had not personally committed the murder). People in modern Western cultures can be aware that they are stained as a result of something they have done, and other people may not want to associate with them or even touch them because they may then come to be affected by the stain. These prophets and priests were stained through their involvement in bringing death to innocent people, and other Judahites would not want to be affected, through colluding with their action, by the stain that attached to them. The more specific idea of the line might then be that other people would not be willing to take hold of the blind prophets and priests in order to help them find their way. Or more likely, the prophets and priests would take hold of other people in order to be able to find their way. While the prophets and priests should not touch people or their clothes because it would convey defilement, they did so.[46]

samek [15] *"Go away, unclean,"*[a]
people called to them.
"Go away, go away, don't touch,"
when they roved,[b] *yes, roamed.*
People said among the nations,
"They should not reside any longer."[c]

45. Salters, *Lamentations*, 318.

46. See L.-S. Tiemeyer, "The Question of Indirect Touch: Lam 4,14; Ezek 44,19 and Hag 2,12–13," *Bib* 87 (2006): 64–74.

a. For singular *ṭāmē'*, 5QLam has *ṭm'w* ("they are unclean"); cf. LXX, Vg. The plural is neater in the context, but MT's text might have been assimilated to Lev 13:45 (Kotzé, *Qumran Manuscripts of Lamentations*, 140).

b. *Nāṣû* looks like a form from *nāṣâ* I (fight) or II (go to ruin). Perhaps the latter verb's meaning has been stretched in order to use a word that alliterates with *nā'û*, which follows. Ibn Ezra (in MG) and Qara in the Breslau version of his commentary (D. Anderson, "Medieval Jewish Exegesis," 96) apparently see it as coming from *nāṣâ* III, or from *nûṣ*, meaning "fly" or "flee" (see BDB, *HALOT*, *DCH*); I translate "roved" to preserve the alliteration with "roamed."

c. The one three-line verse in the poem can be reduced to the usual two lines by omitting the second and fifth cola as explanatory glosses (e.g., Kraus, *Klagelieder*, 72, 79).

15 Once again, the broad point here is clear, but the details regarding who speaks to whom are less so. The broad point is that people affected by a taboo have a responsibility not only to avoid touch but also to make sure that other people know about their taboo so that they do not inadvertently become affected by it. Being affected by most taboos does not matter too much; it matters only if you wish to go to the temple in the near future. In the context of life in the wilderness, people with the taboo that comes from a skin disease are to warn people by shouting out *unclean* and also to stay outside the camp until their ailment has cleared up (Lev 13:45–46). Here in v. 15, it seems that other people are issuing the shout from a distance to the priests and prophets who *roved* and *roamed* about because they were unable to see where they were going. They are urging them to make themselves scarce and thus not transmit their taboo, which is much more serious than the kind to which Lev 15 refers. "Voices out of nowhere cry out: Away! Unclean! 'Get away! Get away! Do not touch!' This interruption of speech bursts abruptly into the poem, bringing with it a very real sense of immediacy and presence. All of a sudden we are there in the streets and are warding off these blind beggars."[47] Ironically, it was in general the priests' job to determine what counted as uncleanness for people (see Lev 13–14); the roles are now reversed.[48]

So the priests and the prophets should *go away*—three times people repeat the exhortation to these poor, pathetic, lost, unseeing religious leaders who do not know where they are and cannot see which way to go. *Don't touch*, they add, repeating the verb from v. 14b—because of the fact that touch transmits defilement. In Isa 52:11, "go away" (*sûr*) refers to Judahites leaving exile to go back to Jerusalem. Here it might encourage the priests and prophets to go away from Judah into exile; they would be free to live as resident aliens in a foreign country (cf. Ezra 1:4).[49] The imaginative picture

47. F. W. Dobbs-Allsopp, *On Biblical Poetry* (New York: Oxford University Press, 2015), 209.

48. Cf. Re'emi, "Lamentations," 123.

49. Koenen, *Klagelieder*, 347–49.

in the one tricolon in the poem thus describes the priests and prophets as having to continue their roaming—"do it somewhere else, please."

But rules about taboo are not confined to Israel. So not surprisingly, the priests and prophets find that even foreigners want nothing to do with them. It is a very different picture from the vision of the response *among the nations* elsewhere (see Joel 2:17; Ps 126:2).[50] The priests and prophets were not even to be able to live as resident aliens in a foreign land. They were to be permanent wanderers. "It is the beginning of the popular theme of the 'wandering Jew.'"[51]

> pe [16]*Yahweh in person—he shared them out,*[a]
> *he would no longer take note of them.*
> *The person of the priests people did not recognize,*
> *to the elders they did not show favor.*

a. For MT *ḥilləqām,* LXX "their share" implies *ḥelqām.*

16 Thus the poem pictures the priests and prophets as the victims of Yahweh's scattering, but the further odd form of expression, *he shared them out* (*ḥālaq hiphil*), carries a biting irony.[52] Israelite families had a share (*ḥēleq*) in the dividing up of land, though strictly this arrangement did not apply to priests. They were not mere resident aliens in the country; they were beneficiaries of land distribution. Here the priests are the victims of distribution or scattering. *Yahweh in person* is literally "Yahweh's face." The face occasionally stands for the person in this way elsewhere (Exod 33:14–15; 2 Sam 17:11; Ps 34:16[17]; Isa 63:9);[53] here the unusual form of expression enables the line to begin with *pe.* "Yahweh's face" is usually a positive image; for the present context, the priestly blessing (Num 6:24–26) would be a significant and ironic example. When the king's face shone on you, it meant his favor; so it is with Yahweh the King. But here Yahweh's face has operated in a hostile fashion toward the priests and the prophets in dividing them up away from the country where land had been divided up among his people. *Take note* of us, Lamentations has repeatedly urged Yahweh (1:11, 12; 2:20; 3:63). He would not take note of these people as he once did.

The *pe* word for face or person repeats in the second line, with another irony. Yahweh's person turned against them; and other people turned against

50. Koenen, *Klagelieder*, 349.

51. *CTAT*, 912 (actually, Hos 9:17 may be the beginning).

52. Renkema, *Lamentations*, 543

53. A. S. Peake, *Jeremiah and Lamentations*, vol. 2, Century Bible (London: Caxton, 1911 [?]), 342.

their person. They did not recognize them—literally, "they did not lift up the priests' face." Lifting the face is, again, especially the action of a king or someone else with power or status toward people without power or status (e.g., Gen 19:21; 32:21; Deut 10:17; 1 Sam 25:35). Someone with less power or status lowers their face toward the other person, who may then lift it up. Likewise to *show favor* (*ḥānan*) is the action of a person with power or resources toward someone who lacks them (Prov 14:31); the one showing favor is usually Yahweh. In a chapter whose warnings Lamentations often reflects, Deut 28:50 applies both verbs to the nation that will swoop down on Israel as a consequence of its ignoring Yahweh's expectations of it, specifically on youths and elders, and will not recognize them or show favor. Thus here, pointedly, *the elders* take the place of the prophets alongside *the priests* as the people who deserve and receive the treatment they get from their own people or from the nations. If the *people* are Babylonians, to say that they did not recognize or show favor is a litotes.[54]

Once again the explicit reference to Yahweh's involvement signals that we are coming to the end of a section.

ayin [17]*Even yet*[a] *our eyes were failing*[b]
for help for us,[c] *in vain.*[d]
In our watchtower[e] *we watched*
for a nation that would not deliver.

a. The *ketiv* has *'wdynh* (lit. "[in] their continuance"); the *qere* has *'ôdênû* ("[in] our continuance"); see BDB, 728.

b. I follow Vg in taking the *yiqtol* verb to have past imperfect significance (LXX has aorist); the verb in the second line makes more explicit the past reference of this stanza, as it recalls the situation before the fall of Jerusalem.

c. Lit. "for our help."

d. I follow LXX in taking *hebel* adverbially (cf. Job 9:29; 21:34); Vg, Tg take it as in apposition, "help for us [that is] vain" (cf. *TTH*, 193), which is also an appropriate idea (see the commentary).

e. For the *hapax legomenon ṣippiyyâ*, LXX, Vg have more abstract expressions denoting being on the watch.

17 As the reference to Yahweh in v. 16 suggested the end of a section, the move from third-person speech to first-person plural speech now signals the start of a new section. The further change from first-person singular speech in vv. 1–6 to first-person plural speech here might also mean that the speaker changes from an individual to a corporate body. Either way, the poem identifies with the people of whom it speaks. The new start also brings a change of theme and

54. Koenen, *Klagelieder*, 351.

a change of perspective. Here the poem again implies the situation of people in Jerusalem itself on the eve of the city's fall, the situation presupposed in vv. 1–11. But there is no more talk about the deprivation of that experience. First, the poem recalls the way people were hoping for support from their allies: "Jerusalem's populace never ceased looking for a political solution to their problem."[55] Presumably the allies are the Egyptians, who did accidentally give Jerusalem some relief when the Babylonian army had to go and sort them out in 589–588; but the help was only momentary (cf. Jer 37:7; Ezek 17:15–17). Yet people kept on hoping, and did so in such a way that *our eyes were failing*. They became used up: the verb occurs elsewhere in connection with looking for Yahweh to act and deliver in a way that one can hope will be fruitful (Ps 119:81, 82, 123). But this looking was *vain* (*hebel*); it had empty results.[56]

The second line restates the point more sharply. Metaphorically speaking, at least, we stood *in our watchtower* (*ṣippiyyâ*); the fact that Mizpah (*ham-miṣpâ*) means "The Watchtower" constitutes a reminder that the authorities in Jerusalem would literally keep watch a little distance from the city for the approach of enemies. *We*, then, might be specifically the nation's political leaders, as opposed to the religious leaders who were in focus in vv. 11–16.[57] This watching is indeed a positive, hopeful straining of the eyes: *we watched* like lookouts hoping that the cavalry would appear over the horizon any day. But straining the eyes hoping for help is an expression that applies to expectations of Yahweh, not of *a nation* like the Egyptians, an expectation against which Jeremiah issued many a warning. They *would not deliver*. That verb, too, only really works with Yahweh as subject. Isaiah had long ago issued the warning: Egypt's so-called help would be vain, empty (Isa 30:7).[58] So did Jeremiah (e.g., Jer 37:7).[59] It transpires that v. 17a was more ironic than we may have noticed. People were not only looking for help in a way that was useless; they were looking for help from a nation whose help would be useless if it materialized.

tsade 18*People hounded our steps*
so that we couldn't go into our squares.
"Our final end[a] *has drawn near, our days are full,*
because our final end has come."

55. House, *Lamentations*, 446.

56. N. C. Lee finds Abel (*hebel*) here in the context of other links with Gen 4, such as the verb "wander" ("Exposing a Buried Subtext in Jeremiah and Lamentations," in *Troubling Jeremiah*, ed. A. R. P. Diamond, K. M. O'Connor, and L. Stulman, JSOTSup 260 [Sheffield: Sheffield Academic, 1999], 121).

57. Koenen, *Klagelieder*, 351.

58. Rashi, in MG.

59. LamR on the passage.

a. Here and in the parallel colon, *qēṣ* is plural (as if signifying "our ends"), though the verbs are singular. LXX has "time," in keeping with the common meaning of *qēṣ* in later Hebrew (S. Talmon, "קֵץ, *qēṣ*," *TDOT* 13:78–86).

18 So no help came, and the siege continued. "We were like animals that were being hunted" (it is the same verb as in 3:52). Maybe the picture is of the attackers building siege towers from which they could fire into the city, so that people did not dare go out into the open squares where people met.

The repetition within the second colon suggests that the poem is quoting words people repeated to one another as the city's fall drew near. *End* (*qēṣ*) can denote an end in an ordinary sense, but it can also denote a cataclysmic end or an end that means we no longer exist. The strange use of the plural for *end* suggests one of the latter meanings (see the translation note). If *our days are full*, it means death (2 Sam 7:12). We've had it.

qoph [19]*Our pursuers were quicker*
than the eagles in the heavens.
On the mountains they were hot after us,
in the wilderness they lay in wait for us.

19 The poem jumps to the aftermath of the city's fall, when the Babylonians pursued Zedekiah and his troops down into the Jordan Valley and overtook them. They were perhaps fitter and better provisioned and thus disarmingly *quicker than the eagles in the heavens* (cf. Jer 4:13), even though they didn't know the territory as the Judahites did.

So down *on the mountains they were hot after us*[60] and then *in the wilderness they lay in wait for us.* In other contexts the parallelism might suggest that mountains and wilderness are general terms for the land as a whole, but here the words point to the sequence of events narrated in Jer 52:7–8.

resh [20]*The breath in our lungs, Yahweh's anointed,*
was captured in their deep pit,[a]
The one of whom we said,
"In his shade we will live among the nations."

a. The plural is intensive, like the only other occurrence of *šəḥît*, in Ps 107:20. LXX "destructions" derives the word from *šāḥat* rather than *šāḥâ* or *šûaḥ*. Vg "our sins" reflects the application of the expression "Yahweh's anointed" (Yahweh's *məšîaḥ*) to Jesus, along with the rest of the verse, which is expounded in this way by writers such as Justin Martyr, Irenaeus, Tertullian, Origen, Cyril of Jerusalem, Ambrose, Rufinus, and Augustine (see Wenthe, *Jeremiah, Lamentations*, 299–304). The application is later reversed with regard to

60. Hillers, *Lamentations*, 144.

the king of England, as the English monarchy is understood in light of the Davidic monarchy (Joyce and Lipton, *Lamentations*, 168–71). As Lancelot Andrewes preached a Gunpowder Treason sermon on 3:22 in 1612 (see the translation note there), following the foiling of the plot in 1605, John Donne preached a Powder Treason sermon on 4:20 in 1622 (*The Sermons of John Donne*, vol. 4 [Berkeley: University of California, 1959], 237–63). And in 1649, Alice Thornton grieved over the execution of Charles I with the same words (R. A. Parry, "Lamentations and the Poetic Politics of Prayer," *TynB* 62 [2011]: 65–66).

20 And there the Babylonians could fulfill their particular aim by capturing the king. He was their particular target because he had defied them and had not fulfilled his obligations to them, and because they wanted to make sure he would not do so again, neither he nor his sons (Jer 52:9–11). To return to the hunting metaphor, the king *was captured in their deep pit*: the metaphor might also suggest the deep pit of death or Sheol, as the word (*šəḥît*) likely does in Ps 107:20 (and cf. *šaḥat* in passages such as Ps 16:10). But for Judah, the significance of Zedekiah was different from his significance for his captors. Yahweh's commitment to David's successors went along with his commitment to Zion itself. It underlay his people's security. Their life depended on him. He was *the breath in our lungs* (lit. "our nostrils"). It is a variant on an image that appears in one of the Amarna Letters, in an inscription relating to Ramesses II from a similar period, and in the Roman writer Seneca,[61] though in their cases they are flattering the rulers they are addressing. Further, the king was *Yahweh's anointed*. That expression is otherwise used mainly of Saul (e.g., 1 Sam 24:6, 10[7, 11]), but it once describes David (2 Sam 19:21[22]). It always appears in contexts that suggest that the king should be honored, though "his anointed" is used more generally of Israel's kings (and of Cyrus in Isa 45:1). The connotations of *Yahweh's anointed* would underline the scandal or outrage of his being captured in the way he was.

To underscore the point further, people had believed that *in his shade we will live among the nations*. He would be like a tree or a rock or a motherbird that provides shade and protection (Pss 17:8; 36:7[8]; 57:1[2]; 121:5; Isa 32:2). It is another ancient Near Eastern image: the king spreads a "beneficial shadow" over his subjects,[62] as Ezekiel pictures Pharaoh doing for his subjects (Ezek 31:1–6, 12, 17). In theory, Judahites would not trust in the aforementioned shade of Egypt (Isa 30:2–3). They knew that their national and international life could continue and flourish as long as they had Yahweh's anointed as their head. They were secure. But Yahweh's commitment

61. *ANET*, 484; A. Spalinger, *The Great Dedicatory Inscription of Ramesses II: A Solar-Osirian Tractate at Abydos*, CHANE 33 (Leiden: Brill, 2009), 30–31; Seneca, *On Clemency* 1.4.

62. A. L. Oppenheim, "Assyriological Gleanings IV: The Shadow of the King," *BASOR* 107 (1947): 8.

to David expressed in Ps 132 collapsed, as Yahweh's commitment to Zion expressed in the same psalm collapsed. The people had forgotten the expectation of the psalm ("if your sons keep my covenant"). As a consequence, their disappointed hopes of foreign help are accompanied by disappointed hopes of their God-appointed king.[63] Thus this section reaches its high point.[64] Yet again the reference to Yahweh signals the end of a section.

shin [21]*Be happy and celebrate, Ms. Edom,*
you who live[a] *in the country of Uz.*[b]
To you, too, the chalice will pass,
you will get drunk and expose yourself.

a. The *ketiv's ywšbty* is an archaic form (GK 90n), presumably original.
b. LXX lacks "of Uz," a nice reading if *the country* then means Judah; see the commentary.

21 After that reference to *Yahweh's anointed*, one final time the subject and the perspective change. There are no more first-person verbs or suffixes, but for the first time there is an addressee. Who speaks? Is it the "I" of vv. 1–6? "Be happy and rejoice," Isa 65:18 will bid the Judahites a little later, "celebrate with Jerusalem" and "be happy" (Isa 66:10), "rejoice and celebrate" (Joel 2:21, 23). Here, the invitation will turn out to be ironic, as perhaps is the polite address to *Ms. Edom*. Neither the First Testament nor other sources provide explicit information on the location of Uz, but circumstantial evidence (e.g., the mention of an Uz in Esau's genealogy in Gen 36:28) fits with the obvious inference from this verse that Uz stands for Edom's homeland, southeast of the Dead Sea.[65] Rather oddly, the Edomites are the first foreign people explicitly to be mentioned in Lamentations[66] (Assyria and Egypt will feature in 5:6); the uniqueness of this reference and the naming of Uz might suggest that Uz is of archetypal and not simply literal significance, which supports the subsequent interpretation whereby Edom signifies Rome.[67] The bidding to rejoice perhaps implies that Lamentations does not begrudge Edom its land or have designs on it (cf. Num 20:14–21).

Yet there might be two reasons for Judah to expect Yahweh to take action against Edom. According to Obadiah 13, the Edomites had joined with other peoples in marching into Jerusalem when the city fell. They will have been inclined to *be happy and celebrate* on that occasion, no doubt, which would

63. Koenen, *Klagelieder*, 356.

64. Berges, *Klagelieder*, 263.

65. See, e.g., D. J. A. Clines, *Job 1–20*, WBC 17 (Dallas: Word, 1989), 10.

66. R. B. Salters suggests that there was hardly need to name Babylon and Egypt ("Text and Exegesis in Lamentations 4:21–22," in *Shai le-Sara Japhet: Studies in the Bible, Its Exegesis and Its Language*, ed. M. Bar-Asher et al. [Jerusalem: Bialek Institute, 2007], 331*).

67. Joyce and Lipton, *Lamentations*, 171–72.

give another nuance to the ironic encouragement in v. 21.[68] Yet they were not alone, or even the main party, in doing so; more significance may therefore attach to the Edomites' increasing occupation of Judahite territory, which is also the background to Obadiah. In this period, the Edomites themselves were under pressure from Arabian tribes to their east and south, and the Babylonian devastation of Judah will have made it easier for them to move into Judahite territory (cf. Ezek 35). Within a handful of years, for practical purposes they were effectively occupying an area including Beersheba and Hebron and thus reaching near Bethlehem, which became Judah's effective southern boundary. Lamentations knows that Yahweh will not simply leave Edom occupying much of Judah. While rhetorically Lamentations here addresses Edom, it will be Judah that actually hears the poem, which will encourage it to remember that Edomite occupation of its land will not go on forever. In the context of Lamentations as a whole, one might see vv. 21–22 as the beginning of a positive response to the pleas in 1:21–22; 3:64–66.[69] The verses then complement and compromise the fact that this poem is the only one in which Yahweh is not addressed, and the fact that Yahweh does not explicitly respond to the pleas, protests, and laments in Lamentations as a whole.

While Edom, then, may *be happy and celebrate* the disaster that came to Jerusalem that freed it to occupy much of Judah, Lamentations knows that the time will come for Edom, too. Following on the encouragement to rejoice, the announcement about *the chalice* might also initially not sound like bad news. But this chalice from which Edom will *get drunk* is the one of which Jer 25:15–29 speaks at length (where Uz features). The two closing verbs *you will get drunk and expose yourself* correspond to the two opening ones, *be happy and celebrate*.[70] Exposing oneself as a consequence of the drinking bout is Lamentations' own nuance on the motif of drunkenness, a nice reversal of 1:8 and in a different way a reversal of the words Ps 137:7 attributes to Edom in connection with the fall of Jerusalem.

tav [22]*Your waywardness has come to an end, Ms. Zion,*
he will exile you no more.
He is attending[a] *to your waywardness, Ms. Edom,*
he will reveal your wrongdoings.[b]

a. Here and in the following line, the *qatal* verbs suggest something that is so definite it can be spoken of as already happening—"perfects of confidence" (Provan, *Lamentations*, 123).

b. Whereas MT otherwise has a chapter marker (a *petuhah*) at the end of the poems, in MT^{L} there is only a section marker (a *setumah*) here.

68. Provan, *Lamentations*, 123.

69. Bier, *"Perhaps There Is Hope"*, 162.

70. Salters, *Lamentations*, 336.

22 For a moment, the poem turns to address *Ms. Zion.* Only in this last stanza does it offer any explicit good news to Judah, though at least it finally does so. As the story in Jer 52 that relates the capture of the last king of Judah ends with a little vignette of hope, so before the end, this poem that reflects that capture incorporates a line with magnificent news. The poem had earlier commented that the *waywardness of my dear people* (*bat-ʿammî*) *was greater than the wrongdoing of Sodom* (v. 6; cf. v. 13), but now *your waywardness has come to an end, Ms. Zion* (*bat-ṣiyyôn*). As was the case earlier, *ʿāwōn* hardly denotes simply the consequences of waywardness so that the point would be that Zion has paid the full penalty for its waywardness; in the poem's final line *ʿāwōn* will recur with the emphasis being on *waywardness* itself. On the other hand, while announcements in Jeremiah and Ezekiel envisage Judah becoming a changed people and promise that it will never go into exile again, those ideas are a lot to read into this line. More likely its point is that Zion's waywardness, along with the guilt and calamity attached to it, ran its course in the 587 disaster.[71] Likewise, the point about *he will exile you no more* (presumably the *he* is Yahweh) is not that their exile need not go on any longer (Tg; cf. Isa 40:1–2) nor that he will not exile you ever again, but simply that the necessary exile has happened. It is now a past reality.

Thus, in the context, the parallelism between the two lines suggests that the point about these observations is that the necessary fate has overwhelmed Ms. Zion, and it will now overwhelm Ms. Edom. *Attending* (*pāqad*) is a standard First Testament word for Yahweh taking punitive action, though there is also such a thing as a nice attentiveness; any negative connotations of the word come from the context. Here, the parallel colon confirms the negative connotations. One has sympathy for the Edomites in moving into Judahite land because of the pressure they themselves were under, but it counts as *waywardness* and *wrongdoings* (the pair of words recur again, as in vv. 6 and 13). Perhaps Lamentations implies a principle for international relationships and expansion: my need does not constitute an excuse for appropriating someone else's land. As well as taking up the word *waywardness* from the first colon in v. 22a, the second line takes up the verb (*gālâ*) from the second colon and thus incorporates a paronomasia. Dictionaries assume that there is only one verb *gālâ* but that it has two meanings, *go into exile* and *reveal,* and the final lines of the poem thus juxtapose forms of the verb with the two meanings. Now that the verb no longer applies to Judah in connection with its going into exile, Judah will be able to reoccupy its land, and the verb will come to apply to Edom in that other sense.

71. Salters, *Lamentations,* 337.

A READER'S RESPONSE

Imagine someone who has taken part in reading Lam 4 in a worship gathering at Mizpah or Bethel.

> In our readings in worship, we could have wished they had finished with the third of the poems. In several respects it would have made an ending we could live with. Admittedly, it had begun with such a bleak portrayal of a man suffering the wrath of God, but it then inspired us with the way he turned from his anti-testimony to his declarations of faith and hope, and it inspired us some more with its confirmatory affirmations about Yahweh's goodness and about the priority of compassion and commitment in his character. We knew the man was right that we need to turn to Yahweh, and we were inspired again by his recollection of how Yahweh had responded to prayer on so many occasions, and by the prayer he then prayed.
>
> But this fourth poem just goes back to where we were. The poems won't let us escape from thinking about the events that led to the fall of Jerusalem, about the horror of the event itself and its aftermath, and about what it did to children and mothers. It made us get so angry at the spiritual leaders who had misled us through those years, and not sorry that they were paying a price. Once again, the poem articulated how impossible it had seemed that Yahweh's commitment to Jerusalem would allow the city ever to fall. It also articulated another aspect of Yahweh's commitment that turned out to be something we couldn't rely on: his promises to David that we believed would be our protection. But at least it ended up in more or less the same position as the third poem. It wasn't a prayer—the poem didn't expect us to pray—but it was an expression of certainty that people like the Edomites who had taken advantage of us would pay a price for their own wrongdoing.

LAMENTATIONS 5: "BE MINDFUL, YAHWEH"

The framework of Lam 5 is a prayer for Yahweh to consider the state of the Judahite community and to restore it. While "God-talk permeates Lamentations," in previous chapters there has been more talk about God than talk to God. Now "the entire last chapter invokes God."[1] An "intense"[2] and "insistent"[3] prayer "fills the last chapter of the book."[4] Not that the ethos of Lam 1–4 is missing from this poem; Lamentations has no Hollywood ending. Printed Hebrew Bibles (e.g., NJPS) repeat 5:21 after 5:22 to take the edge off the work's dark closure. If Lamentations were turned into a Hollywood script, the middle chapter would have to become the end. Indeed, arguably this prayer in Lam 4 constitutes "the real articulation of grief on the community's part, to which the earlier poems have been a preamble."[5] As the community speaks for itself, it does so in prayer, which is maybe now possible after grief has been expressed. Inside the framework of the prayer, then, is a further many-sided account of the economic, social, and religious disaster that had happened to the community, which makes this restoration necessary. It is an account of "occupation . . . deprivation, humiliation, and frustration."[6] "Here the Prophet in the name of the people, and to teach them how to plead with the Lord for mercy, further laieth open their miseries in many things like unto a *Lazar* full of sores and sickness to passengers upon the way, or at the rich mans gate, praying the Lord to remember them, and to take pity upon them" (see Luke 16:19–31).[7] It might thus be argued that Lamentations reaches its goal with this prayer for people to pray,[8] which at this point also suggests something that builds on the affirmations in the middle chapter[9] while also responding to the affirmations at the end of Lam 4.[10] It further confirms that the goal of Lamentations is neither theodicy nor antitheodicy. Here, most explicitly, "the lamenting population was shown a way to rebuild their shattered universe by, paradoxically, reaching out to their God who was not there for them anymore."[11]

1. Melton, *Where Is God in the Megilloth?*, 113.
2. House, *Lamentations*, 454.
3. Renkema, *Lamentations*, 589.
4. C. J. H. Wright, *Lamentations*, 149.
5. Allen, *Liturgy of Grief*, 22, 23; cf. Goldingay, "Models for Prayer in Lamentations and Psalms."
6. Berlin, *Lamentations*, 116.
7. Mayer, *Commentary*, 486.
8. Allen, *Liturgy of Grief*, 145.
9. S. Ellington, "De-centering Lamentations," *OTE* 31 (2018): 494–505.
10. Parry, *Lamentations*, 147.
11. B. Wielenga, "The Suffering Witness: A Missiological Reading of Lamentations," *IDS* 41 (2007): 69.

The final poem in the collection again has points of resemblance to the ones that precede it.

- The number of verses corresponds to the number of letters in the alphabet.
- Like Lam 1, 2, and 3, it begins with a strong four-stress colon.
- It is dominated by a recollection of the dismaying and disturbing events associated with a catastrophe that had overwhelmed Jerusalem, which circumstantial evidence identifies as the fall of Jerusalem in 587.
- It thus comes from sometime between 587 and the beginning of Jerusalem's restoring in 537, from someone who identifies with a Judahite community living in some center such as Mizpah or Bethel.
- While its language is less overtly figurative and more concrete than earlier chapters, its function is to combine a kaleidoscope of images to convey the grim experience of the Judahite community.
- Like the testimony of the man in 3:1–18, the varied images thus cannot be turned into a single picture of the experience of the community at one particular time (see the commentary on v. 2).
- It illustrates how Israel's common reaction to suffering is to point out to Yahweh, if necessary at great length, the facts that he knows but is not taking account of.
- Although it does not explicitly mention the temple, it shares with many psalms an assumption of the special significance of Mount Zion, and it thus grieves over its desolate state.
- It shares with Deuteronomy, 2 Kings, and Jeremiah the assumption that the calamity reflects the waywardness of the past and present Judahite community, and it thus incorporates some low-key acknowledgment of wrongdoing and recognition that they need to turn back to Yahweh.
- The author is an able Hebraist and poet.

Its differences from the preceding poems are also striking.

- It does not open the verses with the successive letters of the alphabet,[12] though in itself there might not be any significance in this fact; the First Testament includes other twenty-two unit compositions of this kind.

12. S. Bergler finds a sentence about Yahweh's rejection behind the initial letters of the lines in the verses ("Threni v," *VT* 27 [1977]: 304–20); cf. P. Guillaume, "Lamentations 5," *JHebS* 9/16 (2009). H. Heater finds a "mini-acrostic" in vv. 19–20 ("Structure and Meaning in Lamentations," *Bibliotheca Sacra* 149 [1992]: 310–11).

- In incorporating address to Yahweh, an appeal for a hearing, a substantial account of affliction, a low-key acknowledgment of wrongdoing, an affirmation of trust, and a plea, it is closer to the form of a protest psalm (specifically, a communal protest) than the other poems. If it appeared in the Psalter, it would not look out of place in the company of Pss 44; 74; 79 and other psalms with twenty-two lines (Pss 33; 38; 103). It thus works for its audience by sticking close to a familiar form of prayer rather than by using poetic creativity to construct a new form.
- It comprises only twenty-two lines. "The brevity of the poem (half the length of Lam 4 and one-third as long as Lam 1, 2 and 3) and the abandonment of the acrostic form focus the attention on the desperate plea contained within."[13]
- If the alphabetic structuring of the other poems about the disaster enables them to combine a sense of disorder with a sense of order, a possible effect of placing this poem at the end of the collection is to take a step away from that balance. This poem "serves as a summation of the pain of the people, the city, the nation, and a final demand that God pay attention to them," though to speak of "accelerating hopelessness" is to read more into it than is evidently there.[14]
- The hint of a lack of order is counterbalanced by the fact that every line in the poem is a self-contained bicolon, that every line apart from v. 16 manifests some parallelism, and that the poem's language is straightforward and manifests less ellipsis. It also lacks any parallelism between lines, except in vv. 9–10. In addition, the lines do group: vv. 2–4 belong together, as do vv. 5–7 and vv. 8–10.
- On the other hand, the poem uses a distinctive word order in which the verb comes second or third in the sentence rather than first (see especially vv. 2, 3, 4a, 4b, 5a, 6, 7a, 7b, 8, 9, 10, 11, 12a, 12b, 13a, 13b, 14), which is elsewhere usually a mark of emphasis or of the subordination of one clause to another.
- Surprisingly, the dominant rhythm of the poem is 3-3, the regular rhythm for more upbeat poetry; only vv. 2, 3, 14, and 18 have a two-beat second colon.[15] It is another hint that we are coming to the end

13. B. D. Giffone, "The Timeless, Unifying Rhetoric of Lamentations," *OTE* 25 (2012): 544–45.

14. The first quotation is from K. M. O'Connor, "Lamentations," *NIB*, in her introduction to Lam 5; the second is from K. M. O'Connor, *Lamentations and the Tears of the World*, 71.

15. A syllable count produces even more striking differences (D. N. Freedman, "Acrostics and Metrics in Hebrew Poetry," *HTR* 65 [1972]: 367–92); it also shows how Lam 5 is similar to other alphabetical compositions (see further D. N. Freedman, "Acrostic Poems in the Hebrew Bible," *CBQ* 48 [1986]: 408–31).

of this sequence of poems; we are about to return to the ordinary, familiar world.

- Whereas other poems intersperse protest with prayer, this poem sets protest in the context of prayer.[16]
- No "I" speaks in this poem; and whereas Lam 1 and 2 never spoke in first-person plural terms and Lam 3 and 4 did so only when they were past the halfway point, Lam 5 speaks throughout in "we/our/us" terms except in vv. 11–14 and thus speaks explicitly in identification with and explicitly on behalf of the community.[17] It thus most systematically draws the community into its formulation of prayer and its articulation of loss and anguish. "The text of Lamentations did not come about without the real or ideal presence of community, more precisely, of a responsive congregation."[18] Whereas reading the preceding poems might confuse the reader because of the mixed voices presented in the text, in Lam 5 "the reader recognises a plural speech now unifying both the narrator and Jerusalem."[19]
- There are only a few verbal links with preceding poems: e.g., the *heart* becoming *faint* in 5:17 and 1:22; *pursue* in 5:5 and 1:3, 6; 3:43, 66; 4:19. These links also manifest a move from "I" to "we."[20]
- It opens and closes with appeal to Yahweh to *be mindful, take note*, and *look*, and to *turn us back*. The last appeal is especially distinctive. It shares the assumption in Jeremiah that Judahites need Yahweh to take action to bring them back but that they also need to come back.
- Its closing appeal incorporates questions and protests that make it end on as dark a note as any of the poems (only Lam 2 is its equal), so that it closes the collection as a whole on this bleak note, and indeed it thus combines with Lam 1 as a whole in constituting a dark framework for the collection. Its woeful end contrasts in particular with the close of Lam 4, which would have provided a more upbeat ending to the poems.[21]
- Its description of the people's affliction focuses on the down-to-

16. Renkema, *Lamentations*, 576.

17. Bailey ("Lamentations," 61) counts thirty-two instances of the closing syllable *-nû* ("us" or "our").

18. E. Gerstenberger, "Elusive Lamentations: What Are They About?," *Int* 67 (2013): 123.

19. Kang and Venter, "Canonical-Literary Reading of Lamentations 5," 260. Bier (*"Perhaps There Is Hope"*, 165–91) does include Lam 5 in her polyphonic reading of Lamentations.

20. Cf. P. E. Koptak, "Identity and Identification in the Book of Lamentations," *Covenant Quarterly* 72 (2014): 206.

21. Koenen (*Klagelieder*, 374–75) suggests it once did.

earth practicalities of their economic and social position (e.g., their loss of homes).

- It does not hold Yahweh responsible for any of the afflictions the community has experienced. The only *qatal* verbs of which Yahweh is the subject are *discarded* and *raged* in the closing line.
- It makes no explicit reference to the sanctuary or to worship. While features such as its allusion to Mount Zion constitute implicit references, its lack of something explicit along these lines is significant alongside its not referring to Yahweh as the cause of the people's affliction.
- Like Jeremiah and 2 Kings, it sees its affliction as reflecting both the present generation's wrongdoing and its ancestors' wrongdoing (e.g., Jer 14:20; 32:18; 2 Kgs 23–25).

While everything in vv. 2–18 may refer literally to things that happened to Judah and Jerusalem, it is more than a simple portrait of the way things were in 587 or in the period that immediately followed. To a greater extent than Lam 4, it incorporates a compilation of flashes from over the decades. For instance,

- the account of pursuit (v. 5) indeed relates to events that followed the city's fall, but those events were the experience of Zedekiah and his men, not of the entire community;
- the lament that people found no rest (v. 5) relates to the experience of people who sought refuge outside Judah in the preceding years;
- reaching out to Egypt (v. 6) was a feature of Judahite policy in those same years in the context of Babylonian pressure; and
- reaching out to Assyria (v. 6) belongs to a time some decades earlier, when Assyria was still a major power.

Other motifs in the anti-testimony are easy to imagine as features of the situation in 587 and the aftermath (see vv. 2, 3, 7, 8, 11, 14, 15, 16, 17, 18). Yet others may also belong to that time period (see vv. 4, 9, 10, 12, 13), and the commentary will seek to relate them to this experience, but more imagination is required. Yet other elements in the accounts combine motifs that do not seem to belong together as straightforward accounts of events (see vv. 5 and 6). Yet others raise puzzling questions concerning what they describe in that they combine images that do not seem to fit together as straightforward reports of events (see vv. 9, 10, and 13). The entire report in vv. 2–18 is a kaleidoscope of images.

The poem outlines:

5:1 "Be Mindful, Yahweh"

v. 1 Our opening plea, urging Yahweh to look to the past and present
vv. 2–10 Our affliction: the concrete things that were taken away
vv. 11–14 The affliction of particular groups
vv. 15–18 Our affliction: our mourning and sense of loss
vv. 19–22 Our closing plea, urging Yahweh to think about the present and future

1*Be mindful, Yahweh, of what happened to us,*[a]
take note[b] *and look at our reviling.*

a. Some MSS of LXX and Vg preface the first line with a heading describing what follows as a prayer, as a prayer of Jeremiah, or some such.

b. The *ketiv* implies the more direct imperative *habbēṭ*; the *qere* and 5QLam have the more deferential *habbîṭâ*.

1 Whereas Lam 4 was distinctive for incorporating no speaking to Yahweh, Lam 5 offers a contrast in immediately addressing him. *Be mindful* specifically picks up the bidding in 3:19; it is a characteristic plea in a protest psalm (e.g., Ps 74:2, 18, 22). So from the beginning, in contrast to all the preceding poems, Lam 5 articulates a prayer, and from the beginning it speaks in terms of *us* and *our*. *Take note and look* then pick up the bidding in 1:11; 2:20, while *reviling* is what Ps 89:50(51) urges Yahweh to be mindful of. In the parallelism, the lack of specificity in the expression *what happened to us* is complemented by the clarification *our reviling*. The nature and basis of the reviling have been indicated by passages such as 2:15, and the specific content of what happened that issued in reviling will be expounded further in vv. 2–18; one might see reviling as a key motif in the poem.[22] As usual, the idea of other people taking much notice of what had happened to Jerusalem involves more projection on Judah's part than objective reality. It reflects the Judahites' shame and their contempt for themselves as they look at themselves. In the parallelism, the single verb *be mindful* is also complemented by the double expression *take note and look at*. The implication is that Yahweh is not being mindful or taking note or looking. As the First Testament often implies, Israel is not very interested in or satisfied by the theoretical truth that Yahweh is omniscient. It is more concerned with whether theoretical awareness becomes awareness that issues in action. And Yahweh's unquestionable awareness of what has happened to Jerusalem has not done so. "It is as if Yahweh is afflicted with attention deficit disorder. God cannot focus

22. Provan, *Lamentations*, 123–24.

on 'what has befallen us,' cannot remember, cannot keep it present in the divine mind long enough to act upon it."[23]

> [2]*Our domain—it turned into that of strangers,*[a]
> *our homes into those of foreigners.*

a. English translations render the verb *hāpak* "turned over to," but there is no parallel for that meaning.

2 The poem then goes straight into pointing out to Yahweh the facts that he knows but is not taking into account, which it will do at great length. The further anti-testimony begins with Judah's loss of its land. The word for *domain* (*naḥălâ*) is conventionally translated "inheritance," but the word's thrust does not relate to the process whereby one generation passes ownership to the next, as is indicated by the fact that Yahweh has a "domain." It focuses more on the distinctive and secure possession of something by a family or a people. Thus, here in the parallelism, *our homes* makes more specific the point about a domain. The protest has in mind not so much the city of Jerusalem, which had been devastated rather than appropriated, but the country in general. The problem is that the people's domain as a whole—its land and thus its homes—got *turned* into the possession of other people, the *strangers* and *foreigners* who invaded the country and took it over. They were people such as the Babylonians, whom Obadiah 11 terms "strangers" and "foreigners" in its critique of Edom, and the Edomites themselves. In another respect, then, Lam 5 follows Lam 4 in a way that is apposite (see 4:21–22). For *turned* (*hāpak*), the use of the *niphal* verb (cf. 1:20; 5:15) rather than the *qal* passive (4:6) or *hophal* suggests an intransitive rather than a passive meaning. A passive verb would raise the question of agency and perhaps imply "turned by Yahweh." The *niphal* fits the way the poem does not describe Yahweh as the cause of any of the community's specific afflictions; it makes for a further slight contrast with Lam 4, and a sharp one with Lam 3. Perhaps the poem recognizes that accusation is not calculated to win the sympathy of the accused. Only in the closing lines will it say anything accusatory to him (vv. 20, 22). Otherwise, it relates his agency only to the positive actions it seeks (vv. 1, 21).

> [3]*Orphans*[a] *we became, with*[b] *no father,*
> *our mothers like widows.*[c]

a. Tg's "like orphans" is a plausible interpretation (see the commentary). Strictly, they would not be orphans if they still had mothers as the second colon implies was the case,

23. K. M. O'Connor, "Lamentations," *NIB*, on the verse.

but the looseness of expression (a kind of hyperbole) need hardly suggest that the second colon does not refer to their literal mothers (so J. Renkema, "Does Hebrew *Ytwm* Really Mean 'Fatherless'?," *VT* 45 [1995]: 119–22).

b. The *ketiv* lacks the *w* ("with" here).

c. 5QLam has "our mothers [have] no daughters and [are] like widows" (see Kotzé, *Qumran Manuscripts of Lamentations*, 154–57).

3 The siege of Jerusalem will have meant the death or exile of many of its menfolk, turning children and wives literally or effectively into orphans and widows. And for a wife and mother, the loss of husband and children means the loss of security as well as heartbreak.[24] Children who have lost their father and women who have lost their husband have nowhere to live, no means of livelihood, no security, and no protection, and the loss of land and homes would itself have brought about the disintegration of the stability of family life. But the *like* in the second colon suggests that, following on v. 2, the hyperbolic generalization in the line as a whole speaks metaphorically. The *like* could apply retrospectively to the first colon, as the verb applies to the second as well as the first. The point then is that having no land or homes puts the entire community into a position like that of a collection of orphans and widows.[25] Perhaps there is poetic justice here, as the Judahites had been neglectful of the obligation to care for orphans and widows (Jer 7:6; 22:3).[26] Perhaps also God is the Father who is missing from his children's lives, which would fit with the suggestion that Lam 5 is taken up in Isa 56–66 (see 63:16; 64:8[7]).[27]

[4] *Our water[a]—we drank it for silver;*
our wood—it would come for a price.

a. LXX "since our days" implies *miyyāmênû* for MT *mêmênû*.

4 "The picture moves from the breakup of the family to the daily struggle for survival"; wood-gathering and water-carrying were basic, down-to-earth activities, and the people engaged in them were "low on the occupational hierarchy."[28] The lack of an immediate water supply and of firewood would be another consequence of losing land and homes; vv. 2–4 form a cluster of

24. Mandolfo, "Lamentations," 453.

25. Ibn Ezra, in MG.

26. Lalleman-de Winkel, *Jeremiah, Lamentations*, 370.

27. See L. S. Flesher, "Daughter Zion," in Boda, Dempsey, and Flesher, *Daughter Zion*, 303–20.

28. Berlin, *Lamentations*, 118.

verses. The poem thus continues with the everyday, practical consequences of the catastrophe that befell the city, moving from the people losing their hold on their domain (v. 2) to their losing their self-sufficiency as families (v. 3) and now to their losing free access to basic necessities. The implication would apparently be that the Babylonians had taken control of the supplies of water and of fuel for cooking, so that people had to pay (with what?) for what had been family or community resources—people normally simply drew water and felled trees or chopped up fallen trees. Admittedly, how things were in practice and what exactly the plaint refers to is hard to see. Did the Babylonians set guards at wells and at the edge of forests? Or is this line another hyperbole or metaphor?

> 5 *Upon*[a] *our neck we were pursued,*
> *as we got weary, there was no*[b] *resting for us.*[c]

a. For MT *ʿal*, Sym "[with] a yoke upon" implies *ʿōl ʿal*, which makes for an interesting alternative sense: the line then refers to working hard, which fits the context, though not the use of the verb *rādap*.

b. For the *ketiv*'s *lōʾ*, the *qere* has *wəlōʾ* ("but there was no . . ."); in the *ketiv*, the asyndeton suggests the first verb is subordinate to the second.

c. Lit. "it was not rested for us."

5 The plaint moves to another sort of issue. It begins allusively, but the reference to being *pursued* without *resting* picks up from 1:3 (pursuit recurs in 1:6; 4:19). The two cola are parallel, and the verb suggests that *upon our neck* denotes the closeness of the chase: the pursuers were breathing down our neck. Or perhaps the line as a whole combines the notion of unrelenting pursuit with the image of the unrelenting expectations placed upon an ox that bears a yoke on its neck. There is another possible suggestion of poetic justice here, as the Judahites had been stiff-necked.[29] Further, the allusiveness and the double imagery of yoking and pursuing, suggested by the line, constitute a further indication that the list of afflictions is serendipitous and poetic rather than systematic and prosaic.

> 6 *To Egypt*[a] *we put out a hand,*
> *to Assyria, to get our fill of bread.*

a. "To" needs to be understood in each colon; in contrast, LXX makes Egypt and then Assyria the subject, implying *nātənû* for MT *nātannû*.

29. Calvin, *Jeremiah and Lamentations*, 5:597.

6 This next line adds to the impression that the poem is clustering themes and recounting things in a chronologically unsystematic fashion, as it speaks of the need of protection from adversaries. Jeremiah juxtaposes *Egypt* and *Assyria* in his critique of Judah's recourse to alien support, but it was already an anachronistic reference in his day (Jer 2:18, 36), and any actual relationship with Assyria dated from quite some decades before the situation of Judahites after 587. The two nations are a conventional word pair to signify potential allies or champions who might support or defend Judah.[30] The verse thus combines ideas in the same way as v. 5. Judah had indeed looked at different times to Egypt and Assyria for political and military support and entered into alliance with them, which is the implication of *put out a hand* (see Ezek 17:18);[31] they shook hands on it, as it were.[32] But the poem explicitly refers to looking for food, and Egypt was also a place that might be the destination of the flight to which v. 5 referred (see Jer 43). The implicit recognition that turning to Egypt or Assyria had been subject to the critique of a prophet such as Jeremiah leads into v. 7.

> 7 *Though our ancestors, they did wrong—they were not there;*[a]
> *we ourselves—we carried their wayward acts.*

a. Whereas LXX, Vg have a present-tense verb, the occurrence of this expression compares with that in Gen 5:24. The *qere* again has *wə* before *they were not* and also before *we ourselves.*

7 This rueful comment leads from v. 6. The poem will shortly acknowledge that *we did wrong* (v. 16), so the Judahites are not here claiming that they did not deserve what happened. Rather, they are expressing a wistfulness about the fact that the ancestors escaped the consequences of *their wayward acts* but the current generation did not. It is self-evident: the people have lost their land and their homes.[33] If the ancestors had turned back to Yahweh, the whole story would have been different; the subsequent generations would not have continued along their wayward path under their influence. But the ancestors did not turn back, and neither did their descendants, who thus *carried their wayward acts.* The doleful observation fits with the common human experience that one generation pays the price for a previous generation's stupidity and waywardness, which the First Testament realistically

30. Cf. D. Grossberg, *Centripetal and Centrifugal Structures in Biblical Poetry* (Atlanta: Scholars, 1989), 96.

31. Ibn Ezra, in MG.

32. Cf. Hillers, *Lamentations*, 157.

33. M. L. Mitchell, "Reading of the Imagery of Lamentations," 205–6.

recognizes as an aspect of the way Yahweh makes things work (Exod 20:5; Jer 32:18). There are advantages as well as disadvantages in blaming a previous generation for one's misfortunes.[34] The First Testament combines the awareness that one generation's decisions affect the next generation with the awareness that each generation nevertheless remains responsible for its own decisions. A later generation is not to feel or claim that it is trapped by the decisions of its parents of grandparents (Jer 31:29; cf. Deut 24:16). Psalm 79:8–9 combines the two considerations in a way analogous to vv. 7 and 16 (cf. Jer 3:25; 11:10; 14:20; 16:10–13).[35]

[8]*Servants—they ruled over us,*
there was no one snatching from their hand.[a]

a. Vg assumes that the noun clause thus refers to the past; LXX has a present verb.

8 The *servants* who first gained control of Judah were the "servants of Nebuchadnezzar King of Babylon" whom he commissioned to besiege Jerusalem in 597 (2 Kgs 24:10–11). The underlings whom he commissioned again in 588 could also be described as Nebuchadnezzar's servants; they included people such as Nebuzaradan, "the servant of the king of Babylon" (2 Kgs 25:8), who *ruled over us* in the way implied in 2 Kgs 25, Jer 39, and Jer 52. The people designated as Nebuchadnezzar's servants might also include people such as the Edomites, who had been under Judah's own control in Judah's better days (2 Kgs 8; 14). But asking too specifically about the identity of the servants may again involve some unwise literalism. Being ruled over by people who were your servants is an image, a sad expression of things being upside down (Prov 19:10; 30:22) when the proper thing is to be ruled by your own king. In this line, the parallelism underscores the point by noting that Judah had no allies to rescue it from these "servants," as was indeed the situation in 587.

[9]*At the cost of our life we would bring in our bread,*
in the face of the sword in the wilderness.

9 The poem continues to combine images as it talks about life in Jerusalem and its environs. If acquiring water and firewood was costly, acquiring bread (that is, basic food) was more so. The picture may presuppose the hazards of growing and harvesting grain during the siege, in the region east of the city (which would count as wilderness), and then of getting it into Jerusalem.

34. Joyce and Lipton, *Lamentations*, 178–79.
35. Koenen, *Klagelieder*, 392–93.

Or it may presuppose the situation after the fall of the city when they were permitted to grow food by the Babylonian authorities (cf. Jer 52:15–16) and to bring it into wherever they then had their abode. In the parallelism, *in the face of the sword in the wilderness* explains *at the cost of our life*. The risk to life and this parallel reference to the sword could suggest the risk involved in venturing outside the city during the siege to bring in the grain or the brigand-affected chaos of the region in the period that followed the fall of Jerusalem. On the other hand, in Deut 28:22 the word for *sword* (*ḥereb*) seems to denote heat that can kill, and v. 10 could suggest this meaning here.

> [10]*Our skin, it shriveled*[a] *as in*[b] *an oven,*
> *in the face of the ravages*[c] *of hunger.*

a. Lit. "they shriveled"; that is, *nikmārû* is oddly plural. The verb's meaning is likely more precise than "got hot" (BDB; see *HALOT*; *DTT*; Koenen, *Klagelieder*, 397–98).

b. On the pregnant meaning of *kə*, see the translation note on 2:5.

c. *Zalʿāpâ* occurs only here and in Pss 11:6; 119:53, and its meaning is a matter of guesswork.

10 The imagery continues from v. 9. In summer, and thus in the time of the grain harvest, the heat in the region east of Jerusalem can be deadly. Working out there would be like working in an oven. It baked people's skin. This line is thus parallel to the preceding one. And in the parallelism, in a way comparable to v. 9, in the parallelism, *in the face of the ravages of hunger* explains how *our skin shriveled as in an oven*: the pressure of hunger compelled people to venture out in the heat of summer to ensure that they had something to eat, despite the toll it took on them.

> [11]*Women in Zion—men humbled them,*
> *girls in the towns of Judah.*

11 The theme changes again, as does the grammatical form of expression. Whereas vv. 2–10 lamented the experience of the community as a whole, vv. 11–14 lament the experience of different groups of people, and thus do so in the third person. *Humbled* (*ʿānâ*) does as the Hebrew word for rape (e.g., Deut 22:24–25; Judg 20:5; 2 Sam 13:12, 14, 22, 32), and the rape of a nation's women is a feature of invasion and defeat. If the authors of Lamentations were women, it might not be surprising that this horrific aspect of war comes first in vv. 11–14. The parallelism will imply that both in Jerusalem and in other Judahite towns, the invading army raped both married women and girls who were not yet married, who might thus become unmarriable.

"In a traditional society, disruption of marriage seems to be one function of widespread rape in wartime."[36] Like some other aspects of traditional society presupposed in Lamentations, in modern societies one of the aims of rape in wartime is the disruption of marriage and family.

> [12]*Leaders, they hung up by their hand,*
> *the faces of the elders, they did not find honor.*

12 After lamenting the women who have been violated and battered, the poem moves on to the community's senior men; *leaders* and *elders* are overlapping or identical people. "It is unlikely that hanging by itself ever served as a form of capital punishment in Israel. The relevant texts appear to suggest instead that those who were condemned, above all blasphemers, were first killed and then hung up, so that hanging was more an additional punishment"[37]—a further shaming and a warning to other people after execution (Deut 21:22; Josh 10:26). But here, the second colon would be an anticlimax after a reference to hanging that also presupposed execution, as it would also be if the colon denoted some form of torture.[38] The parallelism suggests some form of time-limited hanging *by their hand* that might be a means of shaming, a little like putting someone in the stocks. Thus the image is accompanied by the critique that the senior members of the community were not treated as worthy of honor.

> [13]*Young men, they carried the millstone,*[a]
> *youths, they collapsed with wood.*

a. Vg takes this expression as a euphemism for sexual abuse.

13 What happened to the *young men* now follows. What was so problematic about carrying the millstone? In the home, the regular grinding of meal with millstones was undertaken by the women in the family while the men were working in the fields (Exod 11:5; Job 31:10). But there's no indication that Israel was uptight about gender roles; in Num 11:8 it is simply "the people" who grind the manna. For Ms. Babylon to undertake this task would be humiliating, but the Judahite young men's being involved in it would hardly deserve a place in a list of afflictions like the one in this poem. So what could be signified by the expression *they carried the millstone*? There is evidence from elsewhere in the ancient Near East that holding a hand-mill could suggest the

36. M. L. Mitchell, "Reading of the Imagery of Lamentations," 214.
37. M. J. Mulder, "קטר, *qṭr*," *TDOT*, 16:669.
38. Cox and Paulsell, *Lamentations and the Song of Songs*, 99.

work of a slave.[39] In addition, there was a kind of grinding done by a big guy like Samson as required by his overlords (Judg 16:21), if not done by animals manipulating the millstones. They would contrast with domestic millstones, which were not too tricky to lift and carry or throw (Judg 9:53; 2 Sam 11:21!). The poem uses a word for a millstone (*ṭəḥôn*) that comes only here and is thus not one of the regular words. Perhaps it refers to an industrial-strength type of millstone, so that lifting it up might be an overwhelming task for an ordinary young man. Such an implication would fit with the picture in the parallel colon. If the *youths collapsed with the wood*, perhaps they were doing the work that donkeys or oxen would normally do or were being required by their overlords to carry impossible loads. Both cola would then suggest young people having to undertake tasks of disabling magnitude, undertaking them not just for the community but for their overlords.

> [14]*The elderly men, they ceased from the gateway,*
> *the young men from their strings.*

14 Here *the elderly men* may simply be the senior citizens, as opposed to the elders in the sense of people with a recognized leadership position in the community. The picture would then be of them no longer hanging about in *the gateway* as a meeting place, talking and whiling away their time. The *young men* are then similarly no longer enjoying themselves making music; the description suggests a fulfillment of Yahweh's threat to make the sound of celebration cease (Jer 16:9). But the gateways are consistently the places where people who have authority gather for decision-making and for the conduct of public business (e.g., Deut 21:19; 22:15). The squares are more the places where people might gather to hang out (4:18). Likewise the young men's ceasing from their music could imply they are no longer fulfilling their role in community celebrations such as weddings and harvests (to which Jer 16:9 actually refers). Either way, the elderly and the young men *ceased*. It is a doubly significant verb. It recalls the ceasing to which 1:7 refers, which Jerusalem's adversaries laughed at. And it rather suggests that they ceased to exist. They are dead and gone.

> [15]*The joy in our heart ceased,*
> *our dancing turned into mourning.*

15 The poem reverts to first-person plural, though the verb *ceased* and the motif of *joy* (or rather, the termination of joy) follow on from v. 14 and will continue through the first-person plural section that takes up vv. 15–18. The

39. G. R. Kotzé, "Holding up a Hand-Mill in Lamentations 5:13," *JNSL* 45 (2019): 73–87.

anti-testimony returns, then, to the experience of the community as a whole. They had regarded their city as "joy to all the earth" (2:15), but *the joy in our heart ceased* when it fell, and *our dancing turned into mourning*, the mourning to which previous poems have referred (1:4; 2:8). In the Jeremianic warning recalled by v. 14, Yahweh had told the prophet, by way of hyperbole, that he was not to join in mourning rites in Jerusalem. There was going to be too much to mourn and not enough mourners (Jer 16:5–9). And the community's dancing indeed gave way to mourning. Whereas Ps 30:11[12] testifies, "you turned my lament into dancing, . . . you clothed me with rejoicing," the people's experience has been the reverse. Yahweh has promised, "I will turn their mourning into joyfulness" (Jer 31:13), but it certainly hasn't happened yet.

> [16]*The crown on our head fell off;*
> *alas, us, please, because we did wrong.*

16 "So lament can be the only form of song left to the people."[40] The implication of the opening image is that the people of Judah had a claim to royal honor (cf. Job 19:9; Prov 12:4), but it sure does not look like it now. Perhaps there is a link with the way the (supposed) status of Jerusalem in the eyes of the world (e.g., 2:15) disappeared with the city's destruction (cf. v. 18).

The line is the only one in this poem where there is no explicit or distinctive link between the two cola. The inarticulate cry *alas, us, please* (*'ôy-nā' lānû*) parallels the cry of a woman in childbirth and the cry of Baruch (Jer 4:31; 45:3). Without the *please*, it is the cry of Jerusalem in a state of panic at the disaster that is coming (4:13; 6:4; 10:19). The subsequent acknowledgment *because we did wrong* is then a surprise. There are situations in which the people of God can appeal to the fact of their commitment, which means there is no warrant for the disaster that has come to them (e.g., Ps 44). These poems know that the fall of Jerusalem in 587 was not such an occasion. They parallel the kind of psalm that acknowledges waywardness even while protesting the calamity that has come to the community (e.g., Pss 38; 39; see the commentary on 1:9; 3:39). And they presuppose that when calamity does issue from wrongdoing, acknowledging the wrongdoing opens up the way to Yahweh's pardon (1 Kgs 8:46–51).[41] It is here that the poem makes clear how the conviction that *our ancestors did wrong* but *we carried their wayward acts* (v. 7) does not imply being able to make the claim that comes in Ps 44, that the community does not itself deserve its suffering. Indeed, here, the *we* can cover both the community of the present and the community of the past. It is one community. The poem also compares with Ps 79:8–9, which

40. C. J. H. Wright, *Lamentations*, 155.
41. Koenen, *Klagelieder*, 406.

both urges Yahweh not to be mindful of the waywardness of former generations and acknowledges the wrongdoings of the present generation. And it thereby compares with the stance of 2 Kings and Jeremiah, where both the wrongdoings of the past and the wrongdoings of the present find their retribution in the present.[42]

> [17]*Because of this our heart became faint,*
> *because of these things our eyes became dark.*

17 The poem's expression of affliction continues to work toward its closure. *Because of this* and *because of these things* would usually refer to what precedes, but the occurrence of another *because of* in the next verse suggests that here the expressions at least include reference to what follows (it thus parallels the *this* in 3:21, though not in its encouraging implications). It makes little difference because v. 18 will be summarizing what the poem has said so far. *My heart became faint* reformulates the closing colon of Lam 1 (1:22) with a transition to plurals and the addition of the verb that makes explicit the past reference of these words about the heart being faint. In turn, 2:11 referred to how *my eyes failed with much crying*, and here *our eyes became dark* suggests either the way crying can affect the appearance of the eyes or the way it can make them unable to see and thus to look toward any possible future.

> [18]*Because of Mount Zion, which became desolate,*[a]
> *as foxes*[b] *thronged*[c] *onto it.*[d]

a. In isolation, *šāmēm* could be an adjective meaning "desolate" or a *qatal* verb with stative significance, which in either case would imply the meaning "is desolate." With LXX, Vg, I take it rather as referring to the past event of desolation (cf. Ibn Ezra, in MG), which links with the way the asyndetic second colon with the subject before the *qatal* verb looks as if it is subordinate to this colon.

b. Here the creatures are *šûʿālîm*, which LXX, Vg take to be foxes; in 4:3 they were *tannîn*. Renkema (*Lamentations*, 620) argues for jackals because apparently foxes are solitary creatures; they do not "throng." But Lamentations might not be worrying too much about zoological precision; cf. D. Grossberg, *Centripetal and Centrifugal Structures in Biblical Poetry* (Atlanta: Scholars, 1989), 98.

c. The *piel* of *hālak* suggests "throng," "tramp," or "prowl" (BDB).

d. MT has a chapter break after v. 18. Otherwise in Lamentations (with the qualification made in the translation note at 4:22), the chapter breaks come at the end of each poem, with a section break at the end of each stanza when the letter changes.

42. G. Brunet takes the difference between vv. 7 and 16 as a sign that they come from two originally separate poems ("La cinquième Lamentation," *VT* 33 [1983]: 152); T. Wagner suggests a redaction-critical explanation of the relationship between the verses ("Die Schuld der Väter (er-)tragen: Thr 5 im Kontext exilischer Theologie," *VT* 62 [2012]: 622–35).

18 "The final scenario says it all."[43] The reference to Mount Zion (not just Zion as in v. 11) is the closest thing in the poem to an explicit reference to the temple, though the temple is not thought of separately from the city.

> Lam 5:18 implies that the temple has been destroyed and creates the impression that chaos has infiltrated YHWH's abandoned earthly residence. The invasion of chaos into culture forms part of the well-known *topos* of a world turned upside down (*mundus inversus*) in ANE literature. The image of desert-dwelling wild animals, which represent the chaotic, anti-human world, becoming the new occupants of ruined sites that once embodied the pinnacle of culture, communicates the inversion of normal conditions well. In Lam 5:18, the poet uses this established image to describe the disaster of the desolate divine dwelling place.[44]

[19] *You,*[a] *Yahweh—you sit*[b] *for all time,*
your throne is to generation after generation.

a. LXX, Vg have "but you."
b. For *tēšēb*, Vg has "remain," LXX "dwell."

19 In MT, the beginning of a new chapter at this point overdoes the transition to v. 19, but the transition is marked, as LXX and Vg also make explicit (see the translation notes on vv. 18, 19). The anti-testimony has come to an end, and this new verse makes for a startling contrast. So far, Yahweh has been the subject of no verbs, which is a comfort but also a discomfort. The desolation and trampling of Mount Zion carry no implications regarding Yahweh's reality and sovereignty.[45] Over against the chaos that has enveloped Mount Zion despite its God-given security, the poem now sets the infinite throne of Yahweh,[46] who had always been Israel's sole hope.[47] The temple itself is not the most important thing about Jerusalem or about Yahweh.[48] In theory, Judahites knew it to be so, though perhaps they sometimes forgot. The verb translated *sit* (*yāšab*; cf. Ps 102:12[13]) is ambiguous (see the translation note); the parallelism clarifies that the poem is talking about the fact that Yahweh sits enthroned over the universe. Yahweh is King. Although

43. Salters, *Lamentations*, 366.
44. G. R. Kotzé, "Comments on the Expression of Hope in LXX Lamentations 5:19–22," *OTE* 28 (2015): 128–29.
45. Salters, *Lamentations*, 368.
46. Berges, *Klagelieder*, 296.
47. K. M. Hawtrey, "The Exile as a Crisis for Cultic Religion," *RTR* 52 (1993): 80.
48. C. Frevel, "Zerbrochene Zier: Tempel und Tempelzerstörung in den Klageliedern (Threni)," in Frevel, *Im Lesen Verstehen*, 177–231.

there is a sense in which city or temple is Yahweh's throne (Jer 3:17; 14:21; 17:12), Yahweh is not enthroned there now. Yet his earthly throne was always an earthly representation or extension of his heavenly throne (see, e.g., Ps 103:19; Isa 6:1; Ezek 1:26), as his earthly house was an earthly equivalent to his heavenly palace, and the imperiling of the earthly version need say nothing about the heavenly version. To make the point more explicit, the poem adds a declaration about the throne that is not endangered by an event of the kind that has happened. That throne is *to generation after generation*, and there *you sit for all time*. Literally, Yahweh sits there "to age," which implies "forever," though the poem is perhaps more focused on the fact that there will never be a time within history when Yahweh ceases to be king and therefore ceases to be involved with Israel. This second occurrence of the familiar expression (*ləʿôlām*) pairs nicely with the one in 3:31.

> When we fix our eyes on present things, we must necessarily vacillate, as there is nothing permanent in the world; and when adversities bring a cloud over our eyes, then faith in a manner vanishes, at least we are troubled and stand amazed. Now the remedy is, to raise up our eyes to God, for however confounded things may be in the world, yet he remains always the same.[49]

[20] *Why do you put us out of mind forever,*[a]
abandon us for length of days?

a. On LXX's "until victory," see the translation note on 3:18; K. J. Youngblood finds an eschatological reading of the text here ("The Character and Significance of LXX Lamentations," in Parry and H. A. Thomas, *Great Is Thy Faithfulness?*, 68).

20 The expressions *forever* and *for length of days* take up the *for all time* and *to generation after generation* of v. 19. While the multiplicity of expressions points up the importance of Yahweh's eternity, the overlap between them suggests that he himself needs to recognize a tension between the eternity of his being and the perpetuity of his abandonment of his people. *Length of days* is usually a characteristic of something that counts as good news (Pss 21:4[5]; 23:6), but not here. Is there perhaps a worrying link between the two pairs of similar expressions? Is he the eternal God who is therefore eternally wrathful? As it draws near the end, the poem returns to its beginning: *put us out of mind* (*šākaḥ*) is the antithesis of *be mindful* (v. 1), though that fact is not explicit in Hebrew as it is in those English expressions. The poem has implied a recognition of the answer to the question of why Yahweh put his people out of mind

49. Calvin, *Jeremiah and Lamentations*, 5:616.

and abandoned them, but why does he continue to do so?[50] And whereas that initial exhortation to be mindful (conventionally, "remember") related specifically to recent events, to the calamity that had come upon Judah, the question *why do you put us out of mind* (conventionally, "forget") relates not to those events in particular but to the people—its object is *us* not *what* recently *happened to us*. More explicitly than was the case in v. 1, the closing verses presuppose that Yahweh was committed to a relationship with Judah whose obligations he could surely not continue to neglect. "Did you not swear to us yourself: as you exist, so your oath exists?"[51] As usual, *put out of mind* is not only a mental act but one that issues in action; it leads to *abandon*.

> Zion said:
>
> "Yahweh abandoned me,
> the Lord—he put me out of mind." (Isa 49:14)

Really? Yahweh responds,

> "Could a woman put her baby out of mind,
> so as not to have compassion on the child of her womb?
> Even these might put out of mind,
> but I—I would not put you out of mind." (Isa 49:15)

In effect, Lamentations has been talking about divine abandonment all the way through, but only here, virtually at the end, does it come out with the word, which spells out the implications of *put out of mind*. And as usual, the poem's question is not the kind that looks for an answer; it rather looks for a different form of action from abandonment.

> 21 *Turn us back, Yahweh, to yourself, so that we may turn back,*[a]
> *make our days new,*[b] *as of old.*

a. The *ketiv* has *wnšwb*, the *qere* has *wənāšûbâ* ("and may we come back") as in 3:40; cf. the variation in 5:1 (Koenen, *Klagelieder*, 373).

b. Tg makes the plea more explicit by adding "for good."

21 As in substance v. 20 returns to v. 1 with its reference to putting out of mind, in form v. 21 returns to v. 1 in its imperatives, as well as in the invocation of *Yahweh*, the God who had entered into that relationship with Judah. Thus whereas 3:40 put the emphasis on the Judahites turning back to Yahweh (cf.

50. Salters, *Lamentations*, 370.

51. Rashi, in MG.

Deut 4:29–30; 30:2–3), here a return to Yahweh depends on Yahweh's gift.[52] The appeal then corresponds to that of Ephraim in Jer 31:18. It is still the case that the turning has to be reciprocal, and arguably by praying this way in the context of acknowledging wrongdoing, Judah *is* turning back to Yahweh. Judah is like a husband who has been wayward and is now pleading with his wife, "Please take me back," which means, "Agree that we may reestablish the relationship between us." He is coming back but asking that she may be willing for him to come back, because only then can he do so. The dynamics of reconciliation between two parties are always hard to analyze—maybe impossible to analyze. Verse 21 also neatly contrasts with and complements Yahweh's words in Zech 1:3: "Turn back to me . . . and I will turn back to you," though John 6:44 coheres with it. The theme is prominent in Thomas Aquinas's reflection on divine grace and human free will.

> Do people come to God by free will, or do they come by grace alone? For the mature Thomas, *both* are true. The authority of all Scripture forces him to expand his search for truth beyond mere formal compliance. Truth must be located positively in both statements held without compromise at the same time. Conversion must be entirely the work of grace, and at one and the same time entirely the product of free will.[53]

The poem does not speak in terms of turning from serving other gods or from serving Yahweh in the wrong way or anything else specific.[54] It does imply, "We will return to serve you."[55] The parallel colon indicates what will issue from Yahweh's being willing to have Judah back. Again there is no talk about renewing the altar or renewing the temple or even of renewing the city.[56] The plea is quite unspecific: "Make things the way they were before." "When were the good old days?"[57] One would have to go back quite a long way to find some days that one would want to emulate (cf. Jer 2:2), though 1:7; 2:17 could suggest that the expression *of old* refers to the days when the temple was first built, and 1:1 would take us back to some great days.[58]

52. Berges, *Klagelieder*, 299.

53. M. A. Abril, "Lamentations 5:21 within the Development of Thomas Aquinas' Theology of the Grace of Conversion," *International Journal of Systematic Theology* 16 (2014): 254. The Geneva Bible has a note drawing attention to the priority of God's action; the KJV omits such notes (J. A. Naudé and C. L. Miller-Naudé, "Lamentations in the English Bible Translation Tradition of the King James Bible (1611)," *Scriptura* 110 [2012]: 223).

54. I. G. P. Gous, "Lamentations 5 and the Translation of Verse 22," *OTE* 3 (1990): 297–98.

55. Ibn Ezra, in MG.

56. Koenen, *Klagelieder*, 413.

57. Renkema, *Lamentations*, 629.

58. Grossberg, *Centripetal and Centrifugal Structures in Biblical Poetry*, 104.

[22]*Even though*[a] *you actually discarded*[b] *us,*
raged against us so much.

a. For this meaning of *kî ʾim*, cf. 3:32 (R. Gordis, "The Conclusion of the Book of Lamentations (5:22)," *JBL* 93 [1974]: 289–93; cf. Gordis, *Song of Songs and Lamentations*, 196–98). Vg has "but," an established meaning of *kî ʾim* that is not so different in implications from *even though*. Sym "but if" opens up the possibility of an open-ended non-closure to the poem and the scroll (cf. T. Linafelt, "The Refusal of a Conclusion in the Book of Lamentations," *JBL* 120 [2001]: 340–43); again, the implications would not be so different. LXX has "because," but this translation ignores the *ʾim*. NRSV, NIV have "unless"; one would then expect there to have been a statement that the poem was denying, though a passage such as Jer 14:19 might constitute the background. See the discussion in Koenen, *Klagelieder*, 414–15.

b. The verb's infinitive absolute precedes the finite verb, emphasizing the actuality of the action.

22 Lamentations ends as it begins; it is shaped by woe "da capo al fine."[59] It is a tragedy rather than a comedy.[60] It has no plot and its tells no story.[61] The ending of Lam 5 constitutes a radical and confrontational break with the form of a communal lament and an implicit reinterpretation of vv. 2–18 with their holding back from accusing Yahweh of failing to honor his relationship with them.[62] How woeful is the woe depends somewhat on how one understands the opening conjunction (see the translation note). *Discarded* (*māʾas*) implies the reversing of "chose"; it has a more precise implication than "rejecting" (*zānaḥ*; 2:7; 3:17, 31), which also covers an initial non-choice. Yahweh's recalling that he chose and his denying that he has discarded is a key feature of the response in Isa 41:8–9 to this challenge or question. Lamentations itself implies that Yahweh did worse than he threatened, because he had said, "I will not discard them" (Lev 26:44). The poems thus close with one final protest that Yahweh not only did what Deuteronomy and Leviticus threatened; he did more.[63] In light of events in his own day (before the fall of Jerusalem to the Romans), Paul will ask the question whether God has abandoned his people (reflecting language such as that in Ps 94:14) and will vehemently deny the possibility in a way that parallels Isa 41:8–9: after all, God acknowledged this people ahead of time (Rom 11:1–2). This form of expression recalls his declarations about acknowledging Abraham and acknowledging Israel (Gen 18:19; Amos 3:2). That acknowledgment by Yahweh issues in expectations,

59. U. Bail, "Die entsetzte Leserin: Ein Essay vom Ort Gottes in der Gewalt (Klgl 1,12–13)," in *Gretchenfrage: von Gott reden—aber wie?*, Jabboq 2 (Gütersloh: Kaiser, 2002), 104.

60. Dobbs-Allsopp, "Tragedy, Tradition, and Theology," 31–45.

61. Janzen, *Trauma and the Failure of History*, 94.

62. R. Williamson, "Lament and the Arts of Resistance," in Lee and Mandolfo, *Lamentations in Ancient and Contemporary Cultural Contexts*, 73–74.

63. Flanders, "Covenant Curses Transposed," 107–8.

and it can issue in taking action about waywardness and thus in temporary discarding, but it surely cannot issue in rejection or discarding for all time.

The parallel colon links an attitude with an action. Rage might seem more worrying than discarding; but "anger, in all its manifestations, need not be lasting. Angry people can change their minds, change their behavior, even change their personalities; anger in humans is an emotion, not an attribute."[64] The same will be true of Yahweh.

In theory, mourning can lead to hope for a future.[65] And there is some reflection in Lamentations of an order that corresponds to the stages of grief, with Lam 5 suggesting a kind of acceptance.[66] Lamentations actually ends with protest and then with silence. Its appeal meets with no response from God within the book.[67] Yet that observation is tautologous. Lam 5 is a prayer. Prayers as prayers do not incorporate responses. The prayers in the Psalms do not. It is because they are—well, prayers. Lam 5, with its more free-form structure has even been read as a hopeful, Sabbath-like ending to the scroll.[68]

A READER'S RESPONSE

Imagine someone who has taken part in reading Lam 5 in a worship gathering at Mizpah or Bethel.

> My brother and I were in Jerusalem when Zedekiah and his soldiers slipped out and left us to the mercy of the Babylonians. They made him help with the devastation of the temple, trying to pull down those huge stone blocks. He was glad that it was virtually impossible. Two of them raped me. I never really understood why men did that. I still feel the pain and the shame of it.
>
> We used prayers like this in prayer gatherings when we were teenagers, and we carried on praying like this when we were middle-aged,

64. Joyce and Lipton, *Lamentations through the Centuries*, 187.

65. A. Labahn, "Trauern als Bewältigung der Vergangenheit zur Gestaltung der Zukunft: Bemerkungen zur anthropologischen Theologie der Klagelieder," *VT* 52 (2002): 513–27; but it's not evident that this process is taking place in Lamentations.

66. D. J. Reimer, "Good Grief? A Psychological Reading of Lamentations," *ZAW* 114 (2002): 542–59.

67. See, e.g., B. Harris and C. Mandolfo, "The Silent God in Lamentations," *Int* 67 (2013): 133–43.

68. See J. H. Prouser,"Darkness on the Face of the Deep: Lamentations as Midrash on Creation," *Conservative Judaism* 56/4 (2004): 37–42; as cited in L. Rong, *Forgotten and Forsaken by God*, 23, 42.

and we're still praying like this now that we're getting older. But we've heard rumors about the Persians marching across the Middle East and threatening the Babylonians' control of their empire, and we've heard rumors about a prophet who says he's heard a voice:

> Comfort, comfort my people,
> your God says.
> Speak to the heart of Jerusalem,
> cry out to her,
> That she has fulfilled her term of service,
> that she has paid for her waywardness,
> That she has received from Yahweh's hand
> double for all her wrongdoings.
>
> (Isa 40:1–2)

It is almost as if Yahweh has heard our lament and protest. We've kept hoping he would, but for years he hasn't, so we have just carried on praying like this until he would.

* * *

> Grant, Almighty God, that as thou didst formerly execute judgments so severe on thy people,—O grant, that these chastisements may at this day teach us to fear thy name, and also keep us in watchfulness and humility, and that we may so strive to pursue the course of our calling, that we may find that thou art always our leader, that thy hand is stretched forth to us, that thy aid is ever ready for us, until, being at length gathered into thy celestial kingdom, we shall enjoy that eternal life, which thine only-begotten Son has obtained for us by his own blood.—Amen.[69]

69. Calvin, *Jeremiah and Lamentations*, 5:624.

Index of Authors

I am grateful to Amy Pahlen for compiling the Index of Authors and the Index of Scripture and Other Ancient Texts.

Index of Subjects

Index of Scripture and Other Ancient Texts

Ancient Near Eastern Texts

Deutero-canonical Books